PRAISE FOR *TURN! TURN! TURN!*

· ·

"Steve Turner is a splendid writer whose deep and ranging musical knowledge blends inextricably with his understanding of how songs can touch—and save— people's souls. Those virtues come fully into play in this book, which taught me a great deal and moved me even more."

Anthony DeCurtis | Contributing editor at *Rolling Stone,* distinguished lecturer of creative writing at the University of Pennsylvania, author of *Lou Reed: A Life*

· ·

"In *Turn! Turn! Turn!,* a single thread unravels into a beautiful tapestry of art, music, and passion. The words of the Bible are lyrical at their core, and Steve Turner discovers new depth and vision by exploring the evolutional combination of its offerings into the heart and fabric of some of our most intriguing songs and how over time they have told the enduring story of . . . us."

Ken Mansfield | Author of *The Roof: The Beatles' Final Concert* and former US manager of Apple Records

· ·

"Steve Turner's *Turn! Turn! Turn!* is a comprehensive analysis of popular songs influenced by the Bible. Some of the stories are rather surprising, such as the motivation behind John Lennon's song "Girl," written for the Beatles, being the Christian belief that suffering on earth leads to pleasure in heaven. His story of how Pete Seeger came up with the song "Turn! Turn! Turn! (To Everything There Is a Season)" brought to light ideas that I hadn't heard before, even though I knew Pete and have been singing the song for more than fifty years. In all it's a fascinating look at how the Bible continues to blend into popular culture."

Roger McGuinn | Lead singer and lead guitarist for the Byrds

· ·

"When Andrew Lloyd Webber and I embarked upon the original recording of *Jesus Christ Superstar* in 1969, we were reliably informed that Christianity, or indeed any religious topic, was not a suitable—and certainly not a commercial—subject for contemporary popular music to tackle. However, I am glad to say, as Steve Turner so excellently illustrates in *Turn! Turn! Turn!* from the Carter family in 1935 to Stormzy in 2017, this has never been true."

Tim Rice | Award-winning lyricist of *Joseph and the Amazing Techincolor Dreamcoat* and *Jesus Christ Superstar*

· ·

"Here we have a fascinating investigation into one of the most overlooked sources of inspiration for thousands of songs from the era of rock-and-roll and associated genres. The Bible? Yes—and no better detective of scriptural influence could be found than veteran rock journalist Steve Turner, whose critical insights into popular music have often taken note of the religious (or anti-religious) impulses of artists. Always lucid, and often entertaining, he surveys over eighty years of compositions, taking into account both the obvious and the obscure. Most metal-heads know Iron Maiden derived apocalyptic imagery from the book of Revelation, but do they get that Van Halen's "Fire in the Hole" was an exposition on the epistle of James? And how many Beatles fans know that "Girl" was written to protest the biblical teaching of Genesis? Anyone interested in the intersection of religion and popular culture (or, simply, in contemporary appropriation of classic literature) will want to browse this book—and I suspect most browsers will end up reading the entire tome."

Mark Allan Powell | Editor of *HarperCollins Bible Dictionary*, author of *Encyclopedia of Contemporary Christian Music*, and professor of New Testament at Trinity Lutheran Seminary (Columbus, OH)

. . . .

"Turn! Turn! Turn! is an illuminating, inspiring, and must-read journey through songs (and great artists) that have brought the Bible to life. This beautiful book takes Steve Turner—who wrote *Amazing Grace*, an uplifting biography of the great hymn by John Newton—into the heights and depths of profound Bible-inspired lyrics. Whether at a concert, listening to the radio, or simply learning a Johnny Cash or Leonard Cohen song, we are brought into the poetry, stories, and parables of the Bible. Everywhere in these pages is abundant evidence that the Good Book lives today. Steve is a great writer, and the book is truly magnificent. I love it, and so will you!"

Judy Collins | Singer and songwriter, GRAMMY Award winner for "Both Sides Now"

. . . .

"Most Western songs have their origins in the Bible whether one likes it or not, but only a few openly recognize their source. Here is an intriguing and clear-eyed compendium of some of that. An absolute pleasure to read!"

Nick Cave | Singer-songwriter, musician, and frontman for Nick Cave and the Bad Seeds

. . . .

"Turn! Turn! Turn! demonstrates Steve Turner's gift for meticulous research and penetrating analysis. Some of these singers, songwriters, and musicians are close friends with their Bibles, others are passing acquaintances. There are a hundred examples and, like snowflakes, no two are alike. This book has made me revisit some music I thought I was done with—and listen to some I never thought I needed to bother with in the first place."

Paul Jones | Vocalist with Manfred Mann (1962–1966), lead actor in *Privilege* (1967), presenter of *The Blues Show* on BBC Radio 2 (1986–2018), and vocalist with the Blues Band (1979–   )

TURN!
TURN!
TURN!

TURN!
TURN!
TURN!

Popular Songs
Inspired by the Bible

Steve Turner

Library of Congress Cataloging-in-Publication Data

Names: Turner, Steve, 1949- author.
Title: Turn, turn, turn : popular songs and music inspired by the Bible / Steve Turner.
Description: Franklin, TN : Worthy Publishing, 2018.
Identifiers: LCCN 2018029673 | ISBN 9781945470394 (hardcover)
Subjects: LCSH: Popular music--Religious aspects--Christianity.
Classification: LCC ML3921.8.P67 T87 2018 | DDC 782.42/164--dc23
LC record available at https://lccn.loc.gov/2018029673

Produced with the assistance of Hudson Bible (www.HudsonBible.com)

ISBN: 978-1-94547-039-4

Cover Design: Studio Gearbox

Printed in the United States of America

18 19 20 21 22 23 LBM 8 7 6 5 4 3 2 1

CONTENTS

· ·

INTRODUCTION

I'm indebted to Museum of the Bible for approaching me with the idea of a book looking at popular songs inspired by the Bible. Initially the number forty was mentioned, but I didn't think the topic could be adequately addressed with such a small sample. I knew I couldn't be exhaustive, but I wanted the collection to be representative. That's how I came to a round one hundred.

As long as I've been writing, I've been especially interested in the confluence of popular culture and religion. It shows in the types of people I've written books on—Jack Kerouac, Van Morrison, Marvin Gaye, Johnny Cash—and the topics I've tackled—Christianity and the arts in *Imagine*, redemption and rock music in *Hungry for Heaven*, hymnology and folk music in *Amazing Grace*, and worldview and the Beatles in *The Gospel According to the Beatles*.

My task in this book has not been to investigate signs of personal faith (although, obviously, this can often lead to interest in the Bible) or traces of nonbiblical religion, but to specifically look at how the collection of books we know as the Bible has influenced popular music.

By "influence" I mean that some biblical words, stories, characters, or teachings have made an observable impact. Ideally this impact is specific rather than general so that the word, story, character, or teaching can be traced back to a particular biblical book, chapter, and verse. This necessarily meant the exclusion of songs like Norman Greenbaum's "Spirit in the Sky" and Joan Osborne's "One of Us," which are religious and make mention of Jesus (Greenbaum) or God (Osborne) but can't be shown to have been inspired by the Bible.

For similar reasons, I had to let go of some personal favorites such as "Belle" by Al Green and "I Found the Answer" by Tramaine Hawkins and Mahalia Jackson. These are both great songs, but they arose from personal spiritual experience and don't refer to any specific biblical teaching. This doesn't make them worse songs, but it does mean that they don't fit within the parameters set for this book. Even Kris Kristofferson's "Why Me" and "Jesus Was a Capricorn," which he previewed for me at his Hollywood home in 1972, failed this test.

By "popular music" I am mainly referring to English language Western music of the rock 'n' roll era onward (including folk, soul, rap, rock, country, pop, punk, disco, heavy metal, electronica, and other genres). In order to do that thoroughly, I have briefly gone back to the foundations of these forms of music in folk (Woody Guthrie), blues (Robert Johnson), country (Hank Williams), gospel (Sister Rosetta Tharpe), and ballads (the Carter Family).

I have included some gospel songs that have transcended the genre (such as "Oh Happy Day" by the Edwin Hawkins Singers), but in general have stuck to mainstream music. It would be far too easy to pull in a hundred gospel songs influenced by the Bible and none of it would come as a surprise! For the same reason I've deliberately excluded most songs from the Contemporary Christian Music (CCM) genre, although I have included an entry by Larry Norman ("I Wish We'd All Been Ready"), and worship leader Chris Tomlin gets a look-in because his praise song "How Great Is Our God" was interpolated into Chance the Rapper's "How Great."

My intention has been to reveal an often overlooked or ignored strand of influence in popular music. Because we're dealing with a secular art form, it's often assumed that all traces of the Bible have been extinguished. After all, rock 'n' roll is known for resisting conformity, and many people view the Bible as an agent of repression and backwardness. The Bible was on the side of orderliness, self-restraint, obedience, and sacrifice, whereas rock 'n' roll was on the side of anarchy, indulgence, rebellion, and abandon. In 1957, Chuck Berry sang, "Hail, hail, rock 'n' roll / Deliver me from the days of old," and the Bible, for many rock 'n' roll fans, was an integral part of the old days from which they wanted deliverance.

Early rock 'n' roll largely avoided citing the Bible because many of its practitioners were raised in fundamentalist churches and felt forced to make the choice between religious music (gospel) and "worldly" music (blues). Once they had made their choice, they avoided mingling the two forms of music, although some of them, like Elvis, made separate albums of gospel music.

By the mid-1960s, however, the Bible was entering rock music as part of its normal conversation. When a Bob Dylan song ("Highway 61 Revisited," 1965) started, "Oh, God said to Abraham, 'Kill me a son' / Abe said, 'Man, you must be puttin' me on,'" it didn't sound out of place, and today, in the early twenty-first century, it's acceptable for rap stars like Kanye West and Kendrick Lamar to explicitly quote from the Bible.

I'm not arguing that all good songwriters sit down with a thesaurus, a rhyming dictionary, and a copy of the King James Version of the Bible. Some of the "greats"—including Chuck Berry, Brian Wilson, Pete Townshend, and John Lennon—only alluded to the Bible once or twice in their careers. But I argue that the use of biblical language, the references to Bible stories, and the quotation of biblical texts are more widespread than is usually acknowledged.

Some prominent writers—including Dylan, Leonard Cohen, Johnny Cash, Bono, Patti Smith, Bruce Springsteen, Sting, Van Morrison, Nick Cave, and Sufjan Stevens—have repeatedly returned to the Bible for sustenance, challenge, and a framework from within which to understand themselves.

I'm not primarily interested in personal stories of faith in this book because the texts are the subject of the discussion, not the artists. However, it can be illuminating to know what events provoked a composition. For example, it's interesting to note that "Adam Raised a Cain" is not only a reflection of a well-known story in the fourth chapter of Genesis but also a comment on Bruce Springsteen's relationship with his father. With Bob Dylan, it's interesting to know what happened in his life to provoke the stream of explicit gospel songs between 1979 and 1981.

I've included biographical details about the artists so that their songs can be viewed in the context of their lives and careers and also because I can't assume that my readers necessarily know the backgrounds of the people whose work I am discussing. Someone who is automatically familiar with Woody Guthrie, Hank Williams, and Sister Rosetta Tharpe may not know much about Stormzy, Kanye West, or Chance the Rapper, and vice versa.

Each song is followed by a list of basic information about the recording including release date, studio, producer, writers, and recording company. I've included significant cover versions, if they exist, but only up to a maximum of three. The "Also by…" category was an opportunity to mention other tracks by the same artist that also deal with the Bible or religion in some way and may warrant further investigation by the reader. Again, I've restricted myself to three such songs. Because this is a book about the effect of a collection of writings upon a collection of writers, it necessarily focuses on lyrics rather than music. For that reason I haven't included instrumental music that artists may claim was inspired by God—such as the tracks on John Coltrane's *A Love Supreme* (1965)—or even by a biblical passage. It would be impossible to determine how or whether words inspired a particular melody or riff.

There will be a lot of songs that people think should have been included that aren't. This is true for any book of lists. If I explain my selection process, however, this might make these apparent omissions more understandable.

The songs are listed chronologically because I wanted to illustrate the development of biblical usage. Early on, there was caution about using biblical references in pop songs. Record companies didn't want to alienate potential customers in the mainstream market by coming off too religious or offend churchgoers by mingling the sacred and secular. Even in the 1960s, there was concern among executives over the use of the word *God* in "God Only Knows" by the Beach Boys (1966) and *Jesus* in "Mrs. Robinson" by Simon & Garfunkel (1968). They wanted to avoid accusations of blasphemy.

Because of this I have included "Hallelujah I Love Her So" by Ray Charles (1956). The Bible only influenced it in a tangential way, but it's a good example of how the language of Christian and Jewish religion got worked into love songs, thus paving the way for more serious usage in the decades to follow.

The greater acceptance of Bible references in rock and pop has its origin in the folk revival movement that began in the 1930s and 1940s. As a reaction to mass-produced music and the threat of homogeneity presented by Hollywood, Madison Avenue, and Tin Pan Alley, some influential musicians sought inspiration in the simplicity, authenticity, and humanity of ballads, hillbilly songs, hymns, spirituals, and the blues.

Folklorist John A. Lomax began making field recordings of farm laborers and convicts in 1933 for the Archive of American Folk Song held by the

Library of Congress in Washington, DC. Coincidentally, a lot of the songs he collected were religious and were later picked up on by sixties performers looking for "roots" material.

In 1938 and 1939, the inspirational and influential Columbia Records producer John Hammond mounted two concerts at New York's Carnegie Hall under the title *From Spirituals to Swing* to illustrate the connectivity between spiritual, gospel jazz, blues, and big band music. Swing (Count Basie, Benny Goodman) and blues (Big Bill Broonzy, Sonny Terry) shared the same stage as gospel (Sister Rosetta Tharpe, the Golden Gate Quartet). It gave religious music a new dignity. Hammond went on to sign Mahalia Jackson, Bob Dylan, Bruce Springsteen, and Leonard Cohen to Columbia. (Hammond wanted Robert Johnson to appear at the first Carnegie Hall concert, but the blues singer died just months before.)

Another crucial innovator was musician and activist Pete Seeger, who collected recordings with John Lomax in 1938 and went on to form the Almanac Singers in 1941 (a group that included Woody Guthrie) and the Weavers in 1950. Like Lomax and Hammond before him, Seeger was deeply respectful of hymns and spirituals (and composed the song based on Ecclesiastes 3 that gave this book its title).

In 1952, the Folkways Records label released Harry Smith's influential *Anthology of American Folk Music*.[1] Smith, a somewhat eccentric bohemian from New York, had collected rare 78 rpm discs of folk songs, some dating back to the late nineteenth century, and included the best of his finds on six LPs, the third and fourth of which were titled *Social Music* (on the collective sleeve) and individually "Dance" on both sides of the third disc and "Religious" on both sides of the fourth. Here were tracks such as "You Must Be Born Again" and "Oh Death Where Is Thy Sting" by Rev. J. M. Gates, "John the Revelator" by Blind Willie Johnson, and "Since I Laid My Burden Down" by Elders McIntorsh and Edwards' Sanctified Singers.[2]

In 1957, Martin Luther King Jr. helped found the Southern Christian Leadership Conference, an organization that put its weight behind the civil rights movement. King not only seasoned his own rhetoric with phrases from the King James Version of the Bible, but also encouraged the use of songs when marching, campaigning, sitting in, or resisting arrest. Among the most popular songs were the hymns (or adaptations of hymns) "We Shall

Overcome" ("For everyone born of God overcomes the world" [1 John 5:4 NIV]), "This Little Light of Mine" ("Even so let your light shine before men; that they may see your good works, and glorify your Father who is in heaven" [Matthew 5:16 ASV]), and "Go Tell It on the Mountain" ("How beautiful upon the mountains are the feet of him that bringeth good tidings" [Isaiah 52:7]).

Young singers and songwriters in the 1950s and early 1960s looking for alternative forms of music gravitated to the above treasure troves of folk, blues, and gospel. Attendees at the Newport Folk Festival were treated to bills where the gospel of the Dixie Hummingbirds, Reverend Gary Davis, Alex Bradford, and the Staple Singers would be heard alongside the folk of Pete Seeger, the country of Maybelle Carter, and the blues of Willie Dixon, John Lee Hooker, and Muddy Waters.

This environment where gospel was given its rightful seat at the table of authentic American music made it natural for musicians such as Bob Dylan, Joan Baez, Judy Collins, and Peter, Paul, and Mary to incorporate spirituals into their music or to make biblical allusions in their own songs.

The next big impetus was the atmosphere of spiritual questing that affected the counterculture in the mid-1960s. Disillusioned with both main-line Christianity and atheistic materialism, large numbers of Baby Boomers began to explore other forms of religion ranging from Zen Buddhism and Hinduism to monasticism and the occult. The use of religious language became more commonplace in songs.

One of the unintended effects of this was a reappraisal of the Bible. Maybe there were truths in the teachings of Jesus that had been obscured by the close relationship between organized religion and middle-class Western values. The late 1960s and early 1970s saw the rise of the Jesus Movement in America, the musicals *Godspell* and *Jesus Christ Superstar*, and singles like "Spirit in the Sky," "Jesus Was a Cross Maker," and "Oh Happy Day."

In Jamaica, reggae artists such as Bob Marley and Peter Tosh developed a new music that embraced political rebellion, visionary poetry (often inspired by the smoking of ganja), and chunks of the Old Testament and the book of Revelation. Suddenly words like *redemption, exodus, righteous, Zion,* and *Babylon* gained new currency.

Artists such as Bob Dylan, the Band, Leonard Cohen, Bruce Springsteen, and Van Morrison employed biblical language routinely in the 1970s, yet it was controversial when Dylan spoke of having become a "born again" Christian in 1979 and then released a trio of albums with quite explicitly religious songs.

Some argued that it should have come as no surprise because Dylan had always referred to the Bible, but the difference was that the new songs were not using texts for their literary value or out of a sense of solidarity with the black church, but because they reflected his personal beliefs. It was possible for a Greenwich Village folk group to sing about Armageddon without anyone in the audience concluding that they believed in a literal return of Jesus Christ to earth, but anyone listening to Dylan performing "When He Returns," "Are You Ready," or "Property of Jesus" knew that he meant it.

The albums *Slow Train Coming*, *Saved*, and *Shot of Love* helped create a fresh climate where it was safe to refer to the Bible out of personal belief. There had been isolated examples, like the Canadian singer and songwriter Bruce Cockburn, but most Christians in music either gravitated to the CCM industry where church audiences were the primary market or made a distinction between their commercial (secular) material and their niche market (gospel) material for fellow believers.

Yet for the most part Dylan was in an explicit gospel mode when citing the Bible. It wasn't until songs like "Every Grain of Sand," "Heart of Mine," and "The Groom's Still Waiting at the Altar" that he was comfortable integrating biblical references alongside his normal poetic observations of life without the compulsion to convert his listeners.

U2, who emerged in the 1980s, treated the Bible as a source of both lyrical and personal inspiration. Their landmark album *The Joshua Tree* was steeped in biblical imagery as well as biblical attitudes. The yucca palms that gave the album its title were named Joshua trees by nineteenth-century Mormon pilgrims in the Mojave Desert who thought their branches looked like the outstretched arms of the Old Testament patriarch Joshua: "And the LORD said unto Joshua, Stretch out the spear that is in thy hand toward Ai; for I will give it into thine hand. And Joshua stretched out the spear that he had in his hand toward the city" (Joshua 8:18).

When, in November 2005, *Rolling Stone* publisher Jann Wenner asked Bono how big an influence the Bible was on his songwriting, he answered, "It sustains me." Wenner wanted to know whether he meant in the area of belief or as literature. "As a belief," said Bono, ". . . I'm the sort of character who's got to have an anchor."[3]

> I want to be around immovable objects. I want to build my
> house on a rock, because even if the waters are not high
> around the house, I'm going to bring back a storm. I have that
> in me. So it's sort of underpinning for me. I don't read it as a
> historical book. I don't read it as, "Well, that's good advice."
> I let it speak to me in other ways. They call it the *rhema*. It's
> a hard word to translate from Greek, but it sort of means it
> changes in the moment you're in. It seems to do that for me.[4]

Because of their influence as a major stadium band and a significant force in both singles and albums, U2's approach to art fostered a new openness toward the use of Bible references in rock. It provided the ethos in which artists as varied as Nick Cave and the Bad Seeds, the Waterboys, the Call, Mumford & Sons, and Sufjan Stevens could flourish. It could even be argued that they made possible the directness of rap acts such as Kanye West and Kendrick Lamar.

What is certain is that biblical allusions, references, and quotations in rock music are far more prevalent and acceptable today than they were sixty years ago, despite the fact that biblical literacy is declining. In 1989, George Gallup and Jim Castelli revealed that less than half of American adults could name the four Gospels and that even many Christian Americans could only name two to three of the disciples.[5] In 1998, the Barna Research Group found that 82 percent of Americans thought that "God helps those who help themselves" was a Bible verse.[6]

Yet for most of the history of Western civilization, the Bible has provided an enduring reference point. It has not only affected Western religion and values but also language, imaginations, and the collective fund of stories. Some of the greatest Western poets, novelists, and playwrights—even if they disputed the truth of the Bible—relied on a shared knowledge of its teachings and characters among their readership in order to make their points. The term *fatted calf*, for example, has no resonance unless you know the story of the prodigal son. Even *forbidden fruit* loses its power over an audience unfamiliar with the early chapters of Genesis.

Neil MacGregor, former director of Britain's National Gallery, has pointed out that roughly a third of its paintings are of biblical subjects. Literary critic and philosopher George Steiner has said that recognition of the Old and New Testaments has been "the sinew of literacy, the shared matter of intellect and of sentiment from the late sixteenth century onward. The King James Bible and the Luther Bible provided much of our civilization with its alphabet of referential immediacy, not only in the spheres of personal and public piety but in those of politics, social institutions, and the life of the literary and aesthetic imagination."[7]

Therefore, when writers of rock songs reference Cain as the archetypal cursed person or Judas as the ultimate betrayer, they are joining the tradition of Dante and Shakespeare, Donne and Blake, Rembrandt and Caravaggio in using the Bible both as a receptacle of profound shared mythology and a mirror in which to see one's own fallibility and potential glory.

I'm not claiming that these one hundred songs are necessarily the best one hundred examples I could have gleaned from several decades of recorded music, because I've had self-imposed restrictions. I wanted the entries to be spread over the years rather than be too bunched up in one era, and I wanted them to be spread over the genres rather than only from one style. I tried to ensure that the different parts of the Bible were referred to, as well as have different attitudes represented, from the atheistic skepticism of Randy Newman to the overt evangelism of Andraé Crouch.

When I began the project, I thought of only letting each artist have a single entry, but people like Bob Dylan, U2, Leonard Cohen, Bruce Springsteen, Johnny Cash, the Beatles, and the Stones had too many significant songs that I couldn't ignore. I also wanted the whole book to progressively unveil the changing response to the Bible, from the shy inclusion of Hebraic worship terms in Ray Charles to the overt grime gospel of Stormzy.

The hundred songs covered here reference two-thirds of the books in the Bible and over 350 passages. Even though more authors from the Old Testament got a look in, the New Testament ultimately supplied twice as many quotes. The most frequently cited books were Genesis, Exodus, Psalms, Isaiah, Ecclesiastes, Matthew, Mark, Luke, John, and Revelation. The verses most often quoted were Psalm 23:4; 51:2; John 3:16; 9:25; Philippians 2:9; and Revelation 21:4.

It's been a fascinating journey to uncover, and one in which I have participated over the years both as a fan and a commentator. I have met and spoken with many of the key instigators, from Ray Charles, Jerry Lee Lewis, and Johnny Cash to Bruce Springsteen, Bono, John Lennon, Leonard Cohen, and Van Morrison. The interface of religion and popular culture has been my hunting ground as a writer.

I hope the book prompts, provokes, and intrigues as it reveals this often-hidden history. I hope many will respond the way Johnny Cash responded to my book *Hungry for Heaven* when he said to me, "You told me things I never knew, about people I've known all my life."

Steve Turner, London, March 2018

CAN THE CIRCLE BE UNBROKEN (BYE AND BYE)

THE CARTER FAMILY

1

1935

T he original Carter Family recordings significantly influenced American popular music. A. P. Carter sang with his wife, Sara, and her cousin Maybelle (who was married to A. P.'s brother, Ezra), and they recorded for several labels between 1927 and 1944.

Carter was talented not only as a writer and performer but also as an arranger and "catcher" of songs. He traveled through Appalachia collecting music that had been passed down for generations but was in imminent danger of dying out as recorded entertainment replaced oral culture.

Carter found mountain ballads, hymns, fiddle tunes, and spirituals that contained the history and beliefs of people whose family origins were in Ireland, Scotland, England, and Wales. In archiving this varied material, he pioneered what would later be known as American "roots" music, inspiring the folk, gospel, and country movements of the 1940s and 1950s.

Because these songs weren't usually composed with commercial considerations, they spoke from the heart about primal human issues: love, joy, toil, hardship, faith, loss, regret, love, hope, and death. Singing about religion

11

didn't make you a "religious" singer, because religion was regarded as a part of normal life. The secular embraced the sacred just as the sacred embraced the secular. It was only when commercial interests got involved that music needed to be categorized by genre for the purposes of programming and marketing.

Carter didn't have to go far to find the material for "Can the Circle Be Unbroken." "Will the Circle Be Unbroken," a hymn composed by British lyricist Ada Habershon and American musician Charles Gabriel, had first appeared in the 1908 hymnal *Alexander's Gospel Songs* published in Philadelphia.

Charles M. Alexander was an American singer who met Miss Habershon when he visited London in 1905 with renowned evangelist R. A. Torrey. She was a brilliant theologian, the author of several books, and had lectured in America at the invitation of another evangelist, Dwight L. Moody. Alexander invited her to write words for songs that he could perform at Torrey's large public meetings. She obliged with over two hundred lyrics.

"Will the Circle Be Unbroken" became one of the first recorded gospel hymns. In November 1911, the Scottish singer William McEwan, also a friend of Torrey's, performed it in an operatic style for the Columbia label.

It became a favorite hymn of A. P. Carter's mother, Mollie, who, like the rest of the Carters, worshiped at Mount Vernon Methodist Church in Maces Springs, Scott County, Virginia. Although it hadn't appeared in any official Methodist publications, when first recorded by the Carter Family it was in over twenty nondenominational hymnals ranging from *The Highway Hymnal* (1915) to *Spiritual Songs and Hymns* (1935).

A. P. Carter maintained Gabriel's tune and Habershon's chorus but rewrote the verses to tell the story of a single death through the eyes of a loved one, starting with the sight of the hearse arriving at the front door and ending with the empty home after the funeral.

The question posed by the chorus—"Will (or can) the circle be unbroken?"—referred to the family circle. Does death tear us apart irretrievably from our loved ones, or is there hope of heavenly reunion? In Habershon's hymn, the unsettling question was whether or not you would follow your Christian friends and relatives to heaven or face eternal separation. Pre-1935 hymnals suggested the following Bible verses to accompany the hymn: Matthew 25:32 ("And before him shall be gathered all the nations: and he shall separate them one from another, as the shepherd separateth the sheep from the goats" [ASV]), Luke 16:26 ("And besides all this, between us and you there is a great gulf fixed, that they that would pass from hence to you may not be able, and that none may cross over from thence to us" [ASV]), and Matthew 13:49 ("So shall it be in the end of the world: the angels shall come forth, and sever the wicked from among the righteous" [ASV]).

Habershon's version started:

> There are loved ones in the glory
> Whose dear forms you often miss
> When you close your earthly story
> Will you join them in their bliss?

In Carter's version, the issue was whether the stories he'd been told about a heavenly home were trustworthy. Paul said that, for him, being "absent from the body" would mean being "at home with the Lord" (2 Corinthians 5:8 ASV). Jesus used the domestic metaphor when assuring his disciples that heaven contained "many mansions" and that "I go to prepare a place for you" (John 14:2).

Song: "Can the Circle Be Unbroken (Bye and Bye)"

Artist: The Carter Family

Single: A-side: "Can the Circle Be Unbroken (Bye and Bye)" / B-side: "Glory to the Lamb"

Release: July 1935

Studio: ARC Studios, New York, NY

Personnel: A. P. Carter (vocals), Sara Carter (vocals and autoharp), Maybelle Carter (vocals and guitar)

Writer: A. P. Carter

Producer: Ralph Peer

Record Label: Banner Records

Other Significant Recordings: The Brown's Ferry Four (1946), Johnny Cash (1964), Avett Brothers (2002)

Also by the Carter Family: "Can't Feel at Home" (1931), "Glory to the Lamb" (1935), "Never Let the Devil Get the Upper Hand" (1938)

ME AND THE DEVIL BLUES

ROBERT JOHNSON

2

1937

The character of the devil in rock music owes more to the legendary Mississippi blues player Robert Johnson (1911–1938) than to any other musician. He not only embedded the biblical adversary into his songs but also was said to have done a deal with dark forces in order to acquire his talent.

When Johnson took up the blues, it was already known as "the devil's music" because it had developed outside the church; celebrated activities such as lust, drunkenness, violence, and debauchery that the church opposed; and rarely sought God for forgiveness, guidance, or hope. The music of the church didn't wallow in depression or encourage resentment and self-pity. Instead, it promoted joy, hope, and a spirit of thankfulness.

Some blues music also introduced vestigial African beliefs such as voodoo, hexes, charms, and bad spirits. Some of Johnson's twenty-nine recorded compositions (he only ever took part in five brief recording sessions spread over two years) draw on this heritage. "Stones in My Passway," for example, alludes to the voodoo practice of bringing a curse on someone by having them walk unsuspectingly over an arrangement of stones and a personal possession (a button, for example) in what is known as "foot track magic." In "Hell Hound on My Trail," he mentions another voodoo practice of putting "hot foot powder" around a door in order to banish unwanted visitors. This powder would be a concoction of herbs, minerals, chili, salt, and sometimes soil from a grave.

For reasons that no one now knows, Johnson chose to sing about the devil in a very personal way rather than as a distant spirit or a symbol of evil. This has helped consolidate the rumor that his talent itself was attributable to a Faustian deal.

The famous story is told that he was a musician of no great prowess who disappeared from his hometown for six months (or two years, depending on the source), during which time he met the devil at midnight beside a lonely rural crossroads and sold him his soul in return for musical genius. When he returned to the local music joints, he was transformed. He now played guitar with great skill and composed his own songs.

From this distance it's impossible to know Johnson's beliefs or the way in which his audiences received his songs at the time. Johnson biographer Elijah Wald suggested that in the 1930s, the denizens of Mississippi juke joints could well have seen some of his references to the demonic as little more than jokes.

"Me and the Devil Blues" draws from the Bible rather than the spirit world of African ancestry. It speaks of a personal encounter and implies that the devil is no stranger, but also, in some inexplicable way, in control of him. When Satan comes calling, he has to heed his bidding.

The song is not a straightforward narrative, and it's difficult to unpack the action because of the sudden shifts in voice (he addresses the devil in verse one, the listening audience in verse two, and his woman in verse four) and the inexplicable gaps in the story.

In the first verse, the devil calls on him. In the second verse, the two of them are out walking ("side by side"), and then comes the sudden declaration that he's going to beat his woman "until I get satisfied." One assumes that his planned action is somehow provoked by the devil, but this isn't stated.

In the third verse, the woman complains that he's dogging her around (in African American vernacular, "to treat someone badly"), and in the last line he says that this must be the result of "that old evil spirit so deep down in the ground." Is he again referring to the devil, or is he alluding to his own deeply buried evil nature?

The final verse anticipates his death. He claims he won't mind being buried "by the highway side." It's not clear whether the death is one of punishment—execution perhaps—for beating his woman to death or just his inevitable human end. The song's payoff line says that in any case his "old evil spirit" can "get a Greyhound bus and ride."

The story of the devil knocking on his door and walking out with him is reminiscent of the story told in Job where Satan came to God, and when God asked him where he had come from, he answered, "From going to and fro in the earth, and from walking up and down in it" (Job 1:7 ASV). It's also reminiscent of the gospel story of the temptation in the wilderness where Jesus was personally confronted by the devil.

It's notable that the song refers to the devil knocking on the door, but when Johnson answers he addresses him as "Satan." In the Old Testament, there are several mentions of Satan but none of the devil. In the New Testament, the names become interchangeable, so much so that in Revelation 12:9, the writer referred to him as "the great dragon . . . the old serpent, he that is called the Devil and Satan, the deceiver of the whole world" [ASV]. Although Johnson doesn't claim to be a follower of the gospel lifestyle, he appears to accept biblical categories.

Like his life, Johnson's death is swathed in mystery. It appears that he was playing at Three Forks, Mississippi, where he was poisoned by a jealous club owner and died in a nearby hospital in Greenwood on August 16, 1938. Other versions have him being stabbed. No one is certain where he is buried. Everyone agrees that he was only twenty-seven years old.

At the time of his death he was known only to a few. Not all of his recorded work was then released. It was only when the album *Robert Johnson: King of the Delta Blues Singers* was released in 1961 on the Columbia label that he entered the mainstream. His work was manna for young white music fans newly turned on to gospel, country, folk, and blues.

He became an inspiration to people like Bob Dylan, Mick Jagger, Keith Richards, Eric Clapton, Jimmy Page, Jimi Hendrix, and Robert Plant. He was inducted into the Rock and Roll Hall of Fame in 1986. In a twist of irony, the First Presbyterian Church of Dallas has rescued from demolition the building in Dallas where he recorded "Me and the Devil Blues" and "Hell Hound on My Trail," making it part of Encore Park.

Song: "Me and the Devil Blues"

Artist: Robert Johnson

Single: A-side: "Me and the Devil Blues," take 1 / B-side: take 2

Release: May 1937

Studio: 508 Park Avenue, Dallas, TX

Personnel: Robert Johnson (guitar and vocals)

Writer: Robert Johnson

Producer: Don Law

Record Label: Vocalion

Other Notable Recordings: Peter Green (2001), Eric Clapton (2004), Gil Scott Heron (2010)

Also by Robert Johnson: "If I Had Possession over Judgment Day" (1936), "Hell Hound on My Trail" (1937), "Cross Road Blues" (1937)

JESUS CHRIST

WOODY GUTHRIE

3

1945

Woody Guthrie (1912–1967) became a significant influence on the way rock music developed, particularly in its social and political concerns. His most prominent disciple was Bob Dylan, who tracked him down to a New Jersey hospital in 1961 when he was dying of the degenerative brain disease Huntington's chorea. Musicians as diverse as Billy Bragg, Bono, Joe Strummer (the Clash), Roger McGuinn (the Byrds), Bruce Springsteen, Jackson Browne, Donovan, Wilco, Joan Baez, and Tom Morello of Rage Against the Machine have also celebrated him.

Born in Okemah, Oklahoma, Guthrie documented his times mainly through song and had a particular passion for the downtrodden, excluded, and sinned against. He wrote from his direct experiences of the hobo life, living with migrants, and joining protests against workers' pay and conditions. He consciously made himself a voice for those who had no voice.

During World War II, he railed against fascism—his guitar famously bore the legend "This Machine Kills Fascists"—but was also a communist sympathizer, something that turned him into a controversial figure during the Cold War period. He lived and worked with folk revivalist Pete Seeger and was a close friend of Huddie "Lead Belly" Ledbetter.

His passions were always equality, justice, and peace. In 1940, Irving Berlin's "God Bless America" annoyed him so much that he wrote a riposte he originally titled "God Blessed America" but finally became "This Land Is Your Land."

During the same period, he composed "Jesus Christ." "I wrote this song looking out of a rooming house window in New York City in the winter of 1940," he wrote on his original manuscript. "I saw how the poor folks lived, and then I saw how the rich folk lived, and the poor folks down and out and cold and hungry, and the rich ones out drinking good whiskey and celebrating and wasting handfuls of money on gambling and women, and I got to thinking about what Jesus said, and what if He was to walk into New York City and preach like he used to. They'd lock him back in jail as sure as you're reading this. 'Even as you've done it unto the least of these little ones, you have done it unto me.'"[8]

He set his feelings to the tune of the folk song "Jesse James."

As a child in Oklahoma, Guthrie was baptized into the Church of Christ, but as an adult was interested in many religions without signing up to any. However, the figure of Jesus Christ exercised a particular fascination that never left him. "It ain't just once in awhile that I think about this man," he said. "It's mighty scarce that I think of anything else."[9] Once asked to name the people he most admired, he answered, "Will Rogers and Jesus Christ."[10]

He saw Jesus as a champion of the poor and a scourge of the rich, a fearless challenger of political, religious, and military authority, a promoter of peace and a believer in the power of love. "Jesus Christ" became the template for later popular songs that portrayed Jesus as a political irritant, such as "Ballad of the Carpenter" by Phil Ochs (1965), Kris Kristofferson's "They Killed Him" (1985), "The Rebel Jesus" by Jackson Browne (2005), and "Jesus Was a Democrat" by Everclear (2008). The *Billboard* singles reviewer in 1945 sniffily noted, "'Jesus Christ' is social rather than spiritual."[11]

The story told in the song is simple. Jesus travels around preaching, and part of his message (in Guthrie's retelling) is "sell all of your jewelry, and give it to the poor." This upsets the rich and powerful—Guthrie names them as bankers, preachers, cops, soldiers, and landlords—and, as a result, they arrange for him to be terminated.

The main biblical source is the encounter between Jesus and a wealthy ruler recorded in Matthew and Luke. The man asked Jesus what he needed to do to gain "eternal life" and was told that he should keep the commandments. He argued that he had always obeyed these rules, but Jesus said, "If thou wouldest be perfect, go, sell that which thou hast, and give to the poor, and thou shalt have treasure in heaven: and come, follow me" (Matthew 19:21 ASV).

This statement made the man go away "sorrowful" because, as Matthew put it, "he was one that had great possessions" (v. 22 ASV). The response of Jesus was, "Verily I say unto you, It is hard for a rich man to enter into the kingdom of heaven. And again I say unto you, It is easier for a camel to go through a needle's eye, than for a rich man to enter into the kingdom of God" (vv. 23–24 ASV).

Members of the first church in Jerusalem "had all things common . . . and parted them to all, according as any man had need" (Acts 2:44–45 ASV). This was an inspirational idea to Guthrie. "When there shall be no want among you, because you'll own everything in common," he wrote. "When the rich will give their goods into the poor. I believe in this way. I just can't believe in any other way. This is the Christian way and it is already on a big part of the earth and it will come. To own everything in common. That's what the Bible says. Common means all of us. This is pure old 'commonism.'"[12]

In the hospital at the end of his life, he frequently read the Bible, apparently taking more note of Jesus as Savior and healer than he had done during his active years. "I see my words of soulful healing lots plainer in my bibledy book," he wrote. "God is my best doctor, Jesus is my tippytop best teacher on every work."[13]

Song: "Jesus Christ"

Artist: Woody Guthrie

Single: A-side: "Jesus Christ" / B-side: "New York Town"

Album: *Woody Guthrie* (from "The Asch Recordings," vol. 1)

Release: March 1945

Studio: Asch Recording Studio, New York, NY

Personnel: Woody Guthrie (guitar, vocals)

Writer: Woody Guthrie

Producer: Moses "Moe" Asch

Label: Asch

Other Significant Recordings: Bob Dylan (1960, private recording), U2 (1988), Merle Haggard (2009)

Also by Woody Guthrie: "Ezekiel Saw the Wheel" (1944), "Glory" (1944), "This Morning I Was Born Again" (1945)

4 STRANGE THINGS HAPPENING EVERY DAY

SISTER ROSETTA THARPE

1945

S trange Things Happening Every Day," with its honky-tonk piano and electric lead guitar, is a contender for the title of "first rock 'n' roll record," released almost a decade before Elvis Presley entered a recording studio. It was the first gospel song to get near the top of Billboard's newly created Juke Box Race Records chart (number 2 in April 1945). Jerry Lee Lewis used it as one of his audition pieces when he first met with Sam Phillips of Sun Records.

Sister Rosetta Tharpe (1915–1973) was born in Cotton Plant, Arkansas, but moved to Chicago when she was six. Raised in the Church of God in Christ (COGIC), she learned to play guitar and piano at an early age and accompanied her evangelist mother, Katie, on preaching tours. She honed her skills in tent meetings and revivals, but in 1938 she disappointed her COGIC friends by moving to New York to play in mainstream venues such as the Cotton Club and Apollo in Harlem and Café Society in Greenwich Village. She signed a record contract with Decca and recorded not only gospel music but also secular songs with Lucky Millinder and His Orchestra.

She even appeared in a *Life* magazine feature where she was photographed at a private party with such musical legends of the era as Cab Calloway, Duke Ellington, Billie Holiday, and Bud Freeman.

Sister Rosetta Tharpe was like nothing else on the music scene at the time—a spiritual singer who played in jazz clubs, a woman who played electric guitar, an Arkansas cotton-field girl who'd become the toast of fashionable white society. Her voice was powerful and exuberant, and her guitar style was ragged yet beautiful.

"Strange Things Happening Every Day" was ostensibly a poke at church people, telling them to walk the straight and narrow. The "strange things" of the title and chorus refer to their wayward, but unnamed, activities. She may have been implicitly condemning them for their condemnation of her. She thought them strange for believing she was strange.

However, it could also be an outsider's view of Pentecostal worship—especially in the black community. Doesn't the experience of seeing people speak in unknown tongues, collapse in spiritual reveries, and receive instant healing appear to be strange to the uninitiated? The first outsiders to experience Christian worshipers speaking "with other tongues" mocked them, saying, "They are filled with new wine" (Acts 2:4, 13 ASV).

The origin of the phrase she used in the song comes from the gospel story of a sick man who was lowered through a gap in the tiles on the roof of a house so that he could be placed right in front of Jesus, who then healed him on the spot because of his demonstration of faith. "And immediately he rose up before them, and took up that whereon he lay, and departed to his house, glorifying God. And amazement took hold on all, and they glorified God; and they were filled with fear, saying, We have seen strange things to-day" (Luke 5:25–26 ASV).

Long after the single had left the "race" charts, it had an impact on the pioneer rock 'n' roll musicians when it was played over and over in Memphis by DJ Dewey Phillips on his WHBQ program "Red Hot & Blue." Elvis, Jerry Lee Lewis, Carl Perkins, and Johnny Cash were all big fans of the singing and playing of Sister Rosetta Tharpe.

Song: "Strange Things Happening Every Day"

Artist: Sister Rosetta Tharpe

Single: A-side: "Two Little Fishes and Five Loaves of Bread" / B-side: "Strange Things Happening Every Day"

Release: March 1945

Studio: Decca Recording Studio, New York, NY

Personnel: Rosetta Tharpe (guitar, vocals), Sammy Price (piano), Abe Bolar (bass), Harold "Doc" West (drums)

Writer: Rosetta Tharpe

Label: Decca

Chart Position: 2 (US R&B singles chart)

Other Significant Recordings: Etta James (1960), Johnny Cash (1979), Michelle Shocked (2007), Tom Jones (2010)

Also by Sister Rosetta Tharpe: "God Don't Like It" (1939), "Didn't It Rain" (1948), "Up Above My Head I Hear Music in the Air" (1948) by Sister Rosetta Tharpe and Marie Knight with the Sam Price Trio

5

I SAW THE LIGHT

HANK WILLIAMS

....

1948

One of the first professional recordings ever made by Hank Williams (1923–1953), this song was inspired by a comment his mother made when driving him back home to Montgomery, Alabama, from a show in Fort Deposit. Williams, who'd been drinking, was asleep in the back seat, and when his mother saw the lights of the airport in the distance, she realized they were approaching the city. "I just saw the lights," she announced as she turned to rouse her worse-for-the-wear son. The phrase became the seed of the song he would write on January 26, 1947.

"I Saw the Light" develops a theme that would become characteristic of post-war country music—the reprobate who sees the error of his ways, repents, and seeks to change his life. The world in such songs is viewed in terms of opposites: light/darkness, happiness/sorrow, right/wrong, and sight/blindness. There are no gradations of morality or category confusions. The choices are stark, and our responsibility is total.

Having been brought up a Baptist, Williams knew this world well. His mother played the church organ, and his father was a drunkard who abandoned the family. He heard sermons that warned of the wickedness of sin, the necessity of conversion, and the foolishness of delaying that decision.

It left him with a lifelong fear that he would ultimately be condemned to hell.

Although only twenty-three, he already had a reputation for alcoholism, brawling, gambling, and womanizing, but the transformation outlined in "I Saw the Light" wasn't autobiographical. Although he periodically developed good intentions, he never gave up his godless ways or returned to the church. His attachment to religion was powered by sentiment and fear rather than commitment and joy. When he was feeling boisterous and self-indulgent, he wrote honky-tonk songs like "Backache Blues" and "I'm a Long Gone Daddy." When he was feeling maudlin and remorseful, he wrote hymns like "Are You Walking and A-Talking for the Lord," "Jesus Remembered Me," and "Wealth Won't Save Your Soul."

"I Saw the Light" came from his religious memory and would have pleased his mother. It doesn't specify the particular problems that beset him, opting instead for vague references to sinning and straying. The reasons for the big change are themselves self-indulgent: he wants to avoid worry, fear, and sorrow, and get a sense of direction back into his life.

The particular image of light used comes from the conversion of Saul of Tarsus on the road to Damascus as told in the book of Acts. Saul was a zealous Jew involved in harassing and intimidating members of the Jesus religion, but while traveling to Damascus to cause more havoc he was literally floored by a personal vision of Jesus.

> Now as he journeyed he approached Damascus, and suddenly a light from heaven flashed about him. And he fell to the ground and heard a voice saying to him, "Saul, Saul, why do you persecute me?" And he said, "Who are you, Lord?" And he said, "I am Jesus, whom you are persecuting; but rise and enter the city, and you will be told what you are to do." The men who were traveling with him stood speechless, hearing the voice but seeing no one. Saul arose from the ground; and when his eyes were opened, he could see nothing; so they led him by the hand and brought him into Damascus. And for three days he was without sight, and neither ate nor drank. (Acts 9:3–9 RSV)

Saul's transformation from persecutor of the followers of Jesus to early church theologian and prototypical missionary became the archetypal story of Christian conversion.

Williams, however, links Saul's experience with Jesus's healing of blind people. In particular, he may have been thinking of the man whom Jesus healed by softening clay with spittle and rubbing it into the man's eyes. This man said, "Whether he is a sinner, I know not: one thing I know, that, whereas I was blind, now I see" (John 9:25 ASV), a line that John Newton incorporated into his eighteenth-century hymn "Amazing Grace."

The final biblical reference in "I Saw the Light" comes when he admits that he was a fool to stray, "For strait is the gate and narrow the way." Many song transcriptions present this as "straight is the gate," but Williams is referring to the archaic word *strait* ("of limited spatial capacity") used in the King James Version of the Bible: "Enter ye in at the strait gate: for wide is the gate, and broad is the way, that leadeth to destruction, and many there be which go in thereat: Because strait is the gate, and narrow is the way, which leadeth unto life, and few there be that find it" (Matthew 7:13–14).

Hank Williams was pronounced dead the morning of January 1, 1953, after being driven through West Virginia in his 1952 Cadillac. He had been slumped in the back seat for several hours. The cause of death was "acute right ventricular dilation." He was twenty-nine years old.

Song: "I Saw the Light"

Artist: Hank Williams (with his Drifting Cowboys)

Single: A-side: "I Saw the Light" / B-side: "Six More Miles (to the Graveyard)"

Release: September 1948

Studio: Castle Studio, Tulane Hotel, Nashville, TN

Personnel: Hank Williams (guitar, vocals), Zeke Turner (guitar), Zeb Turner (guitar), Bronson "Barefoot Brownie" Reynolds (bass), Tommy Johnson (fiddle), Dale "Smokey" Lohman (steel guitar)

Writer: Hank Williams

Producer: Fred Rose

Label: MGM

Other Significant Recordings: Roy Acuff (1948), Emmylou Harris (1969), Merle Haggard (1971), Aaron Neville (2003)

Also by Hank Williams: "When God Comes and Gathers His Jewels" (1948), "Jesus Died for Me" (1950), "The Angel of Death" (1954)

JEZEBEL

FRANKIE LAINE

6

1951

F rankie Laine (1913–2007) was one of the best-selling pop artists in the era after World War II and before Elvis. Born in Chicago to Sicilian immigrants, he learned to sing in the choir of the church of the Immaculate Conception and changed his name from Francesco Paolo LoVecchio when he started recording in 1947.

"Jezebel," written by Wayne Shanklin, uses the name of Israelite King Ahab's Phoenician wife recorded in 1 Kings and 2 Kings to describe a wicked woman. The lyrics liken her to the "devil" and a fallen angel, but all that the Jezebel of the song had done was to hold out more promise than she delivered. Her eyes project "paradise" but leave the smitten narrator with grief.

Jezebel has come to represent "an impudent, shameless, or morally unrestrained woman," typically one who schemes and tempts. First Kings doesn't portray Jezebel as a sexual temptress. Her main evil was getting Ahab to worship the idol Baal (of whom she was a devotee) rather than the God of Jacob, Moses, and Abraham. She had prophets executed, and she bumped off Naboth so she could seize his vineyard and gift it to Ahab. Eventually she was trampled to death by horses.

Jezebel's reputation for sexiness originated from the New Testament book of Revelation where God warned the church of Thyatira: "I have this against thee, that thou sufferest the woman Jezebel, who calleth herself a prophetess; and she teacheth and seduceth my servants to commit fornication, and to eat things sacrificed to idols. And I gave her time that she should repent; and she willeth not to repent of her fornication. Behold, I cast her into a bed, and them that commit adultery with her into great tribulation, except they repent of her works" (Revelation 2:20–22 ASV). It appears that this use of the name Jezebel was a biblical example of antonomasia—when a proper name expresses a general idea or archetype (such as referring to a miserly person as Scrooge)—in this case describing someone who had lured people away from God to idol worship, possibly using temple prostitutes as an enticement.

Jezebel has been featured in a lot of rock and pop songs since, including "Lies" by the Rolling Stones (1978), "Stay with Me" (1971) by the Faces (with Rod Stewart), "My Lovely Jezebel" by Elvis Costello (2010), and "Hard Headed Woman" (1958) by Elvis Presley. Song titles with the name *Jezebel* have been recorded by Sade (1985), 10,000 Maniacs (1992), Ricky Martin (2000), Dizzee Rascal (2003), Depeche Mode (2009), and others.

Song: "Jezebel"

Artist: Frankie Laine

Single: A-side: "Jezebel" / B-side: "Rose, Rose, I Love You"

Release: April 1951

Studio: Columbia Studios, New York, NY

Personnel: Frankie Laine (vocals), Carl Fischer (piano), Norman Luboff Choir (vocals), Mitch Miller and His Orchestra

Writer: Wayne Shanklin

Producer: Mitch Miller

Label: Columbia

Highest Chart Position: 2 (US)

Other Significant Recordings: Edith Piaf (1951), Everly Brothers (1962), Tom Jones (2012)

Also by Frankie Laine: "God Bless the Child" (1949), "Let Me Be Ready, Lord" (1954), "Dammit Isn't God's Last Name" (1969)

7

IF YOU BELIEVE
JOHNNIE RAY

1954

I rving Berlin was one of the twentieth century's greatest writers of popular songs. Born in Siberia as Israel Baline in 1888, his father was a cantor in the local synagogue. The family immigrated to America in 1892 and settled in New York, where Berlin remained until his death at the age of 101.

His songs became so ubiquitous and celebrated that it was said of him that he didn't have a place in American music—he *was* American music. Among his best-known songs are "Cheek to Cheek," "Alexander's Ragtime Band," "Puttin' on the Ritz," "Easter Parade," "White Christmas," and "God Bless America."

In 1954, a film was made with Marilyn Monroe and Ethel Merman that took "There's No Business Like Show Business," a 1946 song he'd written for the stage musical *Annie Get Your Gun*, as its title and theme song. The rest of the film's songs were taken from Berlin's back catalog.

It told the story of a show business family troupe, and to appeal to the emerging teenage market, the twenty-seven-year old singer Johnnie Ray (1927–1990) was cast as one of the sons. Ray had come to prominence in 1951 with his hit songs "Cry" and "The Little White Cloud That Cried." Tall and skinny and with large protruding ears, he didn't look like a conventional heartthrob, but his emotionally charged performances that would see him dropping to his knees and even weeping stirred teenage girl fans in the way that Frank Sinatra had done and Elvis Presley would do.

Ray's character turns his back on show business, much to the disapproval of his parents, and declares that he's going to enter the priesthood. At this point, he breaks into song with Berlin's "If You Believe," a most unusual number for an idol of teenagers to be singing because it's a pointed, challenging sermon set to music.

The song seems to say that if you believe in something wholeheartedly, the strength of your belief makes it true—"If you believe that there's a heaven / You'll get to heaven"—and may have been inspired by the recently published bestseller *The Power of Positive Thinking* by Norman Vincent Peale, pastor of the Marble Collegiate Church in New York. Peale promoted the idea of autosuggestion, where people overcame their doubts and fears by focusing on desired outcomes and talking themselves out of negativity.

The body of the song starts with a single New Testament reference to "doubting" Thomas, the disciple who wouldn't accept that Jesus had been resurrected: "Except I shall see in his hands the print of the nails, and put my finger into the print of the nails, and put my hand into his side" (John 20:25 ASV). Appropriately, for a Jewish songwriter, Berlin then continues with four Old Testament stories that have traditionally strained the credulity of rationalists. The first is the story of Jonah being "swallowed up by a whale" (Jonah 1:17), the second is Daniel's ability to survive being thrown in with "lions that roared" (Daniel 6:7–27), the third is Noah and the ark (Genesis 6–9), and the fourth is Moses's encounters with God on Mount Sinai when he received the laws (Exodus 19–32).

Although the song affirmed the Bible, it was considered risky at the time to mix religion and entertainment. The production code that then governed Hollywood deemed that movies should contain no profanity (mentions of God, Jesus, and Lord had to be reverent), and said that the clergy, religious beliefs, and religious ceremonies should not be ridiculed. The production code office monitored the shooting of Ray's rendition of "If You Believe," and a priest was on hand to ensure that nothing about it would be offensive to the Catholic church.

Even so, not everyone was impressed. C. A. Lejeune (Caroline Lejeune), the film critic of London's *Observer* newspaper, called *There's No Business Like Show Business* "an insult to intelligence, religion, music, Ethel Merman, good taste, and the human soul."

Song: "If You Believe"

Artist: Johnnie Ray

Single: A-side: "If You Believe" / B-side: "Alexander's Ragtime Band"

Album: *There's No Business Like Show Business*
(movie soundtrack, various artists)

Release: December 1954

Studio: Twentieth Century Fox Recording Stage, Hollywood, CA

Personnel: Johnnie Ray (vocals), Percy Faith and His Orchestra

Writer: Irving Berlin

Label: Columbia

Highest Chart Position: 7 (US), 5 (UK)

Also by Johnnie Ray: "A Sinner Am I" (1952), "I'm Gonna Walk and Talk with My Lord" (1952), "The Touch of God's Hand" (1952)

HALLELUJAH I LOVE HER SO

8

RAY CHARLES

1956

With his first single, Ray Charles made a musical move that would have deep implications for the development of rock 'n' roll. He took the style of gospel, and in this case some of the language, and made secular music of it.

The African American churches were a powerful breeding ground for entertainers. They schooled their young in vocal performance, harmony, composition, and arrangement. Many of them learned to play instruments to take part in services. They also learned the art of using music to express life's deepest passions and truths. Emotional commitment to the words of a song was stressed.

All the pioneers of black American music during this period—Louis Armstrong, Duke Ellington, John Coltrane, Little Richard, Chuck Berry, Aretha Franklin, Nina Simone—got their start in the church. Where else could you be exposed to so much good music and get a free education as a soloist, group member, choir singer, conductor, or leader?

However, it was frowned on to use such "God-given talents" for mere entertainment or to sing songs about fleshly delights. Yes, gospel was great music, but its purpose was to praise God, consolidate doctrine, and act as a beacon of righteousness. The techniques and skills learned were not to bring glory or wealth to individuals.

Ray Charles was raised in a Baptist church but loved blues and jazz as much as he did gospel. In late 1954, he wrote "I Got a Woman" with his trumpet player, Renald Richard, after hearing the gospel song "It Must Be Jesus" by Bob King and the Southern Tones, which was a reworking of the spiritual "There's a Man Goin' 'round Takin' Names" that was first recorded by Josh White in 1933. He took the structure of the gospel song and filled it with blues-style lyrics. In January 1955, it became the first of his singles to hit the R&B charts. Later that year, he performed the same magic on the hymn "This Little Light of Mine," turning it into the hit "This Little Girl of Mine."

"Hallelujah I Love Her So" was modeled very closely on the song "That's Why I Love Him So" written by James Cleveland and recorded by the Gospel All Stars in 1953 on the Apollo label. Oddly enough, *hallelujah*—a Hebrew term meaning "praise the Lord"—doesn't occur in Cleveland's gospel song. Charles could have totally disguised its origins, but instead chose to openly combine the sacred and the secular.

Actually the word *hallelujah* (or *alleluia* as it is often spelled), occurs a lot in hymns and prayers. The Hebrew term is used only twenty-four times, exclusively in the book of Psalms. Also, there are only four mentions of its Greek form in the New Testament (Revelation 19:1, 3, 4, and 6) and they are all delivered by those gathered around the heavenly throne of God.

Song: "Hallelujah I Love Her So"

Artist: Ray Charles

Single: A-side: "Hallelujah I Love Her So" /
B-side: "What Would I Do without You"

Release: May 1956

Studio: Atlantic Studios, New York, NY

Personnel: Ray Charles (vocals, piano), Don Wilkerson (tenor saxophone), Cecil Payne (baritone saxophone), Joshua Willis (trumpet), Joe Bridgewater (trumpet), Paul West (upright bass), Panama Francis (drums)

Writer: Ray Charles

Producer: Jerry Wexler

Label: Atlantic

Other Significant Recordings: Harry Belafonte (1958), Eddie Cochran (1959), Tony Sheridan and the Beat Brothers (1962)

Also by Ray Charles: "Sinner's Prayer" (1957), "My God and I" (1975), "So Help Me God" (1993)

9   I WALK THE LINE
JOHNNY CASH
1956

When Johnny Cash met producer Sam Phillips at Sun Records in 1955, he wanted to make gospel records, but Phillips wasn't interested because it wasn't a market he understood or had good commercial connections with. He'd had one attempt to sell gospel, but it had failed. He wanted his artists to make music for the expanding teenage market that loved R&B and wanted records that were different from the smooth sounds bought by their parents.

Cash's third single, his first pop chart hit, had the rhythm and beat that Phillips loved, but it was also intrinsically Christian without being overtly religious. Cash had never rejected his Baptist upbringing, loved spirituals and hymns, and still aimed to live and think as a Christian. However, he was aware of the temptations of pride, vanity, and infidelity that came with his newfound fame. He'd played on bills with Elvis and saw how music excited crowds and raised levels of sexual energy.

His intention with "I Walk the Line" was to write a song that was both autobiographical and profound. It was the earliest indication of his major theme of the struggle between good intentions and bad desires. Initiated by his recent marriage to Vivian Liberto, it had a broader application because it was about faithfulness, obedience, and the need for moral vigilance. It was a song that could be sung to Vivian, but it was also a song that could be sung to God. On the human level it was a pledge. On the spiritual level it was a prayer.

"Walking the line" wasn't a phrase that Cash coined. In his 1946 song "Sixteen Tons," Merle Travis sang, "Can't no high-toned woman make me walk the line." It meant keeping the rules, taking responsibility, and not straying.

The song is set up by its opening line, "I keep a close watch on this heart of mine," which establishes the source of the problem (the heart) and his resolution (to guard it). As a Bible reader, Cash was aware of verses such as "The heart is deceitful above all things, and it is exceedingly corrupt: who can know it?" (Jeremiah 17:9 ASV) and "But the things which proceed out of the mouth come forth out of the heart; and they defile the man. For out of the heart come forth evil thoughts, murders, adulteries, fornications, thefts, false witness, railings" (Matthew 15:18–19 ASV).

There were other verses urging the faithful to protect and monitor their hearts: "Keep thy heart with all diligence; for out of it are the issues of life" (Proverbs 4:23 ASV); and to be vigilant: "Watch ye, stand fast in the faith" (1 Corinthians 16:13 ASV).

His reference to "the tie that binds" is ambiguous. In the context of marital fidelity, it would refer to his marriage vows, but the phrase may have come to him from the popular eighteenth-century hymn "Blest Be the Tie That Binds" written by John Fawcett in which the tie is the love of God expressed as the love of Christians for each other:

> Blest be the tie that binds
> Our hearts in Christian love;
> The fellowship of kindred minds
> Is like to that above.

He may even have been thinking more esoterically. Jewish practice, based on teaching in Deuteronomy 11:18, was to put the written laws into small boxes and tie them to their wrists and foreheads as a way of making them visual reminders of their commitment. The biblical wisdom writer said:

My son, keep the commandment of thy father, and forsake
not the law of thy mother: Bind them continually upon thy
heart, tie them about thy neck. When thou walkest, it shall lead
thee. When thou sleepest, it shall watch over thee; and when
thou awakest, it shall talk with thee. For the commandment is
a lamp; and the law is light; and reproofs of instruction are the
way of life. (Proverbs 6:20–23 ASV)

Writing in 1975, Cash admitted that his aim with "I Walk the Line" was
to write something "that says I'm going to be true not only to those who
believe in me and depend on me, but to myself and God—a song that might
give courage to others as well as myself."[16] In 2003, the year he died, he told
Robert Hilburn of the *LA Times*, "Sam [Phillips] never knew it, but 'I Walk
the Line' was my first gospel hit."[17]

Song: "I Walk the Line"

Artist: Johnny Cash

Single: A-side: "Get Rhythm" / B-side: "I Walk the Line"

Release: May 1, 1956

Studio: Sun Records, Memphis, TN

Personnel: Johnny Cash (acoustic guitar, vocals), Luther Perkins
(electric guitar), Marshall Grant (bass guitar)

Writer: Johnny Cash

Producer: Sam Phillips

Label: Sun

Highest Chart Position: 17 (USA)

Other Significant Recordings: Burl Ives (1961), the
Everly Brothers (1963), Brook Benton (1966)

Also by Johnny Cash: "My God Is Real" (1962), "Were You There
(When They Crucified My Lord)" (1963), "Belshazzar" (1964)

10

(THERE'LL BE) PEACE IN THE VALLEY (FOR ME)

ELVIS PRESLEY

1957

Elvis Presley, who attended Assembly of God churches in Tupelo and then Memphis, had early aspirations to be a gospel singer. He was friendly with members of the Blackwood Brothers, one of the leading Southern gospel quartets of the 1940s and 50s, and as a teenager even auditioned for the Songfellows Quartet, a younger group that acted as a feeder group for the Blackwoods.

When he and fellow Sun artists Johnny Cash, Carl Perkins, and Jerry Lee Lewis gathered around the studio piano for a spontaneous singalong on December 4, 1956, they chose predominantly hymns, spirituals, or gospel songs. Among the songs—released decades later on the album *The Million Dollar Quartet*—was "Peace in the Valley."

Thomas A. Dorsey, a blues musician from Atlanta, Georgia, who'd undergone a Christian conversion in the 1920s and had turned his talents toward expressing his faith, had written the song in 1939 while traveling from his home in Chicago to a gospel choir convention.

On the train journey, he was reading about the buildup to the war between Britain and Germany in the morning newspaper and was struck by the contrast between these serious political events and the harmony between animals and nature he was seeing from the window of his carriage. "Horses, cows, sheep, were all grazing together in this little valley and up the hill I could see water falling," he later explained. "Everything seemed so peaceful. It made me wonder what the matter was with us humans. Why couldn't Man live in peace like the animals down there?"[14]

It reminded him of an old spiritual, "We Shall March through the Valley," that was included in the 1867 anthology *Slave Songs of the United States* and was played by Lead Belly as "We Shall Walk through the Valley in Peace" when the Library of Congress recorded him in 1943.

> We shall walk through the valley of the shadow of death
> We shall walk through the valley in peace
> And if Jesus himself will be our savior
> We shall walk through the valley in peace.

Although Dorsey kept the gist of the title, he would take his song in another direction—away from the "valley of the shadow of death" described in Psalm 23 (the basis of the spiritual) and toward the "new heaven and a new earth" described in Revelation 21.

When Dorsey wrote of there being "no more sadness, no more trouble," he was conscious of the verses, "And he shall wipe away every tear from their eyes; and death shall be no more; neither shall there mourning, nor crying, nor pain, any more: the first things are passed away. And he that sitteth on the throne said, Behold, I make all things new" (Revelation 21:4–5 ASV).

He then painted an idyllic scene of gentle bears, tame wolves, lions that coexist with lambs, and children leading wild beasts. These images are taken directly from a prophecy of Isaiah about the future reign of the Messiah.

> The wolf also shall dwell with the lamb, and the leopard shall
> lie down with the kid; and the calf and the young lion and the
> fatling together; and a little child shall lead them. And the cow
> and the bear shall feed; their young ones shall lie down together:
> and the lion shall eat straw like the ox. And the sucking child

shall play on the hole of the asp, and the weaned child shall put his hand on the cockatrice' den. They shall not hurt nor destroy in all my holy mountain: for the earth shall be full of the knowledge of the LORD, as the waters cover the sea. (11:6–9)

Dorsey, known as the "father of gospel music," had a knack not only of matching commercial sounds with orthodox Christian teaching but also of linking personal experience with the stories and language of the Bible. He was always concerned about reaching people where they were and lifting them up to a higher truth. Gospel historian Tony Heilbut said of him in 1971, "Everything contemporary music aims for, Dorsey accomplished, welding gospel, blues, jazz, and country music into a distinctive musical style. In the mid-fifties, rhythm-and-blues groups began using simple, funky melodies swiped from Dorsey tunes. Dorsey, in turn, had adapted the plaintive refrains of the twenties. So longest way round is shortest way home."[15]

Elvis chose to sing "Peace in the Valley" with the vocal backing of the Jordanaires when he appeared on *The Ed Sullivan Show* on January 6, 1957. It seemed a surprising departure for the man best known at that point for gyrations that required careful camera framing to keep him modest, but was in fact an aspect of his background and complex nature that had always been there.

It was Ed Sullivan, not Elvis, who appeared embarrassed by the choice. The producers wanted him to stick to rock 'n' roll, but Elvis—who was now powerful enough to get his own way—insisted that he would only appear if he could do his mother's favorite hymn. Sullivan introduced him by mentioning that Elvis was about to do a charity concert in Los Angeles to raise funds for those affected by the recent Hungarian uprising and then said, "Now he's going to sing a song, er . . . he feels that this is sort of in the mood that he'd like to create. 'Peace in the Valley.' Here is Elvis Presley."

The girls started to scream, as they had done for "Hound Dog," but soon realized that this was not an appropriate response. Whereas he had joked around earlier in the show and deliberately teased his audience, he was deadly serious when delivering gospel.

Exactly a week later, in a Hollywood studio, Elvis reconvened with his trio and the Jordanaires to record the song for what would become a gospel EP. The other songs were "I Believe" (previously recorded by Frankie Laine), "It Is No Secret (What God Can Do)," and Dorsey's classic song "Take My Hand, Precious Lord."

Song: "(There'll Be) Peace in the Valley (for Me)"

Artist: Elvis Presley

Extended Play Record: *Peace in the Valley*

Release: April 1957

Studio: Radio Recorders, Los Angeles, CA

Personnel: Elvis Presley (vocals and acoustic guitar), Scotty Moore (electric guitar), Bill Black (bass guitar), D. J. Fontana (drums), the Jordanaires (background vocals), Gordon Stoker (piano)

Writer: Thomas A. Dorsey

Producer: Steve Sholes

Label: RCA

Highest Chart Position: 39 (US)

Other Significant Recordings: Red Foley (1951), Loretta Lynn (1965), Dolly Parton (2003)

Also by Elvis Presley: "Take My Hand, Precious Lord" (1957), "Crying in the Chapel" (1965), "He Touched Me" (1972)

GREAT BALLS OF FIRE
JERRY LEE LEWIS

11

1957

The title "Great Balls of Fire" was a double entendre. On the one hand it was an expression of amazement; on the other it was a description of male sexual excitement. Jerry Lee Lewis was initially reluctant to sing it. He felt it would be sinful to do so. But after a densely theological conversation with producer Sam Philips in the studio, he relented and tore into it with the feeling that he was doing something damnable, giving his performance an added defiant frisson.

The expression "great balls of fire" originated in the South during the nineteenth century and had its origins in biblical stories of God being revealed as fire. Moses confronted God in a burning bush (Exodus 3:1–17), the Israelites were guided at night through the wilderness by a pillar of fire (Exodus 14:24), and the first Christians encountered the Holy Spirit at Pentecost as tongues of fire (Acts 2:3).

The phrase "great balls of fire" was appearing in print by the 1890s and was spoken several times by the character Scarlett O'Hara in the movie *Gone with the Wind* in 1939. Lyricist Earl Burroughs (a.k.a. "Jack Hammer") was raised in Georgia and had heard his grandmother use the phrase. He coupled it with the phrase "goodness gracious"—also originally a blasphemous term referring to the goodness and graciousness of God: "Gracious is the LORD, and righteous" (Psalm 116:5).

Like Elvis, Jerry Lee Lewis came from an Assembly of God family, and he struggled with the demands of the faith (which he hadn't disavowed), show business, and his carnal desires. He had briefly attended Southwestern Bible Institute in Waxahachie, Texas, and his cousin Jimmy Swaggart was an evangelist. Lewis knew all the relevant Bible teachings, but the desire to obey wasn't as strong as the compulsion to satisfy his appetites. "I was raised a good Christian. But I couldn't make it," he told *Rolling Stone* in 1979. "Too weak, I guess."[18]

Engineer "Cowboy" Jack Clement fortunately recorded the fraught studio conversation with Sam Phillips on the day he cut "Great Balls of Fire."[19] The gist of Lewis's argument was that he knew rock 'n' roll was worldly, sinful, and an impediment to walking with God. Phillips—no admirer of fundamentalism but knowledgeable enough about the Bible—countered by saying that not everything Jesus did was of a purely spiritual nature. In his healing ministry, for example, he tended to bodies. He was concerned for people's physicality, not only their salvation. Didn't Lewis accept that rock 'n' roll had the power to do good?

"You can do good, Mr. Phillips," Lewis conceded. "Don't get me wrong." Phillips then pushed it further. "You can save souls." Lewis exploded at this. It seemed preposterous. The notion went against everything he believed about the gospel. "No. NO! NO! NO! How can the devil save souls? What are you talkin' about? Man, I got the devil in me. If I didn't have I'd be a Christian."

Phillips appeared to be at the point of submitting. "If you believe what you're saying," he began, "you've got no alternative whatsoever—" But Lewis interjected, "Mr. Phillips, I don't care. It ain't what you believe. It's what's written in the Bible. It's what's there, Mr. Phillips."

The alternative that Phillips hadn't considered is that you could sincerely believe you were doing the work of the devil but not allow this to hold you back. Robert Palmer believed that Lewis's conviction that he was doing wrong ("dragging the audience to hell," as he told journalist Todd Everett in August 1957 during an interview for Earth News Radio) introduced a unique creative tension: "Jerry Lee Lewis knew from the first that he was going to hell for playing rock & roll," he wrote, "and he went ahead and rocked anyway."[20]

Song: "Great Balls of Fire"

Artist: Jerry Lee Lewis

Single: A-side: "Great Balls of Fire" / B-side: "You Win Again"

Release: November 11, 1957

Studio: Sun Studio, Memphis, TN

Personnel: Jerry Lee Lewis (piano), Sidney Stokes (bass), Unknown (drums)

Writers: Otis Blackwell (music), Earl Burroughs, a.k.a. "Jack Hammer" (lyrics)

Producer: Sam Phillips

Label: Sun

Highest Chart Position: 2 (USA), 1 (UK)

Other Significant Recordings: The Crickets (1960), Mae West (1972), Chris Isaacs (2011)

Also by Jerry Lee Lewis: "When the Saints Go Marching In" (1958), "The Lily of the Valley" (1970), "Jesus Is on the Main Line (Call Him Sometime)" (1975)

12

COME SUNDAY

DUKE ELLINGTON WITH MAHALIA JACKSON

1958

This song started as an instrumental for a themed Carnegie Hall concert in 1943 and had lyrics added when Duke Ellington revised the material for a 1958 album release. Mahalia Jackson was the world's best-known gospel singer, yet she stoically refused to compromise with jazz—despite many offers. But when Ellington, probably the world's best-known jazz bandleader and composer at the time, asked her to sing this song, she relented.

It became an astonishingly powerful recording that blended their unique talents. There was enough space in Ellington's fluid composition for Mahalia to stretch out and improvise. She imbued every word and phrase with the sincerity of her faith and the weight of her experience, managing to capture the balance between the depths of unfulfilled longing, the passion of pleading, and the outpouring of satisfied praise.

Ellington would go on to compose three albums of sacred music starting in the mid-sixties and had written instrumentals that alluded to his religious convictions, but this was the first time he had voiced them in lyrics. Like Mahalia, he was loath to mix worship and entertainment. He once said, "You can jive with secular music, but you can't jive with the Almighty."[21]

"Come Sunday" sounded like an old spiritual, and deliberately so. His intention with *Black, Brown, and Beige* had been to tell the story of the African American experience in sound. This piece was his interpretation of a church meeting. Specifically, in its song form, it became a plea for strength to get through the backbreaking working week and arrive at the Sabbath day—the special day designated by God for rest: "Remember the sabbath day, to keep it holy. Six days shalt thou labour, and do all thy work: but the seventh day is the sabbath of the LORD thy God: in it thou shalt not do any work" (Exodus 20:8–10).

The early reference in the song to "my people" positions him as a spokesman appealing to God on behalf of his group or tribe. It has an echo of the language used by Moses when appealing on behalf of the enslaved Hebrews in Egypt for their freedom from slavery. Ellington writes (and Mahalia sings), "See my people through." Moses tells Pharaoh, "Let my people go" (Exodus 5:1).

Ellington, who was a daily reader of the Bible, appears to have based the central part of the lyrics on verses from the gospel of Matthew: "Often we feel weary / But he knows our every care" sounds as if it was derived from "your Father knoweth what things ye have need of, before ye ask him" (6:8) just as "Go to him in secret / He will hear your every prayer" comes from "when thou prayest, enter into thy closet, and when thou hast shut thy door, pray to thy Father which is in secret; and thy Father which seeth in secret shall reward thee openly" (6:6).

There can be no doubt where the next lines come from. "Lilies of the valley / They neither toil nor spin / And flowers bloom in spring time / Birds sing" paraphrases the words of Jesus:

> Behold the fowls of the air: for they sow not, neither do they reap, nor gather into barns; yet your heavenly Father feedeth them. Are ye not much better than they? . . . And why take ye thought for raiment? Consider the lilies of the field, how they grow; they toil not, neither do they spin: and yet I say unto you, That even Solomon in all his glory was not arrayed like one of these." (6:26, 28–29)

At the same session, Ellington asked Mahalia to record a version of the Davidic psalm that begins, "The Lord is my shepherd . . ." He hadn't drawn up a score for it, and there had been no rehearsal. He just told her to bring her Bible to the studio, requested that she find Psalm 23, struck a chord, and encouraged her to sing straight from the text.

In its instrumental form, "Come Sunday" became a standard, played by the likes of Johnny Hodges, Dizzy Gillespie, and the Ramsey Lewis Trio. As a song, Ellington incorporated it into the first of his sacred concert albums, recorded at Grace Cathedral in San Francisco and released in 1966. The only one of his musicians to perform at his funeral in May 1974 at the Cathedral Church of St. John the Divine in New York was Ray Nance. He played "Come Sunday" on violin at the close of the service. It has since become accepted as a hymn, entering *Ecumenical Praise* in 1977 and the *United Methodist Hymnal* in 1989.

Song: "Come Sunday"

Artist: Duke Ellington and His Orchestra, featuring Mahalia Jackson

Album: *Black, Brown, and Beige*

Release: December 1958

Studio: Radio Recorders, Hollywood

Personnel: Duke Ellington (piano), Mahalia Jackson (vocals), Sam Woodyard (drums), Ray Nance (violin, trumpet), Jimmy Woode (bass), Bill Graham (alto saxophone), Russell Procope (alto saxophone, clarinet), Paul Gonsalves (tenor saxophone), Harry Carney (baritone saxophone), Jimmy Hamilton (clarinet), William "Cat" Anderson (trumpet), Harold "Shorty" Baker (trumpet), Clark Terry (trumpet), Quentin Jackson (trombone), John Sanders (valve trombone), Britt Woodman (trombone)

Writer: Duke Ellington

Producer: Irving Townsend

Label: Columbia

Other Significant Recordings: Carmen McRae (1964), Gladys Knight (2006), Allen Toussaint, featuring Rhiannon Giddens (2016)

Also by Duke Ellington: "The Lord's Prayer" (1966), "David Danced before the Lord with All His Might" (1966), "Praise God and Dance" (1968)

13

WE ARE CROSSING THE JORDAN RIVER

JOAN BAEZ AND BOB GIBSON

1959

The new Queen of Folk, Joan Baez, crashed onto the scene by singing two spirituals—"Virgin Mary Had one Son" and "We Are Crossing the Jordan River"—at the first Newport Folk Festival in 1959. Previously she had only performed at small folk clubs. Three years later she was on the cover of *Time* magazine. She, in turn, played a significant role in introducing Bob Dylan to the public by covering his songs and giving him spots on her shows in 1963.

The received wisdom was that young people—especially the educated young—had no time for the Bible or gospel music and that popular music was a place of escape from such conventional culture. However, two significant forces were changing the musical landscape. The first was an increasing demand for "authenticity" that resulted in musicians (and fans) looking back to American music that had been created to rejoice, mourn, protest, confess, and tell history. This included the blues, ballads, work songs, and spirituals. Two of the most significant resources for such original material were the field recordings made by father-and-son team John and Alan Lomax for the

Library of Congress and archivist Harry Smith's *Anthology of American Folk Music* (1952).

The second contributing force was the civil rights movement—through the hymns and spirituals that were sung during rallies (such as "This Little Light of Mine," "Go Tell It on the Mountain," and "We Shall Overcome") and through the biblically charged speeches of Dr. Martin Luther King Jr. that frequently compared the plight of blacks in America to that of the enslaved Israelites in Egypt.

It was against this background that eighteen-year-old Joan Baez, the child of a Quaker family, joined veteran folkie Bob Gibson on stage to be introduced to the Newport crowd.

"We Are Crossing the Jordan River" refers to events recounted in the book of Joshua following the Israelites' departure from captivity in Egypt and the death of their leader, Moses. They were headed for the land of Canaan that was beyond the Jordan River. "Moses my servant is dead; now therefore arise, go over this Jordan, thou, and all this people, unto the land which I do give to them, even to the children of Israel" (Joshua 1:2).

Crossing the Jordan was to become a literal term to mean traveling from Egypt to Canaan, but it was also a figurative term for the transition from spiritual slavery to salvation (as in passing through the baptismal water) as well as the journey from this world to the next. It is the latter meaning that predominates in "We Are Crossing the Jordan River."

The song speaks of having a "home on the other side" and says, "I want my crown," a reference to Paul's claim, "I have fought the good fight, I have finished the race, I have kept the faith. Finally, there is laid up for me the crown of righteousness, which the Lord, the righteous Judge, will give to me on that Day, and not to me only but also to all who have loved His appearing" (2 Timothy 4:7–8 NKJV).

"We Are Crossing the Jordan River" then switches to "climbing Jacob's ladder," a story from Genesis where the patriarch Jacob fell asleep in Bethel with his head resting on a stone and dreamed of angels ascending and descending a ladder that stretches from heaven to earth. During this experience, he was given a promise about the land he and his people would inherit.

> And behold, the LORD stood above it and said, "I am the
> LORD, the God of Abraham your father and the God of

Isaac; the land on which you lie I will give to you and to your descendants; and your descendants shall be like the dust of the earth, and you shall spread abroad to the west and to the east and to the north and to the south; and by you and your descendants shall all the families of the earth bless themselves. Behold, I am with you and will keep you wherever you go, and will bring you back to this land; for I will not leave you until I have done that of which I have spoken to you." Then Jacob awoke from his sleep and said, "Surely the LORD is in this place; and I did not know it." (Genesis 28:13–16 RSV)

Martin Luther King Jr. used the language of the "promised land" in his last public speech in 1968, the last words of which were:

I just want to do God's will. And He's allowed me to go up to the mountain. And I've looked over. And I've seen the Promised Land. I may not get there with you. But I want you to know tonight, that we, as a people, will get to the Promised Land. So I'm happy, tonight. I'm not worried about anything. I'm not fearing any man. Mine eyes have seen the glory of the coming of the Lord![22]

Song: "We Are Crossing the Jordan River"

Artists: Joan Baez and Bob Gibson

Album: *Folk Festival at Newport Volume 2* (Various Artists)

Release: November 1959

Studio: Live at the Newport Folk Festival, Newport, RI, July 12, 1959

Personnel: Joan Baez (vocals and acoustic guitar), Bob Gibson (12-string acoustic guitar and vocals), Bill Lee (bass)

Writer: Traditional, arranged by Bob Gibson

Label: Vanguard

Also by Joan Baez: "Gospel Ship" (1962), "What Child Is This" (1966), "Put Your Hand in the Hand" (1971)

14

WHEN THE STARS BEGIN TO FALL

THE WEAVERS

....

1961

The Weavers were a seminal group in the folk revivalist movement in the mid-1950s. Not only were they committed to unearthing the best traditional songs, but also to promoting peace, justice, equality, and progressive politics. Although they had a clean look and sound, they were an inspiration to later folkies like Bob Dylan, who admired them both as curators of music and as political activists.

Founding member Pete Seeger left the group when he felt they were becoming too commercial, and *The Weavers' Almanac* (1961) was their first album without him. "When the Stars Begin to Fall" was the opening track.

It was a nineteenth-century spiritual included in the influential 1867 anthology *Slave Songs of the United States*. It had been collected by one of the book's authors, Charles Pickard Ware, who thought its origin was "probably Edisto Island" (in South Carolina). In other collections, it's known as "Lord, What a Morning" or "Oh, What a Morning" after its opening line. (The 1867 version says "what a mournin'" rather than "what a morning.")

The song warns the unprepared about the climactic end of the earth and the return of Jesus found in two of the Gospels. Jesus said, "But immediately after the tribulation of those days the sun shall be darkened, and the moon shall not give her light, and the stars shall fall from heaven, and the powers of the heavens shall be shaken" (Matthew 24:29 ASV).

The image of falling stars reoccurs in Revelation when a book locked by seven seals is opened to reveal the punishments of the final judgment. When the sixth seal is broken, the text says, "There was a great earthquake; and the sun became black as sackcloth of hair, and the whole moon became as blood; and the stars of the heaven fell unto the earth, as a fig tree casteth her unripe figs when she is shaken of a great wind" (Revelation 6:12–13 ASV).

These verses link with the next stanza of the song that says, "You'll weep for the rocks and mountains." The image is taken from this passage:

> And the kings of the earth, and the princes, and the chief
> captains, and the rich, and the strong, and every bondman and
> freeman, hid themselves in the caves and in the rocks of the
> mountains; and they say to the mountains and to the rocks,
> Fall on us, and hide us from the face of him that sitteth on
> the throne, and from the wrath of the Lamb: for the great day
> of their wrath is come; and who is able to stand? (Revelation
> 6:15–17 ASV)

In the political atmosphere of 1961, a song about stars falling and mountains crumbling suggested nuclear apocalypse. The Weavers may have sung, "Oh sinner what will you do / When the stars begin to fall?" but no one in their audience would have assumed that they were issuing a call for repentance.

Song: "When the Stars Begin to Fall"

Artist: The Weavers

Album: *The Weavers' Almanac*

Release: April 1961

Personnel: Erik Darling (banjo and vocals), Ronnie Gilbert (contralto vocals), Fred Hellerman (guitar and vocals), Lee Hays (bass vocals)

Writer: Traditional, arranged by Erik Darling, Ronnie Gilbert, Fred Hellerman, Lee Hays

Label: Vanguard

Other Significant Recordings: The Blue Sky Boys (1938), Hobart Smith with Preston Smith and Texas Gladden (1961), and the Seekers (1966)

Also by the Weavers: "The Seven Blessings of Mary" (1951), "Michael Row the Boat Ashore" (1957), "True Religion" (1961)

15

STAND BY ME
BEN E. KING

1961

S tand by Me" is one of the songs most recorded (over four hundred versions), most played on radio, and most lucrative (over $22 million in royalties by 2015). It's also one of the best examples of a hymn-like song offering nonspecific comfort; a precursor to songs like "Bridge over Troubled Water" and "Let It Be."

Ben E. King had the idea for "Stand by Me" when he was with the Drifters. He'd heard a song of that name recorded by the Staple Singers in 1955, which was based on a 1905 hymn by Methodist Dr. C. A. Tindley of Philadelphia. Tindley, a big influence on Thomas A. Dorsey and the author of the hymn "I'll Overcome Some Day" that would be transformed into the civil rights anthem "We Shall Overcome," was one of the first African American composers to write songs that gospel historian Tony Heilbut said were "neither spirituals nor hymns" but that "incorporated folk images, proverbs, and Biblical allusions familiar to black churchgoers for over a hundred years."[23]

The first verse of Tindley's 1905 "Stand by Me" is:

> When the storms of life are raging, stand by me,
> When the storms of life are raging, stand by me,

When the world is tossing me,

Like a ship upon the sea,

Thou who rulest wind and water, stand by me.

The next verses follow the same pattern, with verse two starting, "In the midst of tribulation, stand by me"; verse three, "In the midst of faults and failures, stand by me"; verse four, "In the midst of persecution, stand by me"; and the final verse, "When I'm growing old and feeble, stand by me."

The song was first published in Tindley's collection *New Songs of Paradise*, and then entered standard hymn books, including the *United Methodist Hymnal*. The Pace Jubilee Singers recorded a version in 1928, the Norfolk Jubilee Singers in 1937, and Sister Rosetta Tharpe in 1940.

Tharpe kept the basic structure and the refrain of "stand by me" but adapted the verses. Sam Cooke, who left the gospel quartet the Soul Stirrers to go solo, composed a version of the song with J. W. Alexander in 1959 that was also called "Stand by Me."

Ben E. King consciously developed his version of the song as a secular hymn. He explained his technique in a 1986 interview: "Most of my writing in the early days came from the fact that I was singing gospel. I would take a gospel song, think of it, and put it into 'I love you' lyrics."[24]

He initially offered it to the Drifters, but their manager turned it down because the group already had enough material. King showed it to his producers, Jerry Leiber and Mike Stoller, two of the most accomplished and celebrated songwriters in rock 'n' roll. They had already authored "Hound Dog," "Jailhouse Rock," and "King Creole" for Elvis; "Yackety Yak," "Poison Ivy," "Love Potion Number 9," and "Searchin'" for the Coasters; and "There Goes My Baby" for the Drifters; as well as many other songs.

Stoller wasn't there when King arrived at the office, so Leiber worked to improve the lyrics; when Stoller arrived, the melody was written in under two hours. "Ben E. had the beginnings of a song—both words and music," Stoller remembered. "He worked on the lyrics together with Jerry, and I added elements to the music, particularly the bass line. To some degree, it's based on a gospel song called 'Lord, Stand by Me.' I have a feeling that Jerry and Ben E. were inspired by it. Ben, of course, had a strong background in church music."[25]

Ben E. King's "Stand by Me," with its mention of wanting the loved one even if the sky should fall or the mountains should crumble into the sea, was less like Tindley's "Stand by Me" and more like the 46th Psalm: "God is our refuge and strength, A very present help in trouble. Therefore will we not fear, though the earth do change, and though the mountains be shaken into the heart of the seas; though the waters thereof roar and be troubled, though the mountains tremble with the swelling thereof" (vv. 1–3 ASV). When Prince Harry and Meghan Markle chose this song to be sung at their wedding in 2018 by the Kingdom Choir, they were unwittingly returning it to the gospel context out of which it had grown.

Song: "Stand by Me"

Artist: Ben E. King

Single: A-side: "Stand by Me" / B-side: "On the Horizon"

Release: April 1961

Studio: Atlantic Records Studio, New York, NY

Personnel: Ben E. King (vocals), Ernie Hayes (piano), Lloyd Trotman (bass), Al Caiola (guitar), Charles McCracken (guitar), Phil Kraus (percussion), Romeo Penque (sax), Stanley Applebaum (string arranger), Gary Chester (drums)

Writers: Ben E. King, Jerry Leiber (lyrics), Mike Stoller (music)

Producers: Jerry Leiber, Mike Stoller

Label: Atco

Highest Chart Position: 4 (USA), 1 (UK in 1987)

Other Significant Recordings: The Drifters (1962), Muhammad Ali (1963), Otis Redding (1964)

Also by Ben E. King: "Supernatural Thing Part 1" (1975), "Do It in the Name of Love" (1975), "Happiness Is Where You Find It" (1975)

16

YOU'LL NEVER WALK ALONE
GERRY AND THE PACEMAKERS

1963

W ritten by Rodgers and Hammerstein for their 1945 Broadway musical *Carousel*, where it appeared in two scenes, "You'll Never Walk Alone" has gone on to become not only a musical standard sung by artists such as Frank Sinatra, Nina Simone, Mario Lanza, Louis Armstrong, Tom Jones, Elvis Presley, and the Three Tenors (Plácido Domingo, José Carreras, and Luciano Pavarotti), but also, in some parts of the world, a sporting anthem sung by crowds before games (e.g., Liverpool F. C. and Celtic) and a secular hymn performed at times of national tragedy (e.g., the 9/11 terror attacks and Hurricane Katrina). Renée Fleming, celebrated soprano opera singer, sang it at the 2009 inauguration of Barack Obama.

Gerry and the Pacemakers was a Liverpool group managed by Brian Epstein (manager of the Beatles). Gerry Marsden first heard the song when he saw the film *Carousel* in Liverpool in 1959, and later introduced it into the group's repertoire because he saw the success that the Beatles enjoyed by contrasting their raucous rock 'n' roll songs with ballads such as "Till There Was You" (from the musical play and film *The Music Man*). It became Gerry and the Pacemakers' third successive number one hit in the UK after "How Do You Do It?" and "I Like It."

Lyricist Oscar Hammerstein was baptized and raised as an Episcopalian in New York, but the faith expressed in "You'll Never Walk Alone" stops short of faith in God. It suggests a faith in courage itself and in the belief that a better day will dawn, although it gives no grounds for either hope. The advice to "Hold your head up high" ("keep your chin up high" in the original stage production) is no more than advice to "pull yourself together" or "get a grip on things."

In a 1958 TV interview, Hammerstein told Mike Wallace about a time when a New York policeman told him that he'd gotten great inspiration from playing the soundtrack to *Carousel* and that he was certain, despite the fact that Hammerstein then belonged to no church, that he was a religious writer. "He had discovered from the words of my songs that I had faith, faith in mankind, faith that there was something more powerful than mankind behind it all," he told Wallace. "And faith that in the long run good triumphs over evil. If that's religion—I'm religious, and it is my definition of religion."[26]

The song bears similarities to Psalm 23, one of the best-known psalms of consolation, although the difference is that whereas David (to whom the psalm is credited) repeatedly pointed to God as the source of comfort, as in, "The LORD is my shepherd; I shall not want. He maketh me to lie down in green pastures: he leadeth me beside the still waters. He restoreth my soul" (vv. 1–3), "You'll Never Walk Alone" points to nothing more substantial than the "hope in your heart."

The song starts with the image of walking "through a storm," which resonates with "though I walk through the valley of the shadow of death" (v. 4), and ends with the promise that "you'll never walk alone," which in a similar way calls to mind "I will fear no evil: for thou art with me" (v. 4).

The comparison of bad weather—"storm," "wind," "rain," "dark"—to testing times in life is also reminiscent of the Bible. Again, in the Psalms we get, "Then they cry unto the LORD in their trouble, and he bringeth them out of their distresses. He maketh the storm a calm, so that the waves thereof are still" (107:28–29).

The use of the phrase "don't be afraid" echoes the many biblical injunctions spread from Genesis to Revelation. Abraham was told to "fear not" (Genesis 15:1), Moses told the people to "fear not" (Exodus 20:20), Joseph was told to "fear not" (Matthew 1:20), Mary was told to "fear not" (Luke

1:30), Jesus told his disciples to "be not afraid" (Matthew 14:27), and "one like unto the Son of man" appeared before John on the island of Patmos and told him to "fear not" (Revelation 1:13, 17).

Hammerstein climaxed the song with the mention of "hope," but in the context of all that's gone before, it appears to be no more than a hope in the power of hope itself. In other words, faith is in the power of the mind to generate good thoughts and for these positive thoughts to lead to positive outcomes.

Hope is preached in the Bible. Paul listed the three great "gifts" of Christian spirituality as "faith, hope, charity" (1 Corinthians 13:13). Yet the hope expressed in the New Testament was "in Christ" (1 Corinthians 15:19), "in God" (1 Peter 1:21), and "of the promise made of God, unto our fathers" (Acts 26:6). It's never just hope.

The original "You'll Never Walk Alone," as performed by the opera singer and actress Christine Johnson, spoke to the mood of the times. The Broadway opening of *Carousel* was on April 19, 1945, and on May 7, Germany surrendered to the allies. On July 10, Judy Garland recorded the song for Decca while in New York on her honeymoon with Vincente Minnelli. It seemed to offer consolation to those who'd lost loved ones in the fighting.

Gerry and the Pacemakers' version of "You'll Never Walk Alone" was number one on the UK charts the day President John F. Kennedy was assassinated, November 22, 1963 (the same day that writers C. S. Lewis and Aldous Huxley also died). It was also played as a Top Ten hit over the PA system at Anfield, the home ground of Liverpool F. C., and was adopted by fans who have sung it at matches ever since. In 1982, the words YOU'LL NEVER WALK ALONE were spelled out in wrought iron above the ground's Shankly Gates.

Song: "You'll Never Walk Alone"
Artist: Gerry and the Pacemakers
Album: *How Do You Like It?*
Single Release: October 16, 1963 (UK), June 1965 (USA)
Studio: EMI Recording Studio, Abbey Road, London

Personnel: Gerry Marsden (vocals), Les Chadwick (bass guitar), Les Maguire (piano), Freddie Marsden (drums), string quartet

Writers: Richard Rodgers, Oscar Hammerstein II

Producers: George Martin, Ron Richards

Label: Columbia (EMI, UK), Laurie (USA)

Highest Chart Position: 1 (UK), 48 (US)

Other Significant Recordings: Judy Garland (1945), Frank Sinatra (1958), Aretha Franklin (1972)

17

CAN I GET A WITNESS

MARVIN GAYE

. . . .

1963

I n African American churches, "Can I get a witness?" is an interjection used by preachers to solicit affirmation from a congregation. It asks, "Do you affirm this from your own experience?," "Do I have your support?," or "Let me hear you back me up." The response should be a hearty, "Amen!," "Preach it," or "All right!" It's a way of involving people in the sermon and keeping them alert. Such churches are alive with encouraging murmurs that fire up the preacher, who in turn fires up the listeners.

By using the phrase in a pop song about a man who thinks his girlfriend isn't paying him enough attention, writers Lamont Dozier, Eddie Holland, and Brian Holland were bringing the call-and-response language of the church to a wider audience. They were importing the vocabulary of spirituality into lyrics and describing sensuality in the way that Ray Charles had done with "Hallelujah I Love Her So." Marvin Gaye, whose father was a preacher, knew exactly what he was doing.

The question "Can I get a witness?" isn't asked in the Bible, but the concept of witnessing or being a witness is strong. It's used to mean giving evidence or testifying, usually to the power of God or the presence of Jesus. The Lord tells Israel, "Ye are my witnesses . . ." (Isaiah 43:10), Jesus says of his disciples, "ye also shall bear witness . . ." (John 15:27), and speaking of Jesus the apostle Peter said, "we are his witnesses . . ." (Acts 5:32). In 1964, the Isley Brothers would release "Testify Part 1," which was a gospel-influenced song about the power of music. At the beginning of "Testify, Pts. 1 & 2," as heard on the album *West Coast Seattle Boy: The Jimmy Hendrix Anthology*, we hear, "I said I'm a witness / I'm here to testify / I wanna tell you all about it / I ain't gonna tell no lies."

"We had to go to church every Sunday when we were growing up, with a choir rehearsal on Wednesdays," said Lamont Dozier. "We all went to church. It was something you didn't say no to. So when we came to write, the melodies were gospel-based because that's the only kind of melodies we knew. The flavors, the chord progressions, and the words were all influenced by gospel. 'Can I Get a Witness' was the typical Holland-Dozier-Holland gospel background all wrapped up in one song. The phrase is right out of the church."[29]

Song: "Can I Get a Witness"

Artist: Marvin Gaye

Single: A-side: "Can I Get a Witness" / B-side: "I'm Crazy 'Bout My Baby"

Release: September 20, 1963

Studio: Hitsville USA, Detroit, MI

Personnel: Marvin Gaye (vocals), Marcus Belgrave (trumpet), Russell Conway (trumpet), Paul Riser (trombone), Patrick Lanier (trombone), Hank Cosby (tenor saxophone), George Fowler (organ), Eddie Willis (guitar), Clarence Isabel (bass guitar), Benny Benjamin (drums)

Writers: Eddie Holland, Brian Holland, Lamont Dozier

Producers: Brian Holland, Lamont Dozier

Label: Tamla

Highest Chart Position: 3 (US)

Other Significant Recordings: Rolling Stones (1964), Dusty Springfield (1964), Rod Stewart (1984)

Also by Marvin Gaye: "Hello There Angel" (1962), "Seek and You Shall Find" (1969), "Abraham, Martin and John" (1970)

18

THE TIMES THEY ARE A-CHANGIN'

BOB DYLAN

1964

B ob Dylan, born into a Jewish family in Duluth, Minnesota, told John Cohen in a 1968 interview for *Sing Out!*: "I have always read the Bible." When Cohen expressed surprise, saying that he didn't think he was the type to pick up a copy of the Gideon's Bible in a hotel room, Dylan responded, "Well, you never know."

When civil rights activist and church minister Bert Cartwright analyzed Dylan's output between 1961 and 1968 for his 1985 booklet *The Bible in the Lyrics of Bob Dylan*, he found that 36 percent of Dylan's songs had biblical references. This added up to 387 individual mentions almost equally split between the Hebrew Bible and the New Testament.

He was also inspired by poets like Dante, William Blake, Walt Whitman, T. S. Eliot, and Allen Ginsberg who had drawn from the Bible. From them he absorbed the declamatory tone that affected songs like "The Times They Are a-Changin'."

Although his immediate influence was the post-war folk music movement exemplified by people like Pete Seeger and Woody Guthrie, he had also learned from Hank Williams, Johnny Cash, Sister Rosetta Tharpe, Robert Johnson, Little Richard, Chuck Berry, and Elvis.

In 1963, he was poised to become not just the leader of the folk-rock movement, injecting literacy, spirituality, and concern for justice into commercial rock 'n' roll, but also the conscience of the Baby Boomer generation. It wasn't a role he sought but came as a consequence of writing songs that started with phrases like "come gather 'round people" and issued warnings to those who refused to adapt to changing times.

"The Times They Are a-Changin'" was deliberately biblical in tone. The words and phrases came from the pages of a seventeenth-century translation of the Bible rather than the *New York Times*—"heed ye the call," "sink like a stone," "the battle outside is raging," "beyond your command," "the curse it is cast"—and he positioned himself as a prophet or teacher.

The song is general rather than particular. He doesn't name any specific sin other than the sin of impeding progress. The message is directed at the older generation—critics (verse two), politicians (verse three), parents (verse four)—and warns them that their options are either to get on board or be left behind.

There is the thinly veiled threat that today's restless young will soon be governing those who are currently in power. The roles will be reversed. For this, he turns to the words of Jesus (spoken in another context) that "many shall be last that are first; and first that are last" (Matthew 19:30 ASV) or "So the last shall be first, and the first last" (Matthew 20:16 ASV).

Dylan's song accurately reflected the turmoil of a period characterized by the assassination of President Kennedy, the arrival of the Beatles, the liberalization of attitudes toward premarital sex and recreational drug use, rising divorce rates, racial unrest, the nuclear arms race, and America's increased military involvement in Vietnam.

Song: "The Times They Are a-Changin'"
Artist: Bob Dylan
Album: *The Times They Are a-Changin'*
Release: January 13, 1964 (album), March 8, 1965 (single, UK)

Studio: Columbia Studios, New York, NY

Personnel: Bob Dylan (vocals, guitar, harmonica)

Writer: Bob Dylan

Producer: Tom Wilson

Label: Columbia

Highest Chart Position: 20 (US), 7 (UK)

Other Significant Recordings: the Byrds (1965), the Hollies (1969), Keb' Mo' (2004)

Also by Bob Dylan: "Quit Your Low Down Ways" (1962), "Blowing in the Wind" (1963), "When the Ship Comes In" (1964)

PROMISED LAND

CHUCK BERRY

1964

C huck Berry took a tune first recorded by the Carter Family as "Wabash Cannonball," matched it with the biblical idea of a promised land, and created a travelogue that took him from Norfolk, Virginia, to Los Angeles on a Greyhound bus, a train, and a plane. He wrote it while serving an eighteen-month sentence for violating the Mann Act, and used an atlas from the prison library to accurately plot his route.

The territory of Canaan in Genesis, Exodus, and Numbers was a land "flowing with milk and honey" (Exodus 33:3) promised first to Abraham (Genesis 15:18–21), then to Isaac and Jacob. In spirituals such as "The Old Ship of Zion," the "promised land" could also refer to heaven or be a slave's code for freedom.

In Berry's song, the "promised land" was California, the epitome of the American Dream with its wealth, glamour, and opportunity. Even in 1991, *Time* magazine could write, "If America is the land where the world goes in search of miracles and redemption, California is the land where Americans go. It is America's America, the symbol of raw hope and brave (even foolish) invention, where ancient traditions and inhibitions are abandoned at the border."[27]

Berry was raised as a Baptist in St. Louis, Missouri, and absorbed not only the ornate language of the Bible but also the rhythm of gospel music. "Long before I learned to walk I was patting my foot to those Baptist beats," he wrote in his autobiography. "Sometimes I wonder if that was the roots of my rockin' rhythm."[28]

His other biblical reference was "Swing low chariot, come down easy," which is addressed to his plane as it descends into LAX. The allusion is to "Swing Low, Sweet Chariot," another spiritual that retold a Bible story while cryptically pleading to be rescued from slavery.

The Bible story in question is that of the prophet Elijah's transportation directly to heaven without having to die. "And it came to pass, as they [Elijah and Elisha] still went on, and talked, that, behold, there appeared a chariot of fire, and horses of fire, which parted them both asunder; and Elijah went up by a whirlwind into heaven" (2 Kings 2:11 ASV).

> Swing low, sweet chariot,
> Coming for to carry me home.
> Swing low, sweet chariot,
> Coming for to carry me home.
>
> I looked over Jordan, what do I see,
> Coming for to carry me home.
> A band of angels coming after me,
> Coming for to carry me home.

Berry was being playful in his adoption of the language of spirituals but helped pave the way for "Promised Land" by Dennis Brown (1980) before Bruce Springsteen's "The Promised Land" (1978), "Wailing Wall" by the Cure (1984), "Across the Borderline" by Ry Cooder (1987), "My Sisters and Brothers" by the Jerry Garcia Band (1991), "Go to Hell" by Kings X (1994), "San Andreas Fault" by Natalie Merchant (1995), "Song of the Century" by Green Day (2009), and many other songs that explored the concept in more depth.

Song: "The Promised Land"

Artist: Chuck Berry

Single: A-side: "Promised Land" / B-side: "Things I Used to Do"

Release: December 1964

Studio: Chess Studios, Chicago, IL

Personnel: Chuck Berry (guitar, vocals), Lafayette Leake (piano), Willie Dixon (bass), Odie Payne (drums)

Writer: Chuck Berry

Producers: Leonard Chess, Philip Chess

Label: Chess

Highest Chart Position: 16 (US)

Other Significant Recordings: Johnny Rivers (1964), the Band (1973), Grateful Dead (1976)

Also by Chuck Berry: "Downbound Train" (1957), "My Little Love Light" (1965), "Some People" (1970)

PEOPLE GET READY

THE IMPRESSIONS

20

1965

C urtis Mayfield (1942–1999) was steeped in gospel music and the church. His grandmother was a minister, and prior to joining the Impressions, Mayfield was a member of various gospel groups, including the Northern Jubilee Gospel Singers. "I credit a lot of my ability to my grandmother, Reverand Annabelle Mayfield," he said. "I was brought up in her church—the Travelling Souls Spiritualist Church. Although I slept through many sermons I think I picked up the touch of being at the pulpit and being able to speak words of inspiration."[30]

The inspiration to write "People Get Ready" for the Impressions was the August 28, 1963, March on Washington for Jobs and Freedom during which Dr. Martin Luther King Jr. delivered his "I Have a Dream" speech. In 1964, Mayfield also wrote "Keep on Pushing," a song that used gospel phrases about moving on up and reaching a higher goal, with interjections of "Hallelujah!" to encourage civil rights campaigners.

Although he often said that the vocabulary and phraseology of "People Get Ready" came from things he'd heard delivered from the pulpit, it was clearly modeled on a specific spiritual, known either as "The Gospel Train" or "Git on Board," first recorded in the hymnal *The Jubilee Harp* in 1866.

When Charles L. Edwards collected "Git on Board" for *Bahama Songs and Stories* (1895), it already referred to "no second class" and "no diffren' in de fare," a view of newly developed rail transport as a social leveler. Mayfield turned this into "don't need no ticket."

By 1921, it was well known enough to be adapted for sheet music as "De Gospel Train (Git on bo'd lit'l children)" and credited to Henry Thacker "Harry" Burleigh (an African American classical composer and singer). Burleigh's version had phrases that Mayfield would use:

> De gospel train am a-comin'
> Hear it jus' at han'
> I hear de car wheels rumblin'
> An rollin' thoo' de lan' . . .
> Git on bo'd lit'l' children
> Dere's room for many a-mo'
> De fare is cheap . . .

In spirituals, the "gospel train" (like the "gospel ship") was an image of salvation. Jesus was the driver, the invitation was to all, there was no segregation once on board, the ticket had already been paid for, the destination was heaven, and only those who took the train would get there.

Slaves may have used such songs as coded information about the "underground railroad," a network of abolitionists and safe houses for slaves escaping from the South to the free states of the North. However, this is difficult to prove since spirituals were only collected after abolition, and there are no first-hand accounts from former slaves as evidence that songs were written or used in this way.

Mayfield spoke of "People Get Ready" as a political song, although there's nothing in the song to prove it unless you take "faith" to mean belief in the civil rights cause and interpret the "train" to mean the general drift of history in the West toward liberal values.

Judged by its words alone, "People Get Ready" is a contemporary spiritual that includes far more doctrine than its folk music ancestors. It starts with a wake-up call to "get ready," says that faith "is the key" ("By grace you have been saved, through faith" [Ephesians 2:8 NIV]), and names Jordan as the destination.

There are even warnings for the "hopeless sinner" who would "hurt all mankind / Just to save his own." This could be a reference to Jesus's saying, "Whosoever shall seek to gain his life shall lose it; but whosoever shall lose his life shall preserve it" (Luke 17:33 ASV). Here is also a warning that "There is no hiding place / Against the kingdom's throne"—a thought that most likely came from John's vision of the final judgment: "And I saw a great white throne, and him that sat upon it, from whose face the earth and the heaven fled away; and there was found no place for them" (Revelation 20:11 ASV).

Mayfield was paralyzed after stage lighting equipment fell on him in 1990. He was confined to a wheelchair for the rest of his life, although he continued to write and record socially conscious songs.

Song: "People Get Ready"

Artist: The Impressions

Single: A-side: "People Get Ready" / B-side: "I've Been Trying"

Release: January 1965

Album: *People Get Ready*

Studio: Universal Recording Studios, Chicago, IL

Personnel: Curtis Mayfield (guitar and vocals), Fred Cash (vocals), Sam Gooden (vocals)

Writer: Curtis Mayfield

Producer: Johnny Pate

Label: ABC-Paramount

Highest Chart Position: 14 (USA)

Other Significant Recordings: the Chambers Brothers (1966), Vanilla Fudge (1967), Aretha Franklin (1968), George Benson (1969), Ladysmith Black Mambazo (1997)

Also by the Impressions: "Amen" (1964), "Keep on Pushing" (1964), "I Thank Heaven" (1964)

21

GATES OF EDEN
BOB DYLAN

1965

B y the mid-sixties, Bob Dylan had moved on from his earlier style of songwriting to an electric rock sound with lyrics that combined surrealism and symbolism. It became harder to determine what a Dylan song was "about," and listener satisfaction now often came from the sensory effect of the words and images rather than any overt meaning.

His use of the Bible similarly became less direct than it had been in early songs like "I'd Hate to Be You on That Dreadful Day," "Quit Your Low Down Ways," "With God on Our Side," and "When the Ship Comes In." In "Desolation Row," Cain and Abel are found with the hunchback of Notre Dame, the good Samaritan dresses for a carnival, and Noah hangs out with Shakespeare's Ophelia. In "Highway 61 Revisited," Abraham prepares to sacrifice his son on US Route 61. In "Gates of Eden," Aladdin and some "hermit monks" sit on the golden calf.

Whatever Dylan's intention, "The Gates of Eden" used the image of Eden in its conventional biblical sense of a place of innocence. Within its gates there are no trials and no sins, whereas outside of it there are "no truths." There are also "no kings" within Eden because it is a place of equality (in an early draft he had written that "all men are kings," which amounts to the same thing).

Genesis doesn't mention Eden having gates (although Revelation pictures heaven with gates), but there is a sense of boundaries. When Adam and Eve were expelled for having eaten the forbidden fruit, their way back to paradise was barred:

> Therefore the LORD God sent him forth from the garden of Eden, to till the ground from whence he was taken. So he drove out the man; and he placed at the east of the garden of Eden Cherubims, and the flaming sword which turned every way, to keep the way of the tree of life. (Genesis 3:23–24)

In another line that may have biblical origins, Dylan wrote that the "kingdoms of experience" rot in the wind. He could have had these words in mind: "My heart hath had great experience of wisdom and knowledge. And I applied my heart to know wisdom, and to know madness and folly: I perceived that this also was a striving after wind" (Ecclesiastes 1:16–17 ASV).

Although Dylan knew enough of the Bible for it to be the sole source for his song about Eden, he was also familiar with the British poets John Milton (*Paradise Lost, Paradise Regained*) and William Blake (*Jerusalem, The Gates of Paradise*), who wrote about Eden. He was also a fan of novelist John Steinbeck, whose 1952 novel *East of Eden* was heavily influenced by the story of Cain and Abel (Genesis 4) and whose title was suggested by the verse "And Cain went out from the presence of the LORD, and dwelt in the land of Nod, on the east of Eden" (Genesis 4:16). The movie of the book, which came out in 1955, starred James Dean—one of Dylan's earliest heroes.

One of the achievements of "Gates of Eden" was that it brought biblical imagery to the forefront of the rock revolution. It would have long-lasting effects.

Song: "Gates of Eden"
Artist: Bob Dylan
Single: A-side: "Like a Rolling Stone" / B-side: "Gates of Eden"
Album: *Bringing It All Back Home*

Release: July 20, 1965

Studio: Columbia Recording Studios, New York, NY

Personnel: Bob Dylan (guitar, vocals, harmonica)

Writer: Bob Dylan

Producer: Tom Wilson

Label: Columbia

Other Significant Recordings: Julie Felix (1967), Arlo Guthrie (1973), Bryan Ferry (2007)

Also by Bob Dylan: "I'd Hate To Be You on That Dreadful Day" (1964, released 2010) and "With God on Your Side" (1964) , "Highway 61 Revisited" (1965)

22

TURN! TURN! TURN! (TO EVERYTHING THERE IS A SEASON)

THE BYRDS

. . . .

1965

I n 1959, Pete Seeger was "just leafing through" the Bible when he came across these verses in the Old Testament book of Ecclesiastes:

> To every thing there is a season, and a time to every purpose
> under the heaven: A time to be born, and a time to die; a time
> to plant, and a time to pluck up that which is planted; a time
> to kill, and a time to heal; a time to break down, and a time to
> build up; a time to weep, and a time to laugh; a time to mourn,
> and a time to dance; a time to cast away stones, and a time to
> gather stones together; a time to embrace, and a time to refrain
> from embracing; a time to get, and a time to lose; a time to
> keep, and a time to cast away; a time to rend, and a time to sew;
> a time to keep silence, and a time to speak; a time to love, and a
> time to hate; a time of war, and a time of peace. (3:1–8)

So moved was he by the ancient poetry that he began creating a melody to which the words could be sung. "I rearranged it very slightly so that it rhymed better," he later explained. "And I added one line of my own."[31]

His additions were the refrain, "Turn! Turn! Turn!" that knit the song together and the final line, "I swear it's not too late," that referred to peace. His rearranging was minor—the dropping of the lines about keeping silence and speaking, keeping and casting away, and the repetition of the line about love and hate.

Why did he have so much affection for the song? In 1964, he explained that it contained a succinct response to the oft-asked question, "What is right and what is wrong about the world?" He said, "The most truthful answer I know comes from Ecclesiastes, that hardboiled section of the Bible."

Ecclesiastes introduces itself as "the words of the Preacher, the son of David, king in Jerusalem" (Ecclesiastes 1:1), which would suggest King Solomon—but this may well have been a dramatic device. Poets of the period often adopted the personae of historical characters to explore issues, in this case the value of wisdom and wealth in the face of the random nature of life and the inevitability of death. The writer of the book of 1 Kings noted that Solomon was well known for his earthly power and glory, his wisdom, and his poetic skills (4:29–34). The early conclusion in the book was "vanity of vanities; all is vanity" (Ecclesiastes 1:2).

The book had a particular relevance in the 1950s and 1960s because of its skepticism and its willingness to look at the possibility of a silent, indifferent, or absent God. It chimed with the often-bleak philosophy of Camus and Sartre, the plays of absurdists like Beckett and Pinter, and the paintings of Jackson Pollock and Francis Bacon.

Although Seeger's tweaks gave the impression of it being a peace song, the words in the third chapter of Ecclesiastes are noncommittal about the things they describe. They simply say that hate and love exist side by side in the world as we find it, as do damage and restoration, war and peace.

Seeger performed the song at The Bitter End in Greenwich Village in May 1962 where his set was recorded. Before the release of the album (*The Bitter and the Sweet*) in January 1963, the Limeliters, a popular New York folk trio (Lou Gottlieb, Alex Hassilev, and Glenn Yarbrough) had already covered it (as "To Everything There Is a Season") for their album *Folk Matinee*.

A year later (January 1964), Judy Collins included it on her album *Judy Collins 3*. The arranger, guitarist, and banjo player on the track was fellow folk musician Jim McGuinn (later known as Roger McGuinn). In 1965 he would form the folk-rock quintet the Byrds in California with the intention of matching the new rock sound pioneered by the Beatles with the lyrical depth and complexity of folk.

In July of 1965, while touring America, McGuinn sang "Turn! Turn! Turn!" on the group's bus, giving the arrangement a new twist because of his fresh experience with rock music. In September, it was included among the songs to record for their second album and was approached with the same rolling arpeggio patterns that had characterized their hit cover of Dylan's "Mr. Tambourine Man." McGuinn estimates the group did seventy-five takes over five days to perfect it.

It was one of the first pop songs to be composed of Bible verses, and the most ancient lyrics ever to top the Billboard charts. Pete Seeger became a huge fan of McGuinn's arrangement, and from 1999 onward donated 45 percent of his royalties from the song to the Israeli Committee Against House Demolitions. He said at the time, "All around the world, songs are being written that use old public domain material, and I think it's only fair that some of the money from the songs go to the country or place of origin, even though the composer may be long dead or unknown."[32]

Song: "Turn! Turn! Turn! (To Everything There Is a Season)"
Artist: The Byrds
Single: A-side: "Turn! Turn! Turn!" / B-side: "She Don't Care About Time"
Release: October 1, 1965
Album: *Turn! Turn! Turn!*
Studio: Columbia Studios, Hollywood, CA
Personnel: Roger McGuinn (lead guitar, vocals), David Crosby (rhythm guitar, vocals), Chris Hillman (bass guitar, vocals), Gene Clark (tambourine, vocals), Michael Clarke (drums)
Writer: Pete Seeger
Producer: Terry Melcher

Label: Columbia

Highest Chart Position: 1 (USA), 26 (UK)

Other Significant Recordings: The Limeliters (1962), Pete Seeger (1963), Judy Collins (1964), Gary Shearston (1964)

Also by the Byrds: "The Christian Life" (1968), "I Am a Pilgrim" (1968), "Jesus Is Just Alright" (1969)

23

GIRL

THE BEATLES

....

1965

I n an interview conducted in 1970, John Lennon told Jann Wenner, the editor of *Rolling Stone*, that the Beatles' song "Girl" had contained a sly dig at the church. "I was just talking about Christianity in that [song]—a thing like you have to be tortured to attain heaven," he said. "I'm only saying that I was talking about 'pain will lead to pleasure' in 'Girl,' and that was sort of the Catholic Christian concept—be tortured and then it'll be alright, which seems to be a bit true but not in their concept of it. But I didn't believe . . . that you *have* to be tortured to attain anything. It just so happens that you were."[33]

"Girl" was a track on *Rubber Soul*, the first Beatles' album to move significantly away from the beat group musical formula and from songs that dealt exclusively with boy-girl love. In "Nowhere Man" and "In My Life," John explored his anxieties.

In a little-known interview just prior to the album's release, Paul told journalist Francis Wyndham a similar story about the composition of "Girl." "John's been reading a book about pain and pleasure, about the idea behind Christianity—that to have pleasure you have to have pain. The book says that's all rubbish; it often happens that pain leads to pleasure but you don't *have* to have it. All that's a drag. So, we've written a song about it, with I suppose a little bit of protest."[34]

Paul's friend (and eventual biographer) Barry Miles believes that the book was *Masochism in Modern Man* (1941) by Theodor Reik, which he'd given to John from the stock at his alternative London bookshop and art gallery, Indica.

Reik, born in 1888, was a psychoanalyst who'd trained under Sigmund Freud in Vienna. He believed that Christianity subjugated people by telling them to endure hardship, frustration, and pain because through suffering came redemption. "The Christian conception of this life as a brief period of affliction, to be replaced by eternal bliss for the righteous, and the exhortations to endure the earthly misery are in this sense undoubtedly formations of mass psychology."[35]

Reik argued that in late Judaism and early Christianity, "suffering was affirmed, even glorified, and its value was acknowledged, for it opened the gates of paradise. Did Jesus not say: 'Be of good cheer. I have overcome the world'? The dying Saviour had found a new way of enjoyment. The steps of suffering became rungs of the ladder to heaven. The warrior-ideal is, by and by, replaced by the ideal of the saint or the martyr. The late Jewish prophets and the Christian faith bring the glorification of masochism."[36]

John raises this issue in the final verse and turns to the creation story. He asks the girl whether she was raised believing that "pain would lead to pleasure." This is commentary on the consequences to Adam and Eve and their descendants of eating the forbidden fruit.

In the Bible story John refers to, God says: "I will greatly multiply thy sorrow and thy conception; in sorrow thou shalt bring forth children; and thy desire shall be to thy husband, and he shall rule over thee" (Genesis 3:16).

John then turns to the consequences for Adam and asks whether the girl was also told that a man must "break his back to earn his day of leisure."

To Adam God said:

> Because thou hast hearkened unto the voice of thy wife, and
> hast eaten of the tree, of which I commanded thee, saying,
> Thou shalt not eat of it: cursed is the ground for thy sake; in
> sorrow shalt thou eat of it all the days of thy life; thorns also

and thistles shall it bring forth to thee; and thou shalt eat the herb of the field; in the sweat of thy face shalt thou eat bread, till thou return unto the ground. (Genesis 3:17–19)

As a child, John attended Sunday school at St. Peter's Church, Woolton, sang in the choir, and was confirmed into the Church of England. Issues of the Christian faith concerned him throughout his life, and his comparison of the Beatles and Jesus in 1966 brought him unwelcome notoriety.

Song: "Girl"

Artist: The Beatles

Album: *Rubber Soul*

Release: December 3, 1965

Studio: EMI Studios, Abbey Road, London

Personnel: John Lennon (rhythm guitar), Paul McCartney (bass guitar), George Harrison (lead guitar), Ringo Starr (drums)

Writers: Paul McCartney, John Lennon

Producer: George Martin

Label: Parlophone (UK) / Capitol (US)

Other Significant Recordings: Chris de Burgh (1995), John Tams (2006), Paul Carrack (2007)

Also by the Beatles: "The Word" (1965), "All You Need Is Love" (1967), "The Ballad of John and Yoko" (1969)

24

BLESSED

SIMON & GARFUNKEL

. . . .

1966

W hile living in London during 1965, Paul Simon stayed in an East End refuge house owned by a central London church, St. Anne's. Running the house was a forty-five-year-old social worker, Judith Piepe, a prewar refugee from Germany who had converted to Christianity and had a passion not only for drug addicts, drifters, and the homeless but also for folk musicians, bohemians, and artists.

The folk musicians she befriended and offered accommodation inevitably ended up knowing the people she cared for and would play at her folk club in the crypt of St. Anne's church in Soho. Through her work, she came to the attention of Roy Trevivian, a religious programs producer for BBC radio, who asked her to contribute to a five-minute, daily devotional slot called *Five to Ten* that was sandwiched between two easy-listening music programs.

The program gave a brief meditation on a relevant social or spiritual issue. Piepe drafted Paul Simon to sing on twelve programs between March and July 1965. He would perform a song, and Piepe would offer an appropriately religious comment. She believed that "The Sound of Silence," "I Am a Rock," "A Most Peculiar Man," and similar songs showed great insight into contemporary problems of loneliness, alienation, and fear.

"Blessed" may have been written for *Five to Ten*. It certainly fit the requirements and was composed during this period. Mention is made in the song of both Soho and the church. He told an interviewer that it came to him after hearing a sermon at St. Anne's. "I was impressed," he said. "What impressed me was that it didn't say anything. Nothing. When you walked out of there, it didn't make any difference whether you'd walked in, unless you dug stained-glass windows. . . . Because the meek are inheriting nothing."[37]

The song (like its title) draws from the Sermon on the Mount. The opening line comes from Matthew 5:5, "Blessed are the meek: for they shall inherit the earth," but halts at the word "inherit," presumably because the meek inherit nothing tangible as far as Simon could see. The next line in the song about the lamb "whose blood flows" derives from "Worthy is the Lamb that hath been slain" (Revelation 5:12 ASV). The fourth line quotes words from Psalm 22:1, "My God, my God, why hast thou forsaken me?," and cited by Jesus on the cross (Matthew 27:46).

His call for the "land and the kingdom" to be blessed could be his paraphrase of "Blessed is the nation whose God is Jehovah" (Psalm 33:12 ASV) or even "Blessed is the kingdom that cometh, the kingdom of our father David: Hosanna in the highest" (Mark 11:10 ASV).

Because the song is deliberately fragmented to mirror the thinking of a confused mind, it's difficult to determine Simon's viewpoint. It's as though he's wandering in and out of a church, hearing a snatch of an uplifting sermon here, experiencing poverty and homelessness there, and questioning whether what is preached in the church has any useful effect on the disenfranchised people outside its walls.

Song: "Blessed"

Artist: Simon & Garfunkel

Album: *Sounds of Silence*

Release: January 17, 1966

Studio: Columbia Studios, New York, NY

Personnel: Paul Simon (vocals, guitar), Art Garfunkel (vocals), Glen Campbell (guitar), Joe Osborn (bass), Hal Blaine (drums)

Writer: Paul Simon

Producer: Tom Wilson

Label: Columbia

Other Significant Recordings: The Tremeloes (1966), Guy Darrell (1966)

Also by Simon & Garfunkel: "Benedictus" (1964), "Go Tell It on the Mountain" (1964), "7 O'Clock News / Silent Night" (1966)

25

GOD ONLY KNOWS
THE BEACH BOYS
....
1966

T he idiom "God only knows" means no more than "I have no idea," but this song restores the cliché to its original meaning. The idea of God knowing and seeing all is there from the beginning of the Bible, but the phrase "God only knows" probably owes most to a saying of Jesus's. After telling his disciples about "the end of the world," he added, "But of that day and hour knoweth no one, not even the angels of heaven, neither the Son, but the Father only" (Matthew 24:36 ASV).

A similar thought about God's omniscience comes in the Psalms.

> O Lord, thou hast searched me, and known me. Thou knowest
> my downsitting and mine uprising, thou understandest my
> thought afar off. Thou compassest my path and my lying
> down, and art acquainted with all my ways. For there is
> not a word in my tongue, but, lo, O Lord, thou knowest it
> altogether. (139:1–4)

The words to "God Only Knows" were written by Tony Asher and set to music by Brian Wilson. The basic song was completed in around forty-five minutes, Wilson said. At the time, both writers worried that it may have been too controversial to use God's name in a pop song. "Unless you were Kate Smith and you were saying 'God Bless America,' no-one thought you could say 'God' in a song," explained Asher. "No one had done it. And Brian didn't want to be the first person to try it. He said, 'We'll just never get any air play.'" Wilson's wife, Marilyn, was also apprehensive. "I thought it was almost too religious," she said. "Too square."[38]

Asher was ultimately convinced that it would be heard as a "legitimately beautiful love song" and that it would be obvious that "it was not saying anything disparaging or blasphemous about God." He said to Wilson, "What are we going to say? Heck only knows? Gosh only knows?"

Wilson asked his brother Carl to sing the lead vocal because he was thought to be the Beach Boy with the most "spiritual" of interests. "At present our influences are of a religious nature," Carl Wilson told an interviewer at the time. "Not any specific religion, but an idea based upon that of a universal consciousness. . . . The spiritual concept of happiness and doing good to others is extremely important to the lyric of our songs, and the religious element of some of the better church music is also contained within some of our new work."[39]

Songwriter Jimmy Webb regarded the song as akin to the church music of J. S. Bach. "It represents the whole tradition of liturgical music that I feel is a spiritual part of Brian's music," he said. "And Carl's singing was pretty much at its pinnacle—as good as it ever got."[40]

It's often said that "God Only Knows" was banned by a handful of radio stations in the South on the grounds that it was blasphemous, but no contemporary news reports are cited as evidence. It's unlikely to have happened because it was released as the B-side of "Wouldn't It Be Nice" in America and, therefore, DJs wouldn't have been compelled to play it anyway.

Song: "God Only Knows"

Artist: The Beach Boys

Single: A-side: "God Only Knows" / B-side: "Wouldn't it Be Nice"

Release: July 22, 1966

Album: *Pet Sounds*

Studio: United Western Recorders & CBS Columbia Square, Los Angeles, CA

Personnel: Bruce Johnston (harmony and backing vocals), Brian Wilson (harmony and backing vocals), Carl Wilson (lead and backing vocals), Hal Blaine (drums, sleigh bells), Jessie Erlich (cello), Carl Fortina (accordion), Jim Gordon (percussion), Bill Green (flute), Leonard Hartman (clarinet), Jim Horn (flute, percussion), Leonard Malarsky (violin), Jay Migliori (clarinet), Frank Marocco (accordion), Ray Pohlman (electric bass), Larry Knechtel (harpsichord, organ), Don Randi (tack piano), Lyle Ritz (string bass), Alan Robinson (French horn), Sidney Sharp (violin)

Writers: Brian Wilson (music), Tony Asher (lyrics)

Producer: Brian Wilson

Label: Capitol

Highest Chart Position: 39 (US), 2 (UK)

Other Significant Recordings: Neil Diamond (1977), Glen Campbell (1977), David Bowie (1984)

26

WITHIN YOU WITHOUT YOU
THE BEATLES

1967

B y the middle of 1967, George Harrison was two years into his exploration of the music, culture, and religion of India. It had started with idle interest in a sitar used on the set of the Beatles' movie *Help!*, progressed into meetings with Asian musicians in London, and eventually led to him spending time in India studying with sitar maestro Ravi Shankar.

Although he had played sitar on "Norwegian Wood" (1965) and "Love You To" (1966), "Within You Without You" was the first time he had combined the sound and philosophy of India. He was enchanted by what he saw of Hinduism not only because it appeared to explain experiences he'd had on LSD but also because the religion was absorbed into every aspect of the lives of its adherents. The Catholicism he'd grown up with in Liverpool was often for Sundays only. Hinduism was 24/7 and affected everything from food and clothing to art and ritual.

The words of "Within You Without You" were written after an intense discussion with friends about the big spiritual issues of the day. They were largely based on what he had absorbed from books by Swami Vivekananda and Paramahansa Yogananda; the Hindu view that "we're all one" and the perception of individuality and separation is the product of illusion.

We can only merge with the whole by freeing ourselves from the illusory world.

However, into this song he dropped two of his favorite Bible references. The first is about the kingdom of God being "within": "And when he was demanded of the Pharisees, when the kingdom of God should come, he answered them and said, The kingdom of God cometh not with observation: Neither shall they say, Lo here! or, lo there! for, behold, the kingdom of God is within you" (Luke 17:20–21).

Bible scholars debate whether Jesus meant the kingdom of God indwelt each follower or whether he meant the kingdom was "among" or "in the midst of" them. Harrison took the former meaning and argued that "God" was already present in everyone but that not everyone had "God realization." This was achievable only through spiritual practices such as meditation, yoga, fasting, and sensory deprivation. In the song, he says, "Try to realise it's all within yourself."

The second biblical quotation is about those who "gain the world and lose their soul." This is again a quote of Jesus and is reported in three of the Gospels:

> Then said Jesus unto his disciples, If any man will come
> after me, let him deny himself, and take up his cross, and
> follow me. For whosoever will save his life shall lose it: and
> whosoever will lose his life for my sake shall find it. For
> what is a man profited, if he shall gain the whole world, and
> lose his own soul? or what shall a man give in exchange for
> his soul? (Matthew 16:24–26; see also Mark 8:34–37 and
> Luke 9:23–25)

Opinion is divided as to whether "Within You Without You" deserved inclusion on *Sgt. Pepper's Lonely Hearts Club Band*. Some critics feel that it's out of place and slows down the flow of the album. Others see it not only as a pioneering example of world music but also as emblematic of the hippie beliefs of 1967, when many young people truly believed that their love would "change the world."

Song: "Within You Without You"

Artist: The Beatles

Album: *Sgt. Pepper's Lonely Hearts Club Band*

Release: May 26, 1967

Studio: EMI Recording Studio, Abbey Road, London

Personnel: George Harrison (sitar, vocals), Anna Joshi (dilruba), Amrit Gajjar (dilruba), Buddhadev Kansara (tamboura), Natwar Soni (tabla), eight violins and cellos of the London Symphony Orchestra

Writer: George Harrison

Producer: George Martin

Label: Parlophone (UK), Capitol (USA)

Other Significant Recordings: Big Jim Sullivan (1967), Sonic Youth (1988), Flaming Lips (2014)

Also by George Harrison: "My Sweet Lord" (1970), "Give Me Love (Give Me Peace on Earth)" (1973), "If You Believe" (1979)

27

I SHALL BE RELEASED

THE BAND

1968

The Band—who had been Bob Dylan's backing group on his 1966 tour of Europe and America and who had later recorded a collection of Dylan's songs at the West Saugerties home of Rick Danko, Garth Hudson, and Richard Manuel—embodied the late 1960s countercultural move from city to country, from pop to tradition, and from colorful kaftans to serviceable work clothes.

The five men in the photo put out to publicize their debut album, *Music from Big Pink*, looked as though they'd come from the nineteenth-century frontier. One had a moustache, three had beards, and four wore hats. They were standing stock-still in a field looking as serious as Victorians posing for a daguerreotype.

They were the antithesis to the wild rock lineups of the era. There was no strutting, no pouting, and no unisex attire. It was as if they'd emerged from the soil along with the trees behind them. Their name—the Band—said it all. It was a matter-of-fact description that singled out no particular performer and signaled serious intention. This was a "band," not a "group." They were men, not boys.

Part of this desire to connect with tradition involved adopting biblical language. Their songs seemed to be about religion even when they weren't. "To Kingdom Come," for example, speaks of "his only son," "false witness," "evil eye," and "haints [ghosts] and saints." "The Weight" is set in Nazareth (Nazareth, Pennsylvania, according to writer Robbie Robertson), mentions "the Devil" and "judgment day," and features characters called "Moses" and "Luke."

Into this mix, they brought the newly written Dylan song "I Shall Be Released," which is about a prisoner awaiting parole but also about redemption. Dylan's central metaphor of seeing a light shining "from the west unto the east," used at the end of each verse, is taken from the description given by Jesus about his return at the end of the age: "For as the lightning cometh out of the east, and shineth even unto the west; so shall also the coming of the Son of man be" (Matthew 24:27).

Although "released" sounds like a biblical word describing freedom from sin's penalty, the only time it is used is when the crowd calling for the death of Jesus is offered the opportunity to release either him or the imprisoned and condemned robber Barabbas. (The crowd opts for the release of Barabbas.) The spiritual equivalent is "redeemed" and the closest a Bible verse comes to saying "Any day now, I shall be redeemed" is when Jesus lists a series of signs of "the end" and adds, "And when these things begin to come to pass, then look up, and lift up your heads; for your redemption draweth nigh" (Luke 21:28).

Song: "I Shall Be Released"

Artist: The Band

Album: *Music from Big Pink*

Release: July 1, 1968

Studio: Capitol Studios, Los Angeles, CA

Personnel: Richard Manuel (lead vocal, piano), Rick Danko (vocal harmony, bass), Levon Helm (vocal harmony, drums), Garth Hudson (drums), Robbie Robertson (acoustic guitar)

Writer: Bob Dylan

Producer: John Simon

Label: Capitol

Other Significant Recordings: Joe Cocker (1969), Nina Simone (1969), Jack Johnson (2012)

Also by the Band: "To Kingdom Come" (1968), "The Unfaithful Servant" (1969), "Daniel and the Sacred Harp" (1970)

28

I AM A PILGRIM

THE BYRDS

1968

B y 1968, the Byrds had lost three founding members and were seeking a new direction now that folk rock had apparently reached its limits. Roger McGuinn was keen to explore all strands of American music, but the group's latest member, twenty-one-year-old Gram Parsons, had a specific vision for melding rock with country music, something he'd explored in two previous short-lived bands. McGuinn willingly succumbed to his fresh ideas, and the resulting album, *Sweetheart of the Rodeo*, announced the arrival of "country rock," a genre that would reach its peak in the mid-1970s with bands like the Eagles.

Although none of the Byrds was a Christian at the time, two of the songs that Parsons urged the band to record were explicitly so. The Louvin Brothers, two close harmony singers from Kentucky, wrote "The Christian Life," and "I Am a Pilgrim" had been popularized by Merle Travis, one of country music's big hitters who'd also played in gospel groups. The Byrds performed both songs with a sense of irony.

Travis, who cut "I Am a Pilgrim" for his 1947 album *Folk Songs of the Hills*, introduces it as follows: "When I first got big enough to start running around by myself at nights, the first place I wanted to go was to the camp

95

meetings and to the brush arbor meetings and hear them singing them good ole songs. I learned a lot of them old songs, but there's one 'specially that I like better than all the rest, and I remember it today just as well as I did the day I learned it. The name of it is 'I Am a Pilgrim.'"

Mose Rager, a guitar player and miner from Kentucky, who taught Travis the thumb-picking style, also taught him this song. Interviewed by folk song scholar D. K. Wilgus in 1961, Rager confirmed Travis's story of its origins. "It's an old song everybody sang," he said. "We'd all get together at the edge of town and just sit out there 'til midnight singing old hymns. As far as I know, 'I Am a Pilgrim' is just an old brush arbor song."[41]

Brush arbor songs were hymns developed during open-air revival meetings in the South that had no attributed authors. Many of them came in different versions as singers and choir leaders added their arrangements and words. The version that Rager adopted in 1930s Kentucky differs from the mid-nineteenth-century hymn attributed to Mary Dana Shindler[42] that can be found in 360 different hymnals ("I'm a pilgrim, and I'm a stranger / I can tarry, I can tarry but a night"), and also from the gospel song recorded by the Soul Stirrers in 1961 ("I'm a pilgrim and a stranger / Travelin' through this ole barren land / I got a home in yonder city, Lord / And I will do the best I can").

All the versions portray the Christian believer as out of place in this world but looking forward to crossing the Jordan, where all burdens will be lifted, all tears will be wiped away, and there will be a homecoming.

The concept of God's chosen people as "strangers" emerges from when the Israelites were held captive in Egypt and later when the Jews were taken to the city of Babylon. In both situations, they risked losing their cultural identity and their religion. As a consequence, they yearned to be "at home" with the freedom to worship. The New Testament writer of Hebrews, commenting on the Israelite patriarchs, said they "confessed that they were strangers and pilgrims on the earth" (11:13).

Members of the early church felt similarly displaced in the cultures of Rome, Ephesus, Athens, and Corinth, where pantheons of gods were followed. They identified with the Jewish feeling of displacement. The letter of 1 Peter advised, "Beloved, I beseech you as sojourners and pilgrims, to abstain from fleshly lusts, which war against the soul" (2:11 ASV).

The reference in "I Am a Pilgrim" to having a home in "yonder city" draws on verses such as "knowing that, whilst we are at home in the body, we are absent from the Lord" (2 Corinthians 5:6) and "I saw the holy city, new Jerusalem, coming down out of heaven from God, made ready as a bride adorned for her husband" (Revelation 21:2 ASV). However, the description of the city as "not made by hand" conflates the concept of the new Jerusalem with the separate but related idea of the new resurrection body, as in knowing "that if the earthly house of our tabernacle be dissolved, we have a building from God, a house not made with hands, eternal, in the heavens" (2 Corinthians 5:1 ASV).

The lines "If I can just touch the hem of his garment, good Lord / Then I know he'd take me home" refer to a woman healed by Jesus. "[She] came behind him, and touched the border of his garment: for she said within herself, If I do but touch his garment, I shall be made whole" (Matthew 9:20–21 ASV). This practice became commonplace. "[The sick] besought him that they might only touch the border of his garment: and as many as touched were made whole" (Matthew 14:36 ASV).

Roger McGuinn and Chris Hillman rearranged Merle Travis's version slightly and a few words were tweaked, but the spirit and sense were kept intact. Although they'd only made it as a tribute to a stream of music, they both admitted it marked a significant step in enlarging the vocabulary of rock music to deal with spiritual topics. Ten years later, McGuinn became a Christian. Subsequently, Chris Hillman also became a Christian: "I accepted him [Jesus], truly accepted him, and proceeded to embrace the church and start learning," said McGuinn. "And learning means I picked up the Bible, and going to church, and was baptized."[43]

Song: "I Am a Pilgrim"

Artist: The Byrds

Album: *Sweetheart of the Rodeo*

Release: August 30, 1968

Studio: Columbia Studios, Nashville, TN; Columbia Studios, Hollywood, CA

Personnel: Roger McGuinn (guitar and vocals), Gram Parsons (guitar), Clarence White (guitar), Chris Hillman (bass), Kevin Kelley (drums)

Writer: Traditional, arranged by Roger McGuinn and Chris Hillman

Producer: Gary Usher

Label: Columbia

Other Significant Recordings: Heavenly Gospel Singers (1936), Merle Travis (1947), Tennessee Ernie Ford (1955)

Also by the Byrds: "Oil in My Lamp" (1969), "Glory, Glory (Lay My Burden Down)" (1971), "My Destiny" (1971)

29 ALL ALONG THE WATCHTOWER
THE JIMI HENDRIX EXPERIENCE

....

1968

O n December 27, 1967, Columbia Records released Bob Dylan's album *John Wesley Harding*, his first since *Blonde on Blonde* in May 1966. A lot had happened between those two dates both in the music business and in youth culture, including the development of psychedelic rock, *Sgt. Pepper* by the Beatles, and the so-called Summer of Love.

The new album was keenly anticipated. Dylan's choice of musical direction was likely to become a significant influence on the music of 1968 and beyond. Each new recording he made responded to the mood of the times and commented on it in oblique ways. The general feeling at the close of 1967 was that rock would become ever more complex and experimental. The day before Dylan's album was launched, the Beatles had premiered their TV film *Magical Mystery Tour* that included the experimental track "I Am the Walrus."

Dylan had spent the previous eighteen months secluded in the arts colony of Woodstock in upper New York State. He'd stopped touring, was rarely seen at music events, and was committed to raising his young family. He hadn't stopped writing, though (as was evidenced by bootlegs of recordings of new songs made with the Band), but he appeared less concerned about competing with his contemporaries in the charts. He was enjoying a time of reflection and restoration. His iconic shock of curly hair was trimmed back, fuzz appeared on his chin, and the Carnaby Street clothing of polka dot shirts and hipster slacks was replaced by more sober attire.

His late-1967 offering confounded everyone's expectations. He'd gone in an opposite direction. His response to the lavishness and color of the *Sgt. Pepper* sleeve was a gray-framed cover with a black-and-white snapshot of him with three unidentified men in a country location. His response to the surrealistic lyrics of the era was a collection of moral tales, parables, puzzles, and ballads rooted in traditional folk forms. There was no reference to turning on, tuning in, or dropping out. Ten years later he would refer to it as "the first biblical rock album."

The language of new songs such as "I Dreamed I Saw St. Augustine," "The Ballad of Frankie Lee and Judas Priest," "Dear Landlord," and "The Wicked Messenger" reflected his new immersion in the Bible. It was as though he was deliberately eschewing the language of pop culture and symbolic poetry for something with a more established heritage. As he commented in one song from this period, "Strap yourself / To the tree with roots / You ain't goin' nowhere" (from "You Ain't Goin' Nowhere").

Within weeks of the album's release, Jimi Hendrix (a huge Dylan fan) went into a London studio to record "All Along the Watchtower," the fourth song on the first side of *John Wesley Harding*. His early attempts were abandoned, but during the summer in New York he revisited it and worked painstakingly on his version.

The result was one of the most inspired singles of the era, a masterful blend of great lyrics and great musicianship. Hendrix dug out meaning from every phrase that Dylan had provided, and Dylan pushed Hendrix to new heights of instrumental imagination.

The song derived its title and imagery from a vision of the fall of Babylon as seen by Isaiah. From the prophet, Dylan found the watchtower, princes, pair of riders, bare feet, talk of confusion, and businessmen.

A grievous vision is declared unto me; the treacherous dealer dealeth treacherously, and the spoiler spoileth. Go up, O Elam:

besiege, O Media; all the sighing thereof have I made to cease. Therefore are my loins filled with pain: pangs have taken hold upon me, as the pangs of a woman that travaileth: I was bowed down at the hearing of it; I was dismayed at the seeing of it. My heart panted, fearfulness affrighted me: the night of my pleasure hath he turned into fear unto me. Prepare the table, watch in the watchtower, eat, drink: arise, ye princes, and anoint the shield. For thus hath the LORD said unto me, Go, set a watchman, let him declare what he seeth. And he saw a chariot with a couple of horsemen, a chariot of asses, and a chariot of camels; and he hearkened diligently with much heed: And he cried, A lion: My lord, I stand continually upon the watchtower in the daytime, and I am set in my ward whole nights: And, behold, here cometh a chariot of men, with a couple of horsemen. And he answered and said, Babylon is fallen, is fallen; and all the graven images of her gods he hath broken unto the ground. (Isaiah 21:2–9)

Dylan's story is enigmatic. It's not possible to say with certainty (as some have) that his "thief" is a reference to one of the crucified thieves, or even to the "day of the Lord" that Paul said would come as "a thief in the night" (1 Thessalonians 5:2 ASV), that "let us not talk falsely" is derived from "the prophets prophesy falsely" (Jeremiah 5:31), or that "a wildcat did growl" comes from the warning, "Be sober, be vigilant; because your adversary the devil, as a roaring lion, walketh about, seeking whom he may devour" (1 Peter 5:8).

Like so much of his work, the song is about imminent collapse and judgment. The line "the hour is getting late" echoes Jesus's warning in answer to the question from the disciples, "What shall be the sign of thy coming, and of the end of the world?" His answer was,

Watch therefore: for ye know not what hour your Lord doth come. But know this, that if the goodman of the house had known in what watch the thief would come, he would have watched, and would not have suffered his house to be broken up. Therefore be ye also ready: for in such an hour as ye think not the Son of man cometh. Who then is a faithful and wise servant, whom his lord hath made ruler over his household, to give them meat in due season? Blessed is that servant, whom his lord when he cometh shall find so doing. Verily I say unto you, That he shall make him ruler over all his goods. But and if that evil servant shall say in his heart, My lord delayeth his coming; and shall begin to smite his fellowservants, and to eat and drink with the drunken; the lord of that servant shall come in a day when he looketh not for him, and in an hour that he is not aware of, and shall cut him asunder, and appoint him his portion with the hypocrites: there shall be weeping and gnashing of teeth. (Matthew 24:42–51)

What makes the song's story so effective is its sparseness. There are only twelve lines, but they tell a story that could fill twelve pages.

Song: "All Along the Watchtower"

Artist: The Jimi Hendrix Experience

Single: A-side: "All Along the Watchtower" / B-side: "Burning of the Midnight Lamp"

Release: September 21, 1968 (US), October 18, 1968 (UK)

Album: *Electric Ladyland*

Studio: Olympic Sound Studios, Barnes, London; Record Plant, New York, NY

Personnel: Jimi Hendrix (vocals, lead guitar, bass guitar), Mitch Mitchell (drums), Brian Jones (percussion), Dave Mason (acoustic 12-string guitar)

Writer: Bob Dylan

Producer: Jimi Hendrix

Label: Reprise (US), Track (UK)

Highest Chart Position: 20 (US), 11 (UK)

Other Significant Recordings: Bob Dylan (1967), U2 (1988), Neil Young (2000)

Also by the Jimi Hendrix Experience: "Castles Made of Sand" (1967), "Voodo Chile" (1968), "Angel" (1971)

30

JOB'S TEARS
THE INCREDIBLE STRING BAND

1968

The Incredible String Band epitomized a whimsical, mystical strain of British 1960s counterculture that spurned the trappings of modern culture, practiced communal living, and sought wisdom in Eastern religions, Gnosticism, legend, and fable. When Mike Heron and Robin Williamson came on stage dressed in their medieval-like clothes to sit on a Persian carpet surrounded by an assortment of acoustic musical instruments from countries like Afghanistan, Morocco, and India, it was as if they'd been beamed in from another dimension. It was hard to imagine them flying on planes or shopping in twentieth-century supermarkets.

For a few years in the late 1960s, they were the hippest of acts, gaining praise from the Beatles and Bob Dylan, appearing at the Woodstock Festival (although edited out of the final film and album), and pioneering a blend of world folk music (instrumentally) and spiritual questing (lyrically).

Heron and Williamson crafted poetic songs in the Romantic tradition that exalted nature, explored myths and dreams, and were rich in symbolism. Heron was more jaunty and melodic, Williamson more reflective and lyrical, but they were united in seeking transcendence and timeless truths behind the apparently random goings-on in the world. In their song "The

Half-Remarkable Question," they sang, "O it's the old forgotten question / What is it that we are part of? / What is it that we are?" In a questionnaire published in their first songbook, Williamson wrote, "Music is prayer. Everything else is interesting in an infinite sort of way."[44]

The Bible was just one of many books they sourced. They were also digging into the Bhagavad Gita, the Tibetan Book of the Dead, *The White Goddess* by Robert Graves, *Life Ahead* by Krishnamurti, the Qur'an, and the Book of Common Prayer. In the space of one song, a reference to Puritan poetry could be linked with Greek myth and New Testament wisdom.

"Job's Tears," the first track on the first disc of their ambitious double album *Wee Tam and the Big Huge*, is typical of this syncretism. It invokes the Bible, hymns, and spirituals while also tipping its hat to alchemy, Greek Orthodoxy, Platonism, Buddhism, and even Groucho Marx.

The title is misleading. It suggests that the song is about the Old Testament story of Job, whom God allowed to be afflicted by Satan, but the phrase was taken from a tropical plant of that name (coix lacryma-jobi) that Williamson was introduced to as a child by an elderly relative. The lyrics instead outline the passion of Jesus, although Williamson admits it was written as a stream of consciousness rather than as a calculated narrative. "The reed they brought him / Sponge and vinegar" refers to a centurion's feeble attempt to allay his pain while on the cross: "And straightway one of them ran, and took a sponge, and filled it with vinegar, and put it on a reed, and gave him to drink" (Matthew 27:48). "The sword that killed him" refers to the wound in his side: "But one of the soldiers with a spear pierced his side, and forthwith came there out blood and water" (John 19:34). "Brother soldiers / Stop your gambling" is an appeal to the Romans who made his seamless garment the prize in a lottery at the foot of the cross: "And they crucified him, and parted his garments, casting lots: that it might be fulfilled which was spoken by the prophet, They parted my garments among them, and upon my vesture did they cast lots" (Matthew 27:35).

The song then comes to the resurrection. "The winter and midnight / could not hold him" alludes to "Whom God hath raised up, having loosed the pains of death: because it was not possible that he should be holden of it" (Acts 2:24), and "The grave was empty / Where they had laid him" speaks of the angel at the tomb: "Do not be alarmed. You seek Jesus of Nazareth, who was crucified. He has risen; he is not here. See the place where they laid him" (Mark 16:6 ESV).

"Job's Tears" ends with references to heaven, most of them taken from the book of Revelation. It speaks of "the old golden land," probably a reference to the "new Jerusalem," where "the street of the city was pure gold, as it were transparent glass" (Revelation 21:21); an angel writing his name in a "golden book," probably a reference to "the book of life" (Revelation 3:5); and "I'll put on my crown / Over in the old golden land," a reference to the twenty-four elders who "cast their crowns before the throne, saying, 'Worthy art thou, our Lord and our God, to receive the glory and the honor and the power: for thou didst create all things, and because of thy will they were, and were created'" (Revelation 4:10–11 ASV).

The first line in the last stanza of "Job's Tears"—"We'll understand it better in the sweet bye and bye"—comes from a spiritual that Heron and Williamson had heard on the album *The Real Bahamas*, released in 1966, where it was sung by the Pinder family (Raymond, Edith, and Geneva) and their friend Joseph Spence.

The author of this song was Charles Albert Tindley (referred to earlier with reference to "Peace in the Valley" and "Stand by Me"), who wrote "We'll Understand It Better By and By" in 1905 during a difficult time in his ministry. It was based on the passage "For now we see through a glass, darkly; but then face to face: now I know in part; but then shall I know even as also I am known" (1 Corinthians 13:12).

> By and by, when the morning comes,
> When the saints of God are gathered home,
> We'll tell the story how we've overcome
> For we'll understand it better by and by.

Song: "Job's Tears"
Artist: The Incredible String Band
Album: *Wee Tam and the Big Huge* (Disc One and Disc Two, respectively)
Release: November 1, 1968

Studio: Sound Techniques, London

Personnel: Robin Williamson (vocals, guitar), Mike Heron (guitar)

Writer: Robin Williamson

Producer: Joe Boyd

Label: Elektra

Also by the Incredible String Band: "A Very Cellular Song" (1968), "The Mountain of God" (1968), "Adam and Eve" (1971)

ASTRAL WEEKS

31

VAN MORRISON

. . . .

1968

Although born and raised in Belfast, Northern Ireland, Van Morrison's exposure to music and religion as a child was closer to that of a contemporary raised in Memphis, Tennessee, or Macon, Georgia. His father collected imported jazz, folk, blues, country, and gospel records, and Morrison tuned his radio to Voice of America and the American Forces Network, where he heard all the contemporary Stateside rock 'n' roll and R&B hits. At the same time, as a resident of protestant East Belfast, he was surrounded by the language of sermons, hymns, and the Bible. He attended Sunday school at a Brethren gospel hall at the end of his street.

As a teenager, he first played skiffle, then Irish showband music, before settling into R&B and eventually becoming commercially successful with the band Them. In his solo career, he embarked on a spiritual quest for transcendence that resulted in such songs as "Into the Mystic," "Full Force Gale," "By His Grace," "Hymns to the Silence," "Haunts of Ancient Peace," and "She Gives Me Religion."

"Astral Weeks," recorded in New York with a group of session musicians he had never met before, was the start of that process. A large part of the lyrics are impressionistic and not meant to be received as commentary. All that can be said for certain is that it's an appeal to a girl to come back to him in order to bring healing and rebirth.

As John Donne's metaphysical poems saw the spiritual in the sensual and the sensual in the spiritual, "Astral Weeks" travels from the earthy—back roads, ditches, viaducts, steel rims—to the heavenly. Morrison likens the experience of having his eyes kissed to being "born again," and this leads him to extemporize on the subject of salvation.

The term "born again" comes from Jesus, who used it in a conversation with Nicodemus, a Pharisee and an official among the Jews, who commended him on his miracles and said they were proof that he was a teacher from God:

> Jesus answered him, "Truly, truly, I say to you, unless one
> is born again he cannot see the kingdom of God." Nicodemus
> said to him, "How can a man be born when he is old? Can
> he enter a second time into his mother's womb and be
> born?" Jesus answered, "Truly, truly, I say to you, unless one is
> born of water and the Spirit, he cannot enter the kingdom of
> God. That which is born of the flesh is flesh, and that which is
> born of the Spirit is spirit." (John 3:3–6 ESV)

Morrison uses mention of "born again" to riff on a number of heavenly metaphors: "another world," "another time," "a home on high," "a stranger in this world," "way up in the heaven." These phrases may have been suggested to him by country songs he heard in his childhood, such as "I Am a Pilgrim" by Merle Travis (1947), "How Far Is Heaven" by Kitty Wells (1950), and "There's a Better Home" by Webb Pierce (1953). As the song ends and he's reduced to moans, hums, and whispers, it sounds as though he's been caught up into the clouds and has left behind the world of corruption.

Song: "Astral Weeks"
Artist: Van Morrison
Album: *Astral Weeks*
Release: November 1968

Studio: Century Sound Studios, New York, NY

Personnel: Van Morrison (vocals), Richard Davis (bass guitar), Jay Berliner (guitar), John Payne (flute), Connie Kay (drums), Warren Smith Jr. (percussion)

Writer: Van Morrison

Producer: Lewis Merenstein

Label: Warner Brothers

Also by Van Morrison: "Full Force Gale" (1979), "Whenever God Shines His Light" (duet with Cliff Richard, 1989), "Be Thou My Vision" (1991)

SYMPATHY FOR THE DEVIL

32 THE ROLLING STONES

1968

The immediate stimuli for "Sympathy for the Devil" were the nineteenth-century poems of French poet Charles Baudelaire and Mikhail Bulgakov's recently translated Russian novel *The Master and Margarita*, which had been gifted to Mick Jagger by his girlfriend, Marianne Faithful. Some of Bulgakov's central scenes, including a suave devil visiting Russia and Pontius Pilate interrogating Jesus, ended up in the song.

Baudelaire's influence most likely came from his 1857 collection *Les Fleurs du mal*, in particular the poem "Les Litanies de Satan," that begins

> O thou of Angels loveliest, most wise,
> O God betrayed by fate, deprived of praise,
> Satan, have mercy on my long distress![45]

Originally titled "The Devil Is My Name," the song is an examination of evil within the devil, who is portrayed as its embodiment without necessarily being an actual spiritual entity. Even so, evil is shown to be more powerful and longer lasting than the people it employs. Jagger catalogs some of history's bloody episodes—the Bolshevik Revolution in Russia, the Hundred Years'

110

War between England and France, the blitz of London by the Germans, the assassinations of John and Robert Kennedy, the crucifixion of Jesus Christ—and places Lucifer at the heart of them all. He is the manipulator, deceiver, and destroyer.

His description of the devil as "a man of wealth and taste" follows Bulgakov, who in turn follows Paul, who warned his readers that the devil is so deceptive that he can be "transformed into an angel of light" (2 Corinthians 11:14). Jagger uses the synonym "Lucifer" ("light bringer"), which acknowledges the traditional Christian belief that the devil was originally an angel, characterized by light, that rebelled against God before the creation of Adam and Eve.

> How art thou fallen from heaven, O Lucifer, son of the morning! how art thou cut down to the ground, which didst weaken the nations! For thou hast said in thine heart, I will ascend into heaven, I will exalt my throne above the stars of God: I will sit also upon the mount of the congregation, in the sides of the north: I will ascend above the heights of the clouds; I will be like the most High. Yet thou shalt be brought down to hell, to the sides of the pit. (Isaiah 14:12–15)

The reference to the devil stealing men's souls may come from "Be sober, be vigilant; because your adversary the devil, as a roaring lion, walketh about, seeking whom he may devour" (1 Peter 5:8).

At the core of the song is the passion of Jesus. This starts with his "moment of doubt and pain," which could refer either to his prayer in the Garden of Gethsemane—"And he went a little farther, and fell on his face, and prayed, saying, O my Father, if it be possible, let this cup pass from me: nevertheless not as I will, but as thou wilt" (Matthew 26:39)—or his abandonment on the cross—"And about the ninth hour Jesus cried with a loud voice, saying, Eli, Eli, lama sabachthani? that is to say, My God, my God, why hast thou forsaken me?" (Matthew 27:46).

During the trial of Jesus, Jagger has the devil ensuring that Pilate sentences Jesus to death but "washed his hands" as an attempt to absolve himself of personal responsibility, clearly a reference to the gospel narrative: "When Pilate saw that he could prevail nothing, but that rather a tumult was made, he took water, and washed his hands before the multitude, saying, I am innocent of the blood of this just person: see ye to it" (Matthew 27:24).

The song concludes with a vision of the world where cops are criminals, sinners are saints, and heads are tails. Jagger later said that it was a world where everything was turned "upside down."[46] If he had needed a supporting verse, he could have found it in the warning of Isaiah: "Woe unto them that call evil good, and good evil; that put darkness for light, and light for darkness; that put bitter for sweet, and sweet for bitter!" (Isaiah 5:20).

Despite its provocative title, the song isn't a celebration of Satan or Satanism but an exposé of evil, with Jagger literally playing devil's advocate. Although he has since said that it's more about human wickedness than a literal devil,[47] it seems that Keith Richards may have a different interpretation. "'Sympathy' is quite an uplifting song," he said in 2002. "I've had very close contact with Lucifer. I've met him several times. . . . You might as well accept the fact that evil is there and deal with it any way you can. 'Sympathy for the Devil' is a song that says—don't forget him. If you confront him, then he's out of a job."[48]

Song: "Sympathy for the Devil"

Artist: The Rolling Stones

Album: *Beggars Banquet*

Release: December 6, 1968

Studio: Olympic Sound Studios, Barnes, London

Personnel: Mick Jagger (vocals), Brian Jones (lead guitar), Keith Richards (rhythm guitar), Bill Wyman (bass guitar, maracas), Charlie Watts (drums), Nicky Hopkins (piano), Rocky Dijon (congas), Anita Pallenberg (backing vocals), Marianne Faithful (backing vocals), Jimmy Miller (backing vocals)

Writers: Mick Jagger, Keith Richards

Producer: Jimmy Miller

Label: Decca (UK), London Records (USA)

Other Significant Recordings: Guns N' Roses (1994), Ozzy Osbourne (2005), Motörhead (2015)

Also by the Rolling Stones: "Shine a Light" (1972), "Dancing with Mr. D." (1973)

33

PRODIGAL SON
THE ROLLING STONES

....

1968

The *Beggars Banquet* album marked a return to simplicity for the Rolling Stones, just as *John Wesley Harding* had done for Bob Dylan and the *White Album* had done for the Beatles. After dabbling in electronic sounds and studio wizardry on *Their Satanic Majesties Request*, they went back to the folk and blues music that had inspired them in their youth.

"Prodigal Son" was one such track—a simple gospel-blues song with finger-picked acoustic guitar and bent notes. The sleeve notes say that all the songs were "written by Mick Jagger and Keith Richard," but advance publicity material noted that "Prodigal Son" was a "traditional blues first recorded in 1927 by Rev. John Wilkinson."

The truth soon emerged that the author was not "John Wilkinson" but the Rev. Robert Wilkins (1896–1987), who'd appeared at the Newport Folk Festival in 1964 and had recorded "The Prodigal Son" in February of that year on an album called *Reverend Robert Wilkins: Memphis Gospel Singer.* What's more, the seventy-three-year-old was still very much alive and, when contacted by journalists, told them that he had no idea that the Rolling Stones had covered his work. A settlement was reached between the group and the preacher.

Although the Stones' version was only a third as long as Wilkins's, the verses left out don't compromise the essence of the parable told by Jesus and collected in the Gospel of Luke. It concerned the younger of two sons, who asked his father to advance him his inheritance and then took off to "a far country" where he squandered the money on "riotous living." When a famine hit the land, the now-penniless boy had to feed pigs to make ends meet. During this time of humiliation, he "[came] to himself" and returned home. The highlight of the story is the reconciliation with his father.

> But while he was yet afar off, his father saw him, and was moved with compassion, and ran, and fell on his neck, and kissed him. And the son said into him, Father, I have sinned against heaven, and in thy sight: I am no more worthy to be called thy son. But the father said to his servants, Bring forth quickly the best robe, and put it on him; and put a ring on his hand, and shoes on his feet: and bring the fatted calf, and kill it, and let us eat and make merry: for this my son was dead, and is alive again; he was lost, and is found. And they began to be merry. (Luke 15:20–24 ASV)

> Well, father said, "Eldest son, kill the fatted calf,
> Call the family round
> Kill that calf and call the family round
> My son was lost but now he is found"
> ("Prodigal Son")

Robert Wilkins was born twenty-five miles outside of Memphis in Hernando, Mississippi, in 1896. He'd recorded blues in the 1920s and 1930s but stopped after becoming a Christian in 1936, partly because of the church's view of the music.

In 1950, he was ordained as a minister for the Church of God in Christ, and when musicologist and record producer Dick Spottswood rediscovered him in 1964, he was running a church in Memphis. He recorded an album (*Memphis Gospel Singer*) for Spottswood's label, Piedmont, that featured blues-style songs with religious lyrics. One of the songs was "Prodigal Son," which was a Christian reworking of his 1929 blues recording "That's No Way to Get Along."[49] Writing in *Blues Unlimited* in July 1964, Spottswood referred to the new version as "one of the most stirring folk hymns ever recorded."

During the mid-1960s blues boom, Wilkins was invited to make a comeback and write more blues material, but he believed that the blues encouraged misery and didn't give adequate thanks to God. "With my type of singing and playing I believe I'd take the world if I was playing blues now," he said in 1968. "That's just the way I feel about it. But my conscience won't let me do it."[50]

Song: "Prodigal Son"

Artist: The Rolling Stones

Album: *Beggars Banquet*

Release: December 6, 1968

Studio: Olympic Sound Studios, Barnes, London, England

Personnel: Mick Jagger (vocals), Keith Richards (slide guitar, rhythm guitar), Bill Wyman (bass guitar, maracas), Charlie Watts (drums)

Writers: Mick Jagger, Keith Richards, Rev. Robert Wilkins

Producer: Jimmy Miller

Label: Decca (UK), London Records (USA)

Other Significant Recordings: Rev. Robert Wilkins (1929, 1964)

Also by the Rolling Stones: "Salt of the Earth" (1968), "I Just Want to See His Face" (1972), "Saint of Me" (1997)

BAD MOON RISING

34 CREEDENCE CLEARWATER REVIVAL

1969

The jaunty beat of his song disguises the dark vision of the lyric—"I know the end is comin' soon." This is John Fogerty's warning of impending doom. It suited the mood of the time. The feelings of optimism generated by the Summer of Love in 1967 were ebbing away by 1969. Not only was the longed-for utopia not being manifested, but there was moral and spiritual darkness.

"Bad Moon Rising" was prompted by its title (which Fogerty had written in his notebook simply because he liked the sound of it), and the 1941 black-and-white film *The Devil and Daniel Webster*, which was based on a short story by Stephen Vincent Benét in which a young farmer sells his soul to Mr. Scratch (the devil) in return for riches and success. "At one point in the movie, there was a huge hurricane," Fogerty told *Rolling Stone*. "Everybody's crops and houses are destroyed. Boom. Right next door is the guy's field who made the deal with the devil, and his corn is still straight up, six feet. That image was in my mind. . . . My song wasn't about Mr. Scratch, and it wasn't about the deal. It was about the apocalypse that was going to be visited upon us. . . . I took it in a biblical sense, meaning hurricanes and lightning—scary, spooky stuff."[51]

Raised and educated as a Catholic, Fogerty would have been familiar with the various omens of "the latter days" mentioned in the Bible, including a darkened sun and moon, shaken planets, and falling stars. The prophet Joel said, "I will shew wonders in the heavens and in the earth, blood, and fire, and pillars of smoke. The sun shall be turned into darkness, and the moon into blood, before the great and terrible day of the LORD come" (Joel 2:30–31).

The first moon landing was imminent as Fogerty worked on the song. Some Christians speculated that the death of an astronaut on the moon could fulfill the prophecy of the moon being turned "into blood." Others thought that if the surface of the moon was disturbed by human contact, it might reveal a red layer beneath surface dust.

The moon also features in New Testament end-times predictions. Jesus said the moon "shall not give her light" (Matthew 24:29), and in Revelation the opening of the sixth seal reveals the sun "black as sackcloth" and the moon "as blood" (Revelation 6:12).

In the rest of the song, Fogerty warned of environmental havoc and general tumult that could have been inspired by the Bible's apocalyptic scenario. The "trouble" could be the predicted "wars and rumors of wars" (Matthew 24:6 ASV), the "famines and earthquakes in divers places" (Matthew 24:7 ASV) and even the "lightning" could be the return of "the Son of man" who will come "as the lightning" (Luke 17:24 ASV).

"I don't think I was actually saying the world was coming to an end," Fogerty said, "but the song was a metaphor. I wasn't just writing about the weather. The times seemed to be in turmoil. Martin Luther King [Jr.] and Robert F. Kennedy had been assassinated. I knew it was a tumultuous time."[52]

Song: "Bad Moon Rising"

Artist: Creedence Clearwater Revival

Single: A-side: "Bad Moon Rising" / B-side: "Lodi"

Release: April 1969 (US); August 1969 (UK)

Album: *Green River*

Studio: Wally Heider's Studio, San Francisco, CA

Personnel: John Fogerty (lead guitar, vocals), Tom Fogerty (rhythm guitar), Stu Cook (bass guitar), Doug Clifford (drums)

Writer: John Fogerty

Producer: John Fogerty

Label: Fantasy (USA)

Highest Chart Position: 2 (US), 1 (UK)

Other Significant Recording: Emmylou Harris (1981), the Reels (1986), Thea Gilmore (2004)

Also by Creedence Clearwater Revival: "Fortunate Son" (1969), "Who'll Stop the Rain" (1970), "Long as I Can See the Light" (1970)

35

OH HAPPY DAY
THE EDWIN HAWKINS SINGERS

1969

Remarkably, in the year of Woodstock, Altamont, and the Manson Family killings, the reworked version of an eighteenth-century hymn written by an English nonconformist preacher and educator became a Top Ten hit in Britain, America, Canada, Ireland, France, Holland, and Germany. Just three years after hesitancy over the use of the word *God* in "God Only Knows" by the Beach Boys and one year after the use of *Jesus* by Simon & Garfunkel, there came a chart song proclaiming, "Oh happy day / When Jesus washed my sins away."

This is partly explained by it being gospel music. Listeners were able to accept a full-frontal gospel message from an African American choir in a way that they wouldn't have been able to from a white rock quartet. They accepted it as an integral part of an art form that they found passionate, uplifting, and worthy. Even so, none of the most revered gospel artists in history, including Mahalia Jackson, Sister Rosetta Tharpe, the Dixie Hummingbirds, and the Soul Stirrers, had enjoyed Top Ten success.

"Oh Happy Day" (or "O Happy Day" as it was originally titled) was first published in the posthumous *Hymns Founded on Various Texts in the Holy Scriptures* in 1755 written by Philip Doddridge (1702–1751), a dissenting minister from Northampton, England. Doddridge set up academies to educate the children of nonconformists at a time when Oxford and Cambridge only accepted Church of England members. His book *Rise and Progress of Religion in the Soul* is considered a spiritual classic and played a part in the conversion of William Wilberforce, the British MP who successfully fought for the abolition of slavery.

Doddridge wrote the words to over four hundred hymns, generally on the themes of his sermons. In a largely illiterate age, it was a way of providing a memorable précis of the message. "O Happy Day" was written for a sermon about a promise made to God by the Israelites: "And all Judah rejoiced at the oath: for they had sworn with all their heart, and sought him with their whole desire; and he was found of them: and the LORD gave them rest round about" (2 Chronicles 15:15). On its first publication, the heading read, "Rejoicing in our covenant engagement to God."

The hymn ran for five verses but had no chorus.

> O happy day, that fixed my choice
> On Thee, my Saviour, and my God!
> Well may this glowing heart rejoice,
> And tell its raptures all abroad.
>
> O happy bond, that seals my vows
> To Him, who merits all my love!
> Let cheerful anthems fill His house,
> While to that sacred shrine I move.
>
> 'Tis done; the great transaction's done:
> I am my Lord's, and He is mine:
> He drew me, and I followed on,
> Charmed to confess the voice divine.
>
> Now rest my long-divided heart,
> Fixed on this blissful centre rest;
> With ashes who would grudge to part,
> When called on angels' bread to feast?

High heaven, that heard the solemn vow,

That vow renewed shall daily hear;

Till in life's latest hour I bow,

And bless in death a bond so dear.

In 1854, while compiling their hymnal *Wesleyan Sacred Harp*, Rev. William McDonald and Stephen Hubbard matched the words to a tune composed almost twenty years before for "Happy Land!," James Burton's poem written in praise of Switzerland. They renamed the tune "Happy Day," and offered a choice of Doddridge's hymn or unaccredited lyrics beginning with, "Jesus, my all to heaven is gone / He whom I fix my hopes upon." Both hymns had the same new refrain:

Happy day, happy day,

when Jesus wash'd my sins away

He taught me how to watch and pray

And live rejoicing every day.

Although sounding like a direct quote from the Bible, the phrase "Jesus washed my sins away" is actually an amalgam of an Old Testament verse, "Wash me thoroughly from mine iniquity, and cleanse me from my sin" (Psalm 51:2 ASV), and a New Testament verse, "But if we walk in the light, as he is in the light, we have fellowship one with another, and the blood of Jesus his Son cleanseth us from all sin" (1 John 1:7 ASV).

"Watch and pray" comes from the words of Jesus to Peter at Gethsemane after he and his fellow disciples had fallen asleep during the crucial build up to Jesus's arrest. "What, could ye not watch with me one hour? Watch and pray, that ye enter not into temptation: the spirit indeed is willing, but the flesh is weak" (Matthew 26:40–41 ASV). "Live rejoicing every day" is a paraphrase of Paul's stirring call to members of the church in Philippi to "Rejoice in the Lord always: and again I will say, Rejoice" (Philippians 4:4 ASV).

From then on, Doddridge's words became attached to this refrain. When Edwin Hawkins (1943–2018) saw the hymn in his mother's hymnbook, he worked on an arrangement that dropped the verses and developed the refrain. All that was left of Doddridge's version now was the phrase "O happy day."

Hawkins's only other alteration was to add the word "fight" between "watch" and "and pray."

Hawkins was the founder and director of the forty-six-member Northern California State Youth Choir, and in June 1968 he funded a live recording to sell at the National Youth Congress Convention in Cleveland. It was taped on a 2-track tape machine and produced by an Oakland man, LaMont Bench, who ran Century Custom Recording Service. The record, titled *Let Us Go into the House of the Lord*, sold six hundred copies on Bench's Century label.

In March 1969, a rock promotion director, John Lingel, heard the record and was impressed enough to send a copy to influential San Francisco DJ Abe "Voco" Kesh at KSAN. Kesh played "Oh Happy Day" on his show *Lights Out: San Francisco*. Within two months, word had spread. The single entered the local Top Ten, got played on other radio stations covering the musical spectrum (Top Thirty, rock, progressive, soul, MOR, and jazz), and in May 1969 *Rolling Stone* reported that it was "the most requested tune of every rock station in LA last week."

Local success led the distributor, Buddah Records, to sign the choir (now known more snappily as the Edwin Hawkins Singers) to a $50,000 contract, retitle the album *Oh Happy Day*, and push the single in markets around the world. Eventually it sold over seven million copies, making it the best-selling gospel track ever. Its success inspired George Harrison to write his hymn to the Hindu god Krishna, "My Sweet Lord."

Hawkins's musical innovations and success in the secular market upset some members of the COGIC community, who thought it was a compromise too far.

> We were pretty okay until we started to do the music that was a little different from what they were used to hearing. . . . [I]n fact, the gospel community did not want to play that because it was played first on rock [radio]. . . . And we were criticized to the point where I said, "Didn't you all teach us that we're supposed to go into the highways and hedges and share the gospel? I'm a little bit confused. What? Do you want us to tell 'em about Jesus or no? . . . We do enough coming to church testifying to each other, you know? I'm saved and sanctified,

and who are you tellin'? Each other—somebody that already knows Jesus Christ. What about those that don't know him? Ain't that what you taught us to do?"[53]

Song: "Oh Happy Day"

Artist: The Edwin Hawkins Singers

Album: *Let Us Go into the House of the Lord*; released also as a single with "Jesus, Lover of My Soul" arranged by Hawkins on the B-side

Release: April 1969

Studio: Live at Ephesian Church of God in Christ, Berkeley, CA

Personnel: Edwin Hawkins (piano, vocals, arrangements, direction), Dorothy Combs Morrison (lead vocal), Betty Watson (soprano vocals), drums, bass, percussion, Northern California State Youth Choir (later known at the Edwin Hawkins Singers)

Writer: Edwin Hawkins

Producer: LaMont Bench

Label: Pavilion, Buddah

Highest Chart Position: 2 (UK), 4 (US)

Other Significant Recordings: Joan Baez (1971), the Golden Gate Quartet (1980), Spiritualized (1998)

Also by the Edwin Hawkins Singers: "Jesus Lover of My Soul" (1968), "Joy, Joy" (1969), "I Heard the Voice of Jesus" (2010)

36

CHRISTMAS

THE WHO

1969

The double album *Tommy*, along with an appearance at Woodstock, helped elevate the Who from a successful British pop group with a hardcore mod following to an international rock band capable of filling stadiums.

Tommy extended the boundaries of what rock could comfortably discuss and suggested new ways of constructing the long-player format. Encouraged by manager Kit Lambert, whose father was the celebrated conductor and composer Constant Lambert, Pete Townshend had developed what at the time was spoken of as a "rock opera"—twenty-four linked songs and instrumental pieces that told the story of a traumatized boy who finds spiritual enlightenment.

"Christmas" was written for Tommy's father, who despairs of his deaf, dumb, and blind child. As the boy "doesn't know who Jesus was or what praying is," the song asks, "How can he be saved?" How can he achieve salvation if he is locked in his own apparently impenetrable world?

The apostle Paul said, "Whosoever shall call upon the name of the Lord shall be saved" (Romans 10:13). He then added, "How then shall they call on him in whom they have not believed? and how shall they believe in him of whom they have not heard? and how shall they hear without a preacher?" (v. 14). Tommy appears to be one of those who can't believe because he can't hear. Christmas celebrates "heaven's generosity," and yet Tommy can't respond to the gift.

It later transpires that Tommy is sensitive to movement and touch—especially to the vibrations of the pinball machine. In his interior monologue, Tommy begs to be cured: "See me, feel me / Touch me, heal me." The language is reminiscent of the healing ministry of Jesus, who restored sight to the blind, hearing to the deaf, and speech to the mute. In one such case, he puts his fingers into a man's ears, spits, then touches his tongue—"And looking up to heaven, he sighed, and saith unto him, Ephphatha, that is, Be opened. And his ears were opened, and the bond of his tongue was loosed, and he spake plain" (Mark 7:32–35 ASV).

Song: "Christmas"

Artist: The Who

Album: *Tommy*

Release: May 23, 1969

Studio: IBC Studios, London

Personnel: Roger Daltrey (vocals), Pete Townshend (lead guitar), John Entwistle (bass guitar), Keith Moon (drums)

Writer: Pete Townshend

Producer: Kit Lambert

Label: Track Records

Highest Chart Position: Album: 4 (US), 2 (UK)

Other Significant Recordings: The Smithereens (2007), Leslie Odom Jr. (2017)

Also by the Who: "The Seeker" (1970), "Love Reign o'er Me" (1973), "Faith in Something Bigger" (1974)

SUPERSTAR

37

MURRAY HEAD

1969

Tim Rice and Andrew Lloyd Webber were two friends with an inter-est in pop music and theater who'd had success with a "pop cantata" they'd based on an Old Testament story. In 1969, *Joseph and the Amazing Technicolor Dreamcoat*, previously only performed at a London school, was recorded.

Buoyed with confidence, Lloyd Webber and Rice set about working on the greatest Bible story of them all—the passion of Jesus. Their ambition was huge. They would write and record the soundtrack of the proposed musical before anyone had committed to finance it as a stage production. Then, ahead of the release of an ambitious double album, they would release the theme song as a single to pique interest.

For the LP they had recruited a number of well-known, British-based musicians, including members of Joe Cocker's Grease Band and singers such as Ian Gillan (Deep Purple), Yvonne Elliman, Mike d'Abo (Manfred Mann), Madeline Bell, John Gustafson (Merseybeats), Gary Glitter (then performing as Paul Raven), Victor Brox (Victor Brox Blues Train), and Lesley Duncan. Murray Head, a twenty-three-year-old actor, then best known for appearing in the controversial stage musical *Hair*, was given the role of Judas.

Jesus Christ Superstar took a skeptical view of Jesus that matched the mood of the times. In an age of stars, superstars, and rock 'n' roll prophets, it posited the idea that Jesus could have been a first-century Bob Dylan or John Lennon—a wise yet fallible leader who came to believe in his own publicity. In Rice and Lloyd Webber's retelling of the story, Judas is transformed from an evil betrayer into a socially conscious whistle-blower. He's the one person who dares to ask uncomfortable questions and challenge the deification of Jesus. He is, in their view, the true believer in the original and untainted message of Jesus.

"Superstar" distils his unease. Judas blames Jesus for letting the simple gospel of love, forgiveness, and generosity become corrupted into a messianic scheme. He suggests that he has sacrificed his principles for fame and directly asks him, "Do you think you're what they say you are?"

The lyrics use deliberate anachronisms—referring to "PR," "mass communication," "Muhammad," and "Buddha"—to raise questions about the efficiency of his salvation plan. Wouldn't he have reached more people and faced less skepticism if he had waited until a time when his words and actions could have been electronically recorded? Were all the great prophets of religion saying the same thing or was Jesus the final and unique word? Was his death vital to our salvation or a tragic accident?

There is no discussion of Judas's motivation in the New Testament. No one suspected him until Jesus singled him out at the Last Supper (Matthew 26:20–25), and so it's safe to assume that he'd voiced no opposition and had been a faithful disciple since being chosen. The only possible reasons appear to be greed (he was paid thirty pieces of silver by the chief priests), satanic influence ("And Satan entered into Judas" [Luke 22:3 ASV]), and fulfilment of prophecy ("But all this is come to pass, that the scriptures of the prophets might be fulfilled" [Matthew 26:56 ASV]).

The *Jesus Christ Superstar* album was released in September 1970, and the first stage production, on Broadway, opened in October 1971. This coincided with a period during which Jesus was being more readily embraced by pop culture. Norman Greenbaum had a hit with "Spirit in the Sky" ("I got a friend in Jesus"), the musical *Godspell* opened off-Broadway, so-called Jesus Freak communities sprung up around the world, religious record labels began pioneering Jesus Rock, and in June 1971, *Time* magazine published a front cover story heralding what it dubbed "The Jesus Revolution."

"I think we did break down a barrier," Tim Rice told me in 1973. "I think that was a good thing. I think if you can't discuss Jesus Christ in contemporary terms then you can't discuss him at all."

Song: "Superstar"

Artist: Murray Head

Single: A-side: "Superstar" / B-side: "John Nineteen Forty-One" (by the Andrew Lloyd Webber Orchestra)

Release: November 21, 1969 (UK), December 1, 1969 (US)

Album: *Jesus Christ Superstar*

Studio: Olympic Studio, Barnes, London

Personnel: Alan Spenner (bass guitar), Neil Hubbard (rhythm guitar), Bruce Rowland (drums), the Trinidad Singers, and orchestra

Writers: Tim Rice (lyrics), Andrew Lloyd Webber (music)

Producers: Tim Rice, Andrew Lloyd Webber

Label: Decca/MCA (UK)

Highest Chart Position: 14 (US)

Other Significant Recordings: Wayne Newton (1972), Allen Toussaint Orchestra (1988), James Taylor Quartet (2003)

Also by Tim Rice and Andrew Lloyd Webber: "Any Dream Will Do" (1970), "Those Canaan Days" (1970), "I Don't Know How to Love Him" (1970)

I WISH WE'D ALL BEEN READY

LARRY NORMAN

38

1969

L arry Norman grew up in San Francisco and San Jose and fully imbibed the musical tastes of his generation, from Elvis and Little Richard in the 1950s to the Beatles, Rolling Stones, and Bob Dylan in the 1960s. He was also a passionate Christian believer and spent his artistic life trying to integrate his spiritual beliefs with his love of pop culture. The result was a body of work that would revolutionize Christian music—leading indirectly to the creation of the Contemporary Christian Music industry (CCM)—and attracting mainstream admirers from Frank Black of the Pixies to Bono of U2.

His recording career started with the San Jose band People! that had a US Top Twenty hit in June 1968 with a cover of the Zombies' song "I Love You." When they recorded their first album later that year, Larry wanted it to be called "We Need a Whole Lot More of Jesus (and a Lot Less Rock and Roll)" after the 1959 country song by Wayne Raney that they'd covered, but Capitol wanted them to use the more commercial-sounding title of the hit single.

Fearing that his beliefs were always going to be edged out by business demands, Larry left People! to go solo and, still under contract to Capitol, cut his first album with the company in 1969. Free to pursue his own interests, he cut eleven songs fusing rock 'n' roll and religious belief with titles such as "Sweet Sweet Song of Salvation," "Moses in the Wilderness," "The Last Supper," and "You Can't Take Away the Lord." The cover was a photo of him looking as though he were ascending to heaven. *Billboard* admitted, "Infusing rock with religious themes is a relatively untried concept."[69]

Norman had what theologians would refer to as a literalist, premillennial dispensationalist eschatology—he believed that Christians will endure a time of "tribulation" before the return of Jesus when they will be taken bodily to heaven without passing through death. The main sources for this view are the prophecies of Daniel and Ezekiel, 1 Thessalonians 4:13–18, and the book of Revelation.

The return of Jesus was a persistent theme in his songs and writings. In a *Hollywood Free Paper* column in 1971, reproduced inside the gatefold cover of his album *Bootleg*,[70] he warned that the church was about to be suppressed and the Bible censored or banned. "The stage is being set," he warned. "It is going to happen right here in America. And while governmental wiretapping, closed circuit television monitors in stores, elaborate credit card and mass identification systems seem harmless enough now, they will be instruments in the coming control and dehumanization prophesied in Orwell's *1984*, Bradbury's *Fahrenheit 451* and Lucas' *THX 1138*, for those who didn't understand it the first time around in John's Revelation (666) from the Isle of Patmos."[71]

"I Wish We'd All Been Ready" is his classic summation of this position. It comprises images and ideas taken from the words of Jesus in Matthew 24 in response to his disciples' question, "What will be the sign of your coming and of the end of the age?" (v. 3 NIV). Norman's song says, "Life was filled with guns and war / And everyone got trampled on the floor." Jesus said,

"You will hear of wars and rumors of wars, but see to it that you are not alarmed. Such things must happen, but the end is still to come. Nation will rise against nation, and kingdom against kingdom. There will be famines and earthquakes in various places. All these are the beginning of birth pains. Then you will be handed over to be persecuted and put to death, and you will be hated by all nations because of me. At that time many will turn away from the faith and will betray and hate each other, and many false prophets will appear and deceive many people." (Matthew 24:6–11 NIV)

Norman's other arresting image is of the "Two men walking up a hill / One disappears and one's left standing still / I wish we'd all been ready," which comes from the same chapter in the Bible:

> "Two men will be in the field; one will be taken and the other left. Two women will be grinding with a hand mill; one will be taken and the other left. Therefore keep watch, because you do not know on what day your Lord will come. But understand this: If the owner of the house had known at what time of night the thief was coming, he would have kept watch and would not have let his house be broken into. So you also must be ready, because the Son of Man will come at an hour when you do not expect him." (vv. 40–44 NIV)

It became Norman's signature song, appearing on at least fifteen of his albums, and was the theme song for the 1972 movie *A Thief in the Night*.

Song: "I Wish We'd All Been Ready"

Artist: Larry Norman

Album: *Upon This Rock*

Release: December 1969

Studio: Studio A, Capitol Records, Hollywood, CA

Personnel: Larry Norman (vocals, guitar), Mike Deasy (guitar), Joe Osborn (bass guitar), Butch Parker (keyboards), Hal Blaine (drums)

Writer: Larry Norman

Producer: Hal Yoergler

Label: Capitol

Other Significant Recordings: Pat Boone (1971), Randy Matthews (1971), the Oak Ridge Boys (1972), DC Talk (1995), the Christian Nightmares Tribulation Band (2015)

Also by Larry Norman: "Why Don't You Look into Jesus" (1972), "Why Should the Devil Have All the Good Music" (1972), "The Rock That Doesn't Roll" (1976)

39

BRIDGE OVER TROUBLED WATER
SIMON & GARFUNKEL

. . . .

1970

P aul Simon had been a longtime fan of gospel music. While listening to the Swan Silvertones's 1959 debut album loaned to him by keyboard player Al Kooper, he heard "Oh Mary Don't You Weep" and was transfixed by the ad-libbed line of lead singer Claude Jeter (1914–2009), "I'll be your bridge over deep water if you trust in my name." He reached for his guitar and began composing a song that built on that image. He later said that it was as though the words and melody had been channeled through him. "I have no idea where it came from. It came all of a sudden. It was one of the most shocking moments in my songwriting career. I remember thinking 'This is considerably better than I usually write.'"[54]

"Oh Mary Don't You Weep" is a spiritual that pre-dates the Civil War. It was recorded by the pioneering Fisk Jubilee Singers of Nashville in 1915, and soon became a classic gospel hymn. The lyrics adopt the voice of Jesus and recreates what he might have said to the sisters Mary and Martha when their brother, Lazarus, fell ill and died. The Bible tells how their neighbors comforted them and how Jesus, who was moved to tears when he arrived at their home in Bethany, brought him back to life. In the song, he tells Mary not to weep (and Martha not to moan) and cites the Old Testament story of Pharaoh drowning in the Red Sea while in pursuit of the Israelites to reassure her that God's power eventually triumphs over all enemies.

During the chorus, Jeter got carried away and made interjections in the style of a preacher (he would become an ordained minister in Detroit's Church of Holiness Science in 1963). He later admitted that it was based on his memory of a Bible verse. This was almost certainly, "When thou passest through the waters, I will be with thee; and through the rivers, they shall not overflow thee: when thou walkest through the fire, thou shalt not be burned, neither shall the flame kindle upon thee" (Isaiah 43:2 ASV).[55]

Paul Simon already had a penchant for biblical-sounding language. He had used it in songs such as "Bleecker Street," "Sparrow," and "Blessed." He advised one young prospective lyricist to raid the Bible for memorable phrases. "Just steal them," he said. "That's what they're there for."[56]

The chorus of "Bridge over Troubled Water," built around the pledge not merely to provide a bridge but to be a bridge, says, "I will lay me down," a phrase that points to such Bible verses as "He maketh me to lie down in green pastures" (Psalm 23:2), "I will both lay me down in peace, and sleep: for thou, LORD, only makest me dwell in safety" (Psalm 4:8), and "Greater love hath no man than this, that a man lay down his life for his friends" (John 15:13).

The opening line, "When you're weary," calls up the words of Jesus in Matthew 11:28, "Come to Me, all who are weary and heavy-laden, and I will give you rest" (NASB), just as "I will comfort you" sounds like, "As one whom his mother comforts, so I will comfort you; and you will be comforted in Jerusalem" (Isaiah 66:13 NASB). Simon later would use verse 12 in Isaiah 66—"For thus says the LORD, 'Behold, I extend peace to her like a river'" (NASB)—as inspiration for his 1972 song "Peace Like a River."

The promise to dry all tears suggests this may have come from "He shall wipe away every tear from their eyes" (Revelation 21:4 ASV) via Bach's use of the image in his cantata BWV 56:

Da wischt mir die Tränen mein Heiland selbst ab
There shall my Saviour wipe the tears from my eyes.[57]

"Bridge over Troubled Water" is a secular hymn in the mold of Ben E. King's "Stand by Me." It promises understanding, comfort, and relief without invoking the divine. The narrator is the savior.

Song: "Bridge over Troubled Water"

Artist: Simon & Garfunkel

Single: A-side: "Bridge Over Troubled Water" / B-side: "Keep the Customer Satisfied"

Release: January 20, 1970

Album: *Bridge over Troubled Water*

Studio: Columbia Studio, New York, NY

Personnel: Paul Simon (guitar and vocals), Art Garfunkel (vocals), Joe Osborn (bass guitar), Larry Knechtel (piano), Hal Blaine (drums)

Writer: Paul Simon

Producers: Paul Simon, Art Garfunkel, Roy Halee

Label: Columbia

Highest Chart Position: 1 (US), 1 (UK)

Other Significant Recordings: Stevie Wonder (1970), Elvis Presley (1970), Aretha Franklin (1971)

Also by Paul Simon: "Silent Eyes" (1975), "Getting Ready for Christmas Day" (2011), "Questions for the Angels" (2011)

WHAT IS TRUTH

JOHNNY CASH

40

1970

Johnny Cash was unusual in being a major star in the traditionally conservative world of Nashville country music who nevertheless had strong sympathies for outcasts, rebels, and the downtrodden. He championed the cause of Native Americans (*Bitter Tears*, 1964) and played for prisoners (*Johnny Cash at San Quentin*, 1969), and when he became host of his own network TV show, he used it to promote the music of the counterculture (Bob Dylan, James Taylor, Derek and the Dominos, Arlo Guthrie, Joni Mitchell, Buffy Sainte-Marie, Neil Young).

He was genuinely interested in the questions asked by the younger generation and saw more potential in the discontent of the radicals than in the complacency of their disapproving elders. Of particular interest to him was their avowed quest to find truth and their intolerance of hypocrisy, prejudice, and ignorance.

"What Is Truth" started life as a twelve-verse poem written for "the youth of America" that he eventually trimmed to a four-verse song and premiered on his show March 18, 1970, two weeks after the birth of his only son, John Carter Cash. The impetus was a disparaging comment about contemporary rock music made by Merle Travis, who said he just couldn't understand it.

Cash had been introducing gospel songs into his show, much to the annoyance of TV executives, and had been criticized for blurring the distinctions between entertainment and religion. "What Is Truth" straddled both worlds with grace. To the secular audience, it was a challenge to get down to the facts. To his Christian fans, it was a call to follow the man who called himself "the way, and the truth" (John 14:6 ASV). To Cash, it was both.

The pivot of the song was Pilate's response to the claims of Jesus at his public trial in Jerusalem: "Pilate therefore said unto him, Art thou a king then? Jesus answered, Thou sayest that I am a king. To this end was I born, and for this cause came I into the world, that I should bear witness unto the truth. Every one that is of the truth heareth my voice. Pilate saith unto him, What is truth?" (John 18:37–38).

Cash was deeply serious about his faith and combined his love of music with an appreciation of fiction, poetry, history, and theology. He took a correspondence course in theology, and in 1986 wrote a novel, *Man in White*, based on the life of the apostle Paul. In 1971, he told *Sunday Times* journalist Philip Norman, "I read a lot. I read novels but I also read the Bible. And study it, you know? And the more I learn, the more excited I get. Some of those stories are as wild as any H. G. Wells could drum up. And that Jesus! He really cuts me up! I worship him, but he tickles me to death."[58]

Song: "What Is Truth"

Artist: Johnny Cash

Single: A-side: "What Is Truth" | B-side: "Sing a Traveling Song"

Release: April 1970

Studio: Columbia Studios, Nashville, TN

Personnel: Johnny Cash (vocals and guitar), Norman Blake (dobro), Marshall Grant (bass guitar), W. S. Holland (drums), Carl Perkins (electric guitar), Bob Wootton (electric guitar), Bill Walker Orchestra

Writer: Johnny Cash

Producer: Bob Johnston

Label: Columbia

Highest Chart Position: 19 (US), 21 (UK)

Also by Johnny Cash: "Jesus Was a Carpenter" (1970), "I See Men as Trees Walking" (1971), "King of Love" (1972)

41

LET IT BE

THE BEATLES

1970

In 1980, shortly before his death, John Lennon said of "Let It Be": "That's Paul. . . . He probably heard a gospel song. No, I think he was inspired by 'Bridge over Troubled Water.' That's my feeling, although I have nothing to go on."[59]

He was wrong because the first recording of "Let It Be" was nine months before Simon & Garfunkel embarked on their classic, even though delays caused by the *Let It Be* film meant that it wasn't released until two months after "Bridge over Troubled Water," and this may have made it appear like an imitator.

However, John correctly identified the song's musical lineage. "Let It Be" was written in the style of a gospel hymn. It offers reassurance, uses images of "darkness" being replaced by "light," and there are gospel chords supplied by former gospel group member Billy Preston.

According to Paul, the song wasn't written intentionally as a hymn, but it has unmistakable Christian imagery probably acquired during his early years in Liverpool. Although his agnostic father never put his sons into a church school, his mother, who died when Paul was fourteen, was a Catholic, and as a result both Paul and his brother had been baptized into the Catholic church.

In a 1964 interview, he claimed, "As a kid I went to all sorts of churches with my friends—Methodist, Baptist, Church of England—everything."[60]

By the end of 1968, the Beatles were drifting apart, and there were repeated arguments about management, taxes, and musical direction. Paul was the Beatle with the strongest desire to keep the group together and also, by default, its leader. Since *Revolver* in 1966, he had been the one to organize the recording sessions, suggest ideas for album covers, and was the primary writer on twice as many singles as John.

He was distressed by the acrimony and the prospect of the Beatles breaking up. During this time, he had a dream in which his mother comforted him, assuring him that everything was going to be all right. On waking, he composed a song. He told his biographer Barry Miles, "I literally started off 'Mother Mary,' which was her name, 'When I find myself in times of trouble,' which I certainly found myself in."[61]

He must have known that referring to his mother as "mother Mary" gave the song a spiritual patina. He admitted that the song became a "quasi-religious thing" and added, "You can take it that way. I don't mind. I'm quite happy if people want to use it to shore up their faith. I have no problem with that. I think it's a great thing to have faith of any sort, particularly in the world we live in."

As "mother Mary" were the first words, they would have suggested the tone and ultimate direction of the song. The language of "speaking words of wisdom," while not directly taken from the Bible, has the feel of invocations such as, "My mouth shall speak of wisdom; and the meditation of my heart shall be of understanding" (Psalm 49:3).

More significantly, the specific words of wisdom cited—"let it be"— have an uncanny resemblance to part of Mary's response to the news that she would conceive a child and that "that holy thing which shall be born of thee shall be called the Son of God" (Luke 1:35). She is recorded in Luke 1:38 as having prayed, "Behold the handmaid of the Lord; be it unto me according to thy word."

Could Paul have absorbed more of the Bible than he realized?

Yet whereas Mary's "be it unto me" was an act of submission to the will of God, the "let it be" of the Beatles' song is another way of saying, "Let it go" or "Don't worry—it's all going to work out fine." As Paul once paraphrased it, "Be gentle. Don't fight things. Just try and go with the flow and it will all work out."[62]

Other phrases in the song—"times of trouble," "brokenhearted people," "the night is cloudy," "a light that shines on me"— suggest other Bible verses. In the version of the song filmed for *Let It Be*, Paul sings "there will be no sorrow" rather than "there will be answer," which makes it closer to "and there shall be no more death, neither sorrow, nor crying" (Revelation 21:4).

Song: "Let It Be"

Artist: The Beatles

Single: A-side: "Let It Be" / B-side: "You Know My Name" (Look Up the Number)

Release: March 11, 1970 (US); March 6, 1970 (UK)

Album: *Let It Be*

Studios: Apple Studio, EMI Studios

Personnel: John Lennon (rhythm guitar), Paul McCartney (bass guitar, vocals), George Harrison (lead guitar), Ringo Starr (drums), Billy Preston (electric piano, organ), Linda McCartney (backing vocals), two trumpets, two trombones, cellos, tenor saxophone

Writers: John Lennon, Paul McCartney

Producers: George Martin (single version), Phil Spector (album version)

Label: Apple

Highest Chart Position: 2 (UK), 1 (USA)

Other Significant Recordings: Aretha Franklin (1970), Joan Baez (1971)

Also by the Beatles: "Eleanor Rigby" (1966), "Lady Madonna" (1968), "The Inner Light" (1968)

42

WOODSTOCK
JONI MITCHELL

1970

The Woodstock Music & Art Fair (to give the event its proper name) was a three-day festival held on the six-hundred-acre dairy farm of Max Yasgur near the town of Bethel in New York State (August 15–18, 1969) that attracted an audience of possibly five hundred thousand, and was headlined by some of the biggest acts of the era: the Who, Santana, Joe Cocker and the Grease Band, the Grateful Dead, the Band, Creedence Clearwater Revival, Janis Joplin, Jimi Hendrix, and Crosby, Stills, Nash & Young.

It was always intended as more than an entertainment spectacular. It was a show of strength by the counterculture to witness to the world that it had found a new way of living that worked. The official posters called it as "An Aquarian Exposition,"[63] reflecting the organizers' optimism that we were moving into a new astrological age characterized by love, unity, integrity, brotherhood, and peace. Indian yogi Swami Satchidananda delivered the opening invocation. He informed the audience that America already led the world materially and it was time for it to offer spiritual leadership.

The documentary movie *Woodstock* (Michael Wadleigh, 1970) and the accompanying triple-disc soundtrack album boosted the message of the festival. Woodstock was now seen as the high point of the hippie dream—the moment in time that captured the ideals of free love, loud music, recreational drugs, self-expression, and freedom from the regulations of "straight" society. Images of young lovers frolicking in fields and seminaked revelers dancing in the mud consolidated the impression of the festival as a time of benevolent abandon when people threw off the shackles of a corrupt civilization and rejoiced in primitive ritual.

Joni Mitchell had been slated to appear, but due to transport problems caused by blocked highways and a commitment to appear the next day on the *Dick Cavett Show*, she stayed behind in a New York hotel and heard about what was happening from TV newscasts and, later, from her boyfriend Graham Nash, who had played there with Crosby, Stills, Nash & Young.

She then wrote a song that framed Woodstock in explicitly spiritual terms. In it she meets a "child of God," who is on his way to the festival to try and "get my soul free." She speculates that the success of the event could be the time of year but also that it could be "the time of man," referring to the popular idea that the love and peace movement could be the result of a spurt in human evolution or a new astrological age.

In the chorus, she repeats her injunction, "We've got to get ourselves back to the garden," which could, on the surface, simply mean moving from city to country (she had earlier mentioned smog and the feeling of being a mere cog in the machine), but has the larger implication of returning to the biblical paradise—the Garden of Eden.

In the story told in Genesis, humans were created for Eden but, after rebelling, were forced to live in exile. The rest of the Bible is the story of God seeking to restore humanity to that original purpose without compromising either his holiness or justice. The eventual destiny is not the old garden made good again but "the New Jerusalem," the "Kingdom of Heaven," or the "new heaven and earth."

In her vision of Woodstock, she dreams that she sees bomber planes "turning into butterflies,"[64] an allusion to Isaiah's prophecy about "the last days" when God will judge the nations "and they shall beat their swords into plowshares, and their spears into pruninghooks: nation shall not lift up sword against nation, neither shall they learn war any more" (Isaiah 2:4).

She later explained to Crosby, Stills & Nash biographer Dave Zimmer[65] that at the time of writing "Woodstock" she had been going through "a kind of born again Christian trip" after leaving the United Church of Canada during her teens. Finding herself as one of the songwriters being looked to for leadership, she again "took it seriously" and "decided I needed a guide and leaned on God. So I was a little 'God mad' at the time."[66]

She had been searching for what she called "modern miracles," and Woodstock seemed to be such an event. "[Woodstock was] like a modern day fishes-and-loaves story," she said.[67]

To the academic and social critic Camille Paglia, Mitchell summarized the message of the song as, "We need to get a grip on our original destiny."[68]

Song: "Woodstock"

Artist: Joni Mitchell

Album: *Ladies of the Canyon*

Release: April 1970

Studio: A&M Studios, Hollywood, CA

Personnel: Joni Mitchell (piano, vocals)

Writer: Joni Mitchell

Producer: Joni Mitchell

Label: Reprise

Other Significant Recordings: Crosby, Stills, Nash & Young (1970), Matthews Southern Comfort (1970), Spin Doctors (1994)

Also by Joni Mitchell: "Jericho" (1977), "God Must Be a Boogie Man" (1979), "Slouching Towards Bethlehem" (1991)

AMAZING GRACE

JUDY COLLINS

43

1970

John Newton, born in England in 1725, was a sailor who became a rebellious atheist, a slave trader on the west coast of Africa, a Christian convert, a slave ship captain, a customs official in Liverpool, an Anglican curate, a hymn writer, the minister of a church in London, and an influential abolitionist. "Amazing Grace," words he wrote in 1772 to accompany a sermon preached at the parish church of St. Peter and St. Paul in Olney, Buckinghamshire, was both autobiographical and biblical.

When working for a slave trader on Plantain Island, off the coast of Sierra Leone, his boss's African mistress chained him up in the open air and had her servants torment him. He'd contracted malaria-like symptoms, was starving, and was now exposed to the direct heat of the sun. The indignity, loneliness, and pain brought him to the lowest point in his life. It was only when his seafaring father sought the help of British slavers headed to Africa that a ship called the *Greyhound* eventually rescued him.

While returning to England, the *Greyhound* was caught in a severe storm that began ripping the sides apart. Newton had to tie himself to a mast to avoid being swept into the sea. During the ordeal, he completed a conversion to Christianity that had been taking place for some time.

Despite popular legend, he didn't immediately renounce the slave trade. In fact, it was after his conversion that he became a slave ship captain and completed three triangular trips between England, Africa, and America. It would be several years before his faith led him to oppose slavery.

"Amazing Grace" wasn't about his regrets over his role in the slave trade. That would come later. It was a meditation on "Who am I, O LORD God, and what is mine house, that thou hast brought me hitherto?" (1 Chronicles 17:16). He used this thought to explore the question of who he was and how God had brought him from the shackles of Plantain Island to the comfort of a vicarage in the small countryside town of Olney.

His lyrical exploration drew him into other portions of the Bible. "Lost" and "found" came from the parable of the prodigal son where the father exclaims, "For this my son was dead, and is alive again; he was lost, and is found" (Luke 15:24). "Blind" and "see" came from a blind man healed by Jesus, who responded, "One thing I know, that, whereas I was blind, now I see" (John 9:25). The concept of being a "wretch" came from Paul's comment, "O wretched man that I am! who shall deliver me from the body of this death?" (Romans 7:24).

No one knows what tune was used when "Amazing Grace" was first sung in 1773. Lyrics with what was known as "common meter" could be sung to a variety of available tunes. The words were first published in *Olney Hymns* in 1779, along with other works of Newton and his poet friend, William Cowper, who also lived in Olney.

By the nineteenth century, "Amazing Grace" was entering American hymnals, initially set to a variety of tunes, and then eventually to the one to which it is most often sung today. By the middle of the twentieth century, it had gained a universal popularity that crossed the normal boundaries of age, denomination, race, political persuasion, class, and even religion.

Judy Collins was part of the generation who knew it both as a church hymn from childhood and as a favorite of folk musicians, gospel singers, and civil rights marchers. Those who had already recorded it included Mahalia Jackson, Sister Rosetta Tharpe, Paul Robeson, Clara Ward, the Weavers, Burl Ives, and Arlo Guthrie. Collins added it to her set list.

She finally recorded "Amazing Grace" after experiencing an incident in a New York encounter group where the song was used to calm participants after a particularly volatile session. Her producer, Mark Abramson, was also there and later urged her to include the song on the album they were making.

To preserve the song's purity, it was recorded acapella at the campus chapel of New York's Columbia University. Friends provided an informal choir to hum on the second verse and sing harmony thereafter. Its release as a single and subsequent chart success in several territories around the world led to a resurgence in the popularity of the song that hasn't stopped. At the end of the twentieth century, 97 percent of the recordings of "Amazing Grace" held by the Library of Congress were made after the success of Collins's version.

Song: "Amazing Grace"

Artist: Judy Collins

Single: A-side: "Amazing Grace" / B-side: "Nightingale 1" (US), "I Pity the Poor Immigrant" (UK)

Release: December 1970 (US), November 20, 1970 (UK)

Album: *Whales & Nightingales*

Studio: St Paul's Chapel, Columbia University, New York, NY

Personnel: Judy Collins (vocals)

Writer: John Newton (lyrics)

Producer: Mark Abramson

Label: Elektra

Highest Chart Position: 15 (US), 5 (UK)

Other Significant Recordings: Rod Stewart (1971), Aretha Franklin (1972), Soweto Gospel Choir (2005)

Also by Judy Collins: "Simple Gifts" (1970), "I Believe in You" (1993), "Joy to the World" (2000)

44

WHOLY HOLY
MARVIN GAYE

. . . .

1971

What's *Going On* was Marvin Gaye's masterpiece. Initially resisted by label owner Berry Gordy for not having the optimistic, bright, young sound that had characterized Motown throughout the sixties, it became the record that defined the new era of funk and politics, and allowed Marvin to reconcile his musical, social, and spiritual aspirations.

As the son of a one-time preacher, he was forced quite early on to decide between "worldly" music that glorified the apparently trivial and the gospel music he'd so enthusiastically sung in church. Initially he threw his lot in with Harvey Fuqua's doo-wop group the Moonglows and then became a significant part of Motown, America's first black-owned independent record label, and eventually married Berry Gordy's sister, Anna.

Marvin's father hoped that his son might become a preacher, or even a gospel singer, and Marvin never completely discounted that possibility. He just worked out another way to do it, and another gospel to sing about. "God is writing this album," he told fellow Motown artist Smokey Robinson as he was recording *What's Going On*: "I'm not writing it. I'm just the catalyst."[72]

"Wholy Holy" (like the album's title track and "Save the Children") was a collaboration between Marvin, Renaldo "Obie" Benson of the Four Tops, and Motown songwriter Al Cleveland. It's unclear who contributed exactly what. Benson spoke of the song as a reggae style number that Marvin transformed into a spiritual.

The message of "Wholy Holy," like so much of the album, is one of reconciliation, understanding, and love. He believed we have a duty to break down barriers but also that it is only with the help of divine power that we can achieve anything substantial. He declares that we need to believe in one another, and yet, as soon as he has made the assertion, his voice comes in singing, "Believe in Jesus" ("Let not your heart be troubled: ye believe in God, believe also in me" [John 14:1]). He says that we can conquer hate and then adds the prayerful plea, "Oh, Lord."

When recorded, the song was known as "Holy Holy" rather than "Wholy Holy." The reason for the late change isn't known. Was it a playful pun to tone down the seriousness or a way of stressing that effective holiness can't be partial?

The phrase "holy, holy" doesn't occur in the Bible, but "holy, holy, holy," known as the "Trisagion," is used twice. Both times it occurs in songs presented to God by angelic figures. The seraphim seen by Isaiah cried, "Holy, holy, holy, is the Lord of hosts: the whole earth is full of his glory" (Isaiah 6:3). The four living creatures seen by John in his vision said, "Holy, holy, holy, Lord God Almighty, which was, and is, and is to come" (Revelation 4:8).

In the nineteenth century, Reginald Heber wrote the popular hymn still sung today and known as "Holy, Holy, Holy." It starts,

> Holy, holy, holy, Lord God Almighty!
> Early in the morning our song shall rise to Thee;
> Holy, holy, holy! Merciful and mighty!
> God in three persons, blessed Trinity!

The verse after the "Holy, holy, holy" announcement in Isaiah reads, "And the foundations of the thresholds shook at the voice of him that cried, and the house was filled with smoke" (6:4 ASV). Could this be the origin in "Wholy Holy" of the line "We can rock the world's foundation"?

Song: "Wholy Holy"

Artist: Marvin Gaye

Album: *What's Going On*

Release: May 21, 1971

Studio: Hitsville USA, Detroit, MI

Personnel: Marvin Gaye (vocals)

Writers: Marvin Gaye, Al Cleveland, Renaldo "Obie" Benson

Producer: Marvin Gaye

Label: Tamla

Other Significant Recordings: Aretha Franklin (1972), Everette Harp (1997), John Legend and the Roots (2010)

Also by Marvin Gaye: "Mercy Mercy Me (The Ecology)" (1971), "Praise" (1981), "The Lord's Prayer" (1995)

45

WEDDING SONG (THERE IS LOVE)

NOEL PAUL STOOKEY

1971

T he acoustic folk trio Peter, Paul, and Mary were at the heart of the folk revival, producing a clean sound that was radio-friendly and penetrated the mainstream market. Albert Grossman, later to be Bob Dylan's manager, had put the group together in 1961 with just such an end in mind.

In 1968, Noel Paul Stookey underwent a spiritual crisis. In order to clear his thinking, he called on Bob Dylan at his home in Woodstock and was given advice that changed his life. Dylan urged him to revisit his old hometown in Michigan to gain a sense of who he was, where he had come from, and how far he had traveled. Then he recommended that he read the Bible (Stookey noticed Dylan had a large family Bible open on a lectern in his living room). Shortly afterward Stookey became a Christian.

When Peter Yarrow became engaged the next year (to the niece of 1968 Democrat presidential candidate Eugene McCarthy), Stookey wrote "Wedding Song" for the marriage at a Catholic church in Willmar, Minnesota. The song was unusual in being about Jesus yet never mentioning his name. Stookey said of it, "Into every songwriter's life comes a song, the source of which cannot be explained by personal experience."[73] Released as a single in 1971, it became a popular music choice for weddings.

Central to the song are the words of Jesus spoken to the Pharisees:

> Have ye not read, that he which made them at the beginning
> made them male and female, and said, For this cause shall a
> man leave his father and mother, and shall cleave to his wife:
> and they twain shall be one flesh? Wherefore they are no more
> twain, but one flesh. What therefore God hath joined together,
> let not man put asunder. (Matthew 19:4–6, citing Genesis 2:24)

With the thought "For whenever two or more of you / Are gathered in his name / There is love, there is love," Stookey joins the idea of marriage with that of Christian fellowship: "For where two or three are gathered together in my name, there am I in the midst of them" (Matthew 18:20).

Consistent to his conviction that the song was given to him, he has never taken any payment for it. He said that the only work involved on his part was to "allow the pencil to move across the page."[74] He set up a company called Public Domain to collect the royalties and distribute them to worthy causes.

Song: "Wedding Song (There Is Love)"

Artist: Noel Paul Stookey

Single: A-side: "Wedding Song (There is Love)" / B-side: "GIve a Damn"

Release: June 28, 1971

Album: *Paul and*

Studio: Record Plant, New York, NY

Personnel: Noel Paul Stookey (12-string guitar, vocals), Jim Mason (bass), Eddie Mottau (guitar)

Writer: Noel Paul Stookey

Producers: Jim Mason, Eddie Mottau

Label: Warner Brothers

Highest Chart Position: 24 (USA)

Other Significant Recordings: The Lettermen (1971), Harry Belafonte (1972), Captain and Tennille (1976)

Also by Paul Stookey: "The 23rd Psalm" (1977), "Know Jesus" (1979), "One and Many" (2008)

46

AFTER FOREVER
BLACK SABBATH

1971

B lack Sabbath created the template for heavy metal: very loud music, screaming vocals, long hair, dark clothing, and an implied affinity with horror, chaos, pain, self-destruction, and evil. It would ultimately spawn everything from Kiss to Marilyn Manson, Poison to Mötley Crüe.

The music was initially a reaction to the love and peace era, with its emphasis on harmony, color, gentleness, and beauty, and yet became a reflection of the disintegration of that very dream. By 1971, communes were breaking up, charismatic leaders became brutal dictators, harder drugs flooded the market, and experiments with alternative spiritual beliefs led to flirtations with the dark side of the occult.

The euphoria surrounding Woodstock was checked four months later at Altamont where, in true hippie spirit, the revelers decided to dispense with the police and security guards and allow the Hells Angels to keep the crowds in order. The Angels turned on some audience members and beat them with billiard cues. During a performance by the Rolling Stones, a black teenager, Meredith Hunter, was stabbed to death close to the stage.

The person who seemed to sum up all that had gone wrong was Charles Manson, a failed musician who'd become the leader of a desert commune, took LSD, believed in the dissolution of the ego, and thought the Beatles were speaking to him through their songs. He argued for a merging of good and evil. In August 1969, his followers committed a series of murders at his request, the most notorious of which was the stabbing of the pregnant movie star Sharon Tate, wife of Polish film director Roman Polanski.

Manson was arrested in October 1969, went to trial in July 1970, and was sentenced to life imprisonment on April 22, 1971, for seven counts of first-degree murder. The case was given extensive coverage because of its cultural significance, and Manson was voted the "Man of the Year" by one underground newspaper and was even featured on the cover of *Rolling Stone*. (Manson died November 19, 2017, aged eighty-three, having served a life sentence at the California State Prison in Corcoran.)

This was the cultural atmosphere when Black Sabbath was formed and recorded its first three albums. Although the group name came from a 1963 Italian horror film and their only intent was to write songs that were an antidote to saccharine pop, they were hailed as the originators of "Devil Rock" or "Satan Rock," a group as in tune with the dark turn of the counterculture as Donovan had been with its enchanted beginning.

"After Forever" was an odd song for a group intent on accentuating the solemn and scary to release as its first single. The lyrics are some of the most overtly Christian and finger-pointingly evangelistic ever recorded by a non-gospel act. It wasn't until Bob Dylan's "Gotta Serve Somebody" and "When You Gonna Wake Up" in 1979 that anything that obvious would make it onto a mainstream record.

Lyricist Geezer Butler, who said he was "brought up strictly Catholic," wrote the words against the backdrop of the conflict in Northern Ireland. "We all believed in Jesus—and yet people were killing each other over it," he said. "To me, it was just ridiculous. I thought that if God could see us killing each other in his name, he'd be disgusted."[75]

Yet the song isn't addressed to the ardent Catholic or Protestant but to the agnostic who never considers religion and the atheist who disbelieves in an afterlife. The narrator claims to be different: to have "seen the truth," seen the light, and changed his ways. He's unafraid of death and berates unbelievers. Are they fearful of being ostracized by friends? Are they slaves to fashion? Are they small-minded? In his view they are no better than those who crucified Christ.

A point made three times in the song is that no one who dies without God is prepared to meet God. "As I live, saith the Lord, every knee shall bow to me, and every tongue shall confess to God. So then every one of us shall give account of himself to God" (Romans 14:11–12). In the words of Black Sabbath (or at least Butler), "He is the one / The only one who can save you now / From all this sin and hate."

Asked in 2015 about who or what was the biggest influence on his lyrics, Butler said, "The Bible. When I first went to school we read the *Iliad* and the *Odyssey*, and I can't remember anything of what they were about, but the Bible stuck with me."[76]

Song: "After Forever"

Artist: Black Sabbath

Album: *Master of Reality*

Release: July 21, 1971

Studio: Island Studio, Basing Street, London

Personnel: Ozzy Osbourne (vocals), Geezer Butler (bass guitar), Tony Iommi (guitar), Bill Ward (drums)

Writers: Terence "Geezer" Butler (lyrics), Tony Iommi (music)

Producer: Rodger Bain

Label: Vertigo

Other Significant Recordings: Deliverance (1992), Biohazard (1997), Aurora Borealis (2000), Stryper (2015)

Also by Black Sabbath: "Heaven and Hell" (1980), "The Sign of the Southern Cross" (1981), "Born Again" (1983)

47

GOD'S SONG (THAT'S WHY I LOVE MANKIND)

RANDY NEWMAN

1972

Although now better known for his movie soundtracks (*Toy Story*, *A Bug's Life*, *Monsters, Inc.*; and many more), Randy Newman's early reputation was as a singer-songwriter capable of biting satire. His particular skill was in being able to write in the voices of those he was skewering and thereby exposing their apparently implausible views. In "Lonely at the Top," it was a world-weary Vegas singer like Frank Sinatra; in "Sail Away," it was a slave owner; in "God's Song (That's Why I Love Mankind)," it was God.

His family were nonobserving Jews, and his father (Irving, a physician) was an atheist who allegedly once took Randy on a hospital visit during which he pointed out sick children in their beds and said, "That's God's will over there, and that's God's will over there, and that's God's will over there . . ."[77]

Randy inherited his religious attitude from his father and his talent and love of music and film from Alfred Newman, his uncle who was a renowned film composer and winner of nine Oscars. In "God's Song," Newman adopts the voice of a deity who has no compassion for humanity and who thinks it's hilarious that no matter how many calamities he visits on his devotees they still worship and adore him. He delights in their gullibility and dogged faithfulness.

This view is called maltheism—the belief in a God who regards humanity not with love but with malice. But this isn't Randy Newman's position. He's merely positing it in order to expose what he sees as the fallacy of (in particular) Christianity and Judaism.

He starts by putting his question in the mouth of the biblical character Seth. Adam and Eve first had two sons, Cain and Abel, but Cain killed Abel in a fit of jealousy after God accepted the sacrifice of Abel rather than the sacrifice of Cain (Genesis 4:2–16). Seth, a third son, was born after the murder and replaced Abel (Genesis 4:25) in the line leading to Jesus as the son of God, according to the genealogy in Luke 3:38.

Although the biblical Seth asked no such question, Randy Newman has him ask God why it was necessary for anyone to die in the process of producing "the children of Israel." God responds curtly, "Man means nothing" to him, saying, "How we laugh up here in heaven at the prayers you offer me / That's why I love mankind."

In the final verse, God tells his followers that when he burns their cities and kills their children, unbelievably they respond not with anger but by saying, "How blessed are we." This probably refers to fire and brimstone raining on Sodom and Gomorrah (Genesis 19:24). The death of children might be a reference to David's son by the widow of Uriah the Hittite: "David said to his servants, 'Is the child dead?' And they said, 'He is dead.' So David arose from the ground, washed, anointed himself, and changed his clothes; and he came into the house of the LORD and worshiped" (2 Samuel 12:19–20 NASB).

Newman didn't see his song as "knocking God" or insulting believers. "I view him like I view the ether. He's just not there," he told me in 1974. "I'm not going to actively go out there and say, 'Stop following false idols,' but I don't believe he's there. Flying saucers—God—I don't believe in them."

Song: "God's Song (That's Why I Love Mankind)"
Artist: Randy Newman
Album: *Sail Away*

Release: May 1, 1972

Studio: Amingo, Western, Poppi Studios, Los Angeles, CA

Personnel: Randy Newman (piano)

Writer: Randy Newman

Producers: Lenny Waronker, Russ Titelman

Label: Reprise Records

Other Significant Recordings: Etta James (1973), Tracy Nelson (1978), Mathilde Santing (1993)

Also by Randy Newman: "I Think He's Hiding" (1968), "He Gives Us All His Love" (1972), "If We Didn't Have Jesus" (2002)

GO LIKE ELIJAH

CHI COLTRANE

48

1972

This unusual song is based on the account of the prophet Elijah being translated directly into heaven without passing through death. Elijah, who knew what was going to happen to him, traveled to the banks of the Jordan River near the city of Jericho with his prophetic heir, Elisha, who would literally and metaphorically pick up his mantle when he had gone.

> Then Elijah took his cloak, and wrapped it together, and
> smote the waters, and they were divided hither and thither,
> and they twain went over on the dry land. Now when they
> were passed over, Elijah said unto Elisha, Ask what I shall
> do for thee before I be taken from thee. And Elisha said,
> I pray thee, let thy Spirit be double upon me. And he said,
> Thou hast asked an hard thing: yet if thou see me when
> I am taken from thee, thou shalt have it so: and if not, it
> shall not be. And as they went walking and talking, behold,
> there appeared a chariot of fire, and horses of fire, and
> did separate them twain. So Elijah went up by a whirlwind
> into heaven. (2 Kings 2:8–11 GNV)

Coltrane, then a twenty-four-year-old funk and blues singer who'd recently been signed by Columbia Records, was driving across America with her mother when the idea for the song inspired by this biblical story came to her. As she held on to the wheel, she dictated the lyrics line by line and her mother wrote them out. She later composed the music for it, and "Go Like Elijah" was recorded for her debut album, *Chi Coltrane.*

> Just let me go, I wanna go
> When my time comes for me to go
> Just let me go like Elijah when I go

The message is that she would love to get to heaven in a similarly triumphant style—no sickness or death, no coffin or tombstone, no funeral or grief. Coltrane said:

> There were a few people in history who didn't die. There was
> Enoch, there was Elijah and there was Methuselah. Elijah and
> Enoch just went up into the air in a whirlwind. God took them
> instead of them having to die. Their bodies were changed.
> They had eternal bodies instead of small, short-time bodies
> like we have here. This is possible for everybody because
> Christ promised that. He said that if you believe in him and do
> what he says the same thing will happen to you. You will "go
> like Elijah." You may go through death but your spirit leaves
> your body and instantly goes to be with him and then when he
> returns the body rises from the dead, just like Elijah did, and
> just goes straight up. The difference is, they didn't taste death.
> That's how I want to go. That's my dream![78]

Song: "Go Like Elijah"

Artist: Chi Coltrane

Single: A-side: "Go Like Elijah" / B-side: "It's Really Come to Nothing"

Release: December 1, 1972

Album: *Chi Coltrane*

Personnel: Chi Coltrane (piano, vocals), Dean Parks (guitar), Larry Knechtel (bass), Jim Gordon (drums), Victor Feldman (percussion), the Billy Barnum Chorus (choir)

Writer: Chi Coltrane

Producer: Toxey French

Label: Columbia

Highest Chart Position: 94 (US)

Other Significant Recordings: Deep River Quartet (2006)

Also by Chi Coltrane: "The Tree" (1972), "Hallelujah" (1973)

49

ECLIPSE
PINK FLOYD

1973

The Pink Floyd album *The Dark Side of the Moon* shares similar concerns to the book of Ecclesiastes—transience ("Breathe"), futility ("Time"), violence ("Us and Them"), wealth ("Money"), madness ("Brain Damage"), and death ("The Great Gig in the Sky").

This could have been coincidence; these are among the perennial themes of all art and literature. Roger Waters, who wrote all the lyrics, said the theme of the album was most directly inspired by the pressures they'd experienced as members of a major band—the drug-induced craziness of founder member Syd Barrett, business squabbles, fame, adulation, wealth, deadlines, travel.

Yet the structure of "Eclipse," the final song on the album, strongly resembles the opening of the third chapter of Ecclesiastes: "All that you love / And all that you hate" sounds a lot like "A time to love, and a time to hate" (v. 8), and "everything under the sun" reminds us of "under the sun," a phrase repeated twenty-nine times in Ecclesiastes.

The author of Ecclesiastes used "under the sun" to define the natural world apart from supernatural intervention. Without a creator, purpose, and eternal life, human activity appears fruitless. Everything comes to nothing: "I have seen all the works which have been done under the sun, and behold, all is vanity and striving after wind" (Ecclesiastes 1:14 NASB).

This bleak picture was the starting point for the quest in Ecclesiastes but was the conclusion for Pink Floyd's Roger Waters. We embellish our days with actions and accumulate achievements, but when the big picture is viewed, our fate remains unchanged. The album's opening track, "Breathe," compares living to cresting waves out of our control, all of them ultimately leading to oblivion. Knowing this is our lot, the song argues, we should make the most of every sensation because "All you touch and all you see / Is all your life will ever be."

The earliest version of what would become *The Dark Side of the Moon* had a composition known as "Religion Song" or "The Mortality Sequence." It was an organ recital by Rick Wright over which was heard the sound of religious talk—a reading of Ephesians 5:15–20 ("Look therefore carefully how ye walk, not as unwise, but as wise" [ASV]), the Lord's Prayer, and comments from journalist and TV personality Malcolm Muggeridge, who'd become a recent Christian convert. This experiment evolved into "The Great Gig in the Sky."

"Eclipse" was the album's summation. Ecclesiastes pairs off opposites (love/hate, war/peace, birth/death), concluding that there is "a time to every purpose under the heaven" (Ecclesiastes 3:1). Waters pairs off opposites (create/destroy) and things similar (touch/see) before concluding, "And everything under the sun is in tune / But the sun is eclipsed by the moon." However harmonious the appearance, all things, even the sun, will one day be extinguished and forgotten.

Song: "Eclipse"

Artist: Pink Floyd

Album: *The Dark Side of the Moon*

Release: March 1, 1973

Studio: Abbey Road Studios, London

Personnel: Roger Waters (vocals, bass guitar), David Gilmour (guitar, backing vocals), Rick Wright (organ, backing vocals), Nick Mason (drums, percussion, sound effects)

Writer: Roger Waters

Producers: Roger Waters, David Gilmour, Rick Wright, Nick Mason

Label: Harvest

Other Significant Recordings: Easy Star All-Stars (2003), Flaming Lips, featuring Henry Rollins (2010), Nick Blessing (2012)

Also by Pink Floyd: "Take Up Thy Stethoscope and Walk" (1967), "Sheep" (1977), "The Post War Dream" (1983)

50

DESPERADO
THE EAGLES

1973

The Eagles' second album took the myth of the Western outlaw gang and sought parallels with the life of a contemporary rock 'n' roll band. Both sets of people lived outside of conventional society, traveled restlessly, valued independence, and found temporary relief in gambling, sex, intoxicants, money, and notoriety.

For the Eagles, however, this wasn't necessarily a cause for unadulterated celebration. While bragging about their exploits and their freedom to satiate their desires, they also bemoaned the hollowness that resulted. They'd gotten a lot less than the promise had held out to them. Too much license led to dissatisfaction. Too many thrills eventually numbed the senses. This was a theme pursued in later songs such as "After the Thrill Is Gone," "Take It to the Limit," "Wasted Time," and "Life in the Fast Lane."

This complaint is summarized in the title track, "Desperado," which, like Pink Floyd's *The Dark Side of the Moon*, is (consciously or unconsciously) a contemporization of parts of Ecclesiastes. Don Henley, the band's main lyricist, was raised a Southern Baptist in Texas and worked on the song with Glenn Frey, whom he credited with filling in some of the gaps and giving structure to it. (The only cover version on the record, "Outlaw Man," written by David Blue, says, "In one hand I've a Bible / In the other I've got a gun.")

"Desperado" begs the wandering outlaw to recognize the diminishing returns of his chosen lifestyle. The excitements that were the initial temptation give progressively less rewards. The lack of responsibility essential to this conception of freedom eventually leads to the prison of loneliness. It's not a call to "remember also thy Creator in the days of thy youth" (Ecclesiastes 12:1 ASV), but a call to come home and be loved.

The opening line asking him to "come to your senses" seems to allude to the parable of the prodigal son, an archetypal desperado who "wasted his substance with riotous living" (Luke 15:13). The turning point in his life took place when he "came to his senses" (Luke 15:17 NIV) and returned home. (The song was originally addressed to a friend of Henley's, and the first line was, "Leo, my God, why don't you come to your senses.")

The line "It seems to me some fine things have been laid upon your table / But you only want the ones that you can't get" is suggestive of "All things are full of weariness; man cannot utter it: the eye is not satisfied with seeing, nor the ear filled with hearing" (Ecclesiastes 1:8 ASV).

In the other songs on the album, the outlaws display pride at having no fixed abode and of descending on towns only to grab pleasure. But in "Desperado," the flip side of this disengaged life is confronted: "Your prison is walking through this world all alone." Ecclesiastes makes a similar calculation: "There is one that is alone, and he hath not a second. . . . For whom then, saith he, do I labor, and deprive my soul of good? This also is vanity, yea, it is a sore travail. Two are better than one, because they have a good reward for their labor" (4:8–9 ASV).

The conclusion of Ecclesiastes is "fear God, and keep his commandments" (12:13 ASV). The conclusion of "Desperado" is "You better let somebody love you before it's too late." It's assumed that the "somebody" is a woman, but it could be God. After all, the song says there is "a rainbow above you," and in the Bible (Genesis 9:8–17) the rainbow symbolizes the covenant between God and "all flesh that is upon the earth" (ASV).

"The songs were really perceptive, but they only identify the truth of the condition," guitarist Bernie Leadon told me in 1981. "They don't offer any real answer. Are we ever going to be satisfied? The ultimate answer must be, no, we're not. We can have all the stuff we want, but ultimately we're trapped. We can't leave. We're victims of our appetites. We need more sex, more money, and better tasting food. I've heard people say, 'Give me more of everything and I'll be satisfied.' But ultimately you're not. So these guys identified the fact that we need, need, need, and are never satisfied."

Song: "Desperado"

Artist: Eagles

Album: *Desperado*

Release: April 17, 1973

Studio: Island Studios, London

Personnel: Don Henley (vocals, drums), Glenn Frey (lead guitar), Randy Meisner (bass guitar), Bernie Leadon (rhythm guitar), Jim Ed Norman (string arranger), members of the London Symphony Orchestra

Writers: Don Henley, Glenn Frey

Producer: Glyn Johns

Label: Asylum Records

Highest Chart Position: 44 (US)

Other Significant Recordings: Linda Ronstadt (1973), Johnny Cash (2002), Diana Krall (2015)

Also by the Eagles: "Outlaw Man" (1973), "After the Thrill Is Gone" (1975), "Long Road Out of Eden" (2007)

JESUS IS THE ANSWER

ANDRAÉ CROUCH AND THE DISCIPLES

51

1973

A ndraé Crouch, the most successful gospel singer of his generation, was a prolific writer, a recording artist, a performer, a choral arranger, a musician, a mentor, and the pastor of a Los Angeles church. He worked with mainstream artists such as Madonna and Michael Jackson, contributed to the soundtracks of the movies *The Color Purple* and *The Lion King*, and has his star on the Hollywood Walk of Fame.

Like Thomas A. Dorsey, he combined the language of the Bible with the latest commercial sounds—in his case the sounds of rock, pop, jazz, and soul. Also, like Dorsey, he was considered a bit too righteous for the mainstream commercial music market and a bit too worldly for the church.

Raised in the Church of God in Christ in Los Angeles, he was powerfully influenced by his father, who was a preacher, pastor, and evangelist. To his dying day, Crouch insisted that his music was a gift from God to be used in the service of God. He didn't mean "gifted" in the conventional sense of being talented, but that his ability to sing and play piano had come to him in an instant when his father asked him to play for him at an evangelistic meeting. He hadn't taken music lessons, had to overcome a bad stammer in order to sing, and had to battle with dyslexia to write.

His first group, COGICS (Church of God in Christ Singers), was formed with his twin sister, Sandra, at Christ Memorial Church in Pacoima. Three of its members would go on to make their mark in the music industry—Gloria Jones as a singer and a writer at Motown ("Tainted Love"), Edna Wright as a member of Honey Cone ("Want Ads"), and Billy Preston as a solo artist ("That's the Way God Planned It") and a keyboard player with the Beatles ("Get Back"), Sly and the Family Stone ("Family Affair"), George Harrison ("My Sweet Lord"), John Lennon ("God"), the Rolling Stones ("Shine a Light"), and many others.

There were two strong influences on his early writing. The first was composing material for a choir of former drug addicts at Teen Challenge, the rehabilitation ministry that employed him. To aid their recovery, he gave them songs that were memorable extensions of his counseling advice—"The Power of Jesus" and "Hallelujah, I Am Free." The second influence came at Bible college when he found the most effective way for him to memorize the Bible was to set it to music. Much of his best music was a combination of counsel and Bible passages along with humble self-analysis.

Andraé Crouch and the Disciples was the next group formed at church. Ralph Carmichael, an innovative and experienced composer and arranger who had worked with the likes of Stan Kenton, Nat King Cole, and Ella Fitzgerald, had formed a record label, *Light*, to tap into the emerging Jesus Movement. He spotted the group and signed them up.

"Jesus Is the Answer" was typically direct. Crouch never hid his beliefs or engaged in subtle preamble. Just as his father, he was a preacher, pastor, and evangelist. The gist of the song is contained in the title, a phrase that is repeated a dozen times. The line coupled to it—"Above him there's no other, Jesus is the way" —is taken from Paul's claim about Jesus that "wherefore God also hath highly exalted him, and given him a name which is above every name" (Philippians 2:9) and the words of Jesus, "I am the way, the truth, and the life: no man cometh unto the Father, but by me" (John 14:6).

He goes on to specify a number of situations where he believes Jesus can supply answers, including discouragement, anxiety, guilt, depression, and apparently insurmountable problems. The comments of Jesus supporting the thesis of his song are likely to have been: "Come unto me, all ye that labour and are heavy laden, and I will give you rest" (Matthew 11:28), "Whatsoever ye shall ask in my name, that will I do" (John 14:13), and "Peace I leave with you, my peace I give unto you: not as the world giveth, give I unto you. Let not your heart be troubled, neither let it be afraid" (John 14:27).

When, after making this series of claims, Crouch says, "Everything he's promised / He will do it for you," he is pointing to a saying of Paul: "Faithful is he that calleth you, who also will do it" (1 Thessalonians 5:24).

"My dad used to tell me not to use any trendy effects," Crouch said, but to instead "stay close to the mic, and then your songs will have staying power. He also used to tell me to give the people at least two chances to hear the lyrics in a song. So that's what I try to do, to make the song repeat the words so you know them. The music is married to the lyrics. The people gotta hear the lyrics, and understand what I'm saying. They may not understand the message at first, but they will hear the lyrics. And maybe the understanding comes later."[79]

The song got a huge boost when it was performed by the Jessy Dixon Singers from Chicago while they toured with Paul Simon, who was riding high on the back of his first two post–Simon & Garfunkel solo albums. A recording by Dixon and his singers was included on Simon's 1974 album *Live Rhymin'*.

Song: "Jesus Is the Answer"

Artist: Andraé Crouch and the Disciples

Album: *Live at Carnegie Hall*

Release: May 1973

Studio: Live at Carnegie Hall, New York, NY

Personnel: Andraé Crouch (vocals, keyboards), Bill Thedford (bass, vocals), Bill Maxwell (drums), Fletch Wiley (flute), Hadley Hockensmith (guitar), Sandra Crouch (tambourine, vocals), Perry Morgan (vocals)

Writers: Andraé Crouch, Sandra Crouch

Producer: Andraé Crouch

Label: Light

Other Significant Recordings: The Archers (1972), Jessy Dixon Singers (1974), Michael W. Smith (1996)

Also by Andraé Crouch: "The Blood Will Never Lose Its Power" (1970), "Through It All" (1971), "Soon and Very Soon" (1976)

52

GIVE ME STRENGTH

ERIC CLAPTON

1974

In February 1974, Eric Clapton began neuroelectric therapy treatment for his heroin addiction at the Harley Street (London) apartment of Dr. Meg Patterson and her husband, George. For the previous three years, he'd been a virtual recluse at his Surrey mansion dependent on regular supplies of the drug, ashamed to go out, and unable to perform or compose to the best of his abilities.

The treatment, based on the principles of acupuncture, required a mild electric current to be passed into the earlobes at regular intervals. This stimulated production of the body's natural opiates—endorphins—allowing the addict to resist temptation as well as staving off the agonies of doing it "cold turkey." Most addicts continue fixing not because they still get a kick but because without their drug they're faced with physical pain and mental terror.

The Pattersons were both evangelical Christians (George had been a missionary to China) and spoke of their faith to Clapton. In her autobiography, Meg recounted a night when George prayed with Clapton during the night when he was distressed and having trouble sleeping. His anguish was partly caused by uncertainty over his future. In the morning Eric asked what he should do when he was free of addiction. "There's you, there's your guitar, and there's God," George told him and then, according to Meg, offered a few lines of a half-remembered hymn:[80]

> Lord, for tomorrow and its needs
> I do not pray.
> Give me, dear Lord, just give me
> Strength for today.

When Eric released his comeback album, *461 Ocean Boulevard*, four months later, "Give Me Strength" was one of only three self-written songs. The Pattersons assumed that it was a result of that experience.

The only flaw in the story is that the lines attributed to George come from a well-known Catholic hymn, "For Tomorrow and Its Needs," that has no request for strength. Written in the nineteenth century by Sybil Farish Partridge (who lived as a nun in Liverpool under the name Sister Mary Xavier), the relevant lines are:

> So, for tomorrow and its needs
> I do not pray;
> But keep me, guide me, love me Lord,
> Just for today.

In his autobiography, published in 2007, Eric gave a completely different version of the song's origin. He explained that it was a song he first heard in a London club during the early 1960s. He said simply, "It seemed to perfectly fit the occasion."[81]

"It's pretty easy to write a song like that because you're not writing anything brand new," he told me in 1975. "It could have been sung by anybody. There is nothing really innovative about the words. I mean—"Dear Lord. Give me strength"—people say that just walking along the street. People say it in exasperation."

Regardless of the origin, it was written in the style of a psalm of confession and supplication to God. In the simplest terms, it admits sin and requests divine strength. There are many biblical psalms that follow this pattern, but the one that comes closest is Psalm 86:

Bow down thine ear, O LORD, hear me: for I am poor and needy. Preserve my soul; for I am holy: O thou my God, save thy servant that trusteth in thee. Be merciful unto me, O Lord: for I cry unto thee daily. Rejoice the soul of thy servant: for unto thee, O Lord, do I lift up my soul. For thou, Lord, art good, and ready to forgive; and plenteous in mercy unto all them that call upon thee. Give ear, O LORD, unto my prayer; and attend to the voice of my supplications. In the day of my trouble I will call upon thee: for thou wilt answer me. (vv. 1–7)

The psalm ends:

But thou, O Lord, art a God full of compassion, and gracious, long suffering, and plenteous in mercy and truth. O turn unto me, and have mercy upon me; give thy strength unto thy servant, and save the son of thine handmaid. Shew me a token for good; that they which hate me may see it, and be ashamed: because thou, LORD, hast holpen me, and comforted me. (vv. 15–17)

In his autobiography, Clapton explained how he picked up the prayer habit again in 1987 after several relapses into alcoholism. "From that day until this, I have never failed to pray in the morning, on my knees, asking for help, and at night, to express gratitude for life and most of all, for my sobriety. I choose to kneel because feel I need to humble myself when I pray, and with my ego, this is the most I can do."[82]

Song: "Give Me Strength"
Artist: Eric Clapton
Single: A-side: "I Shot the Sheriff" / B-side: "Give Me Strength"
Album: *461 Ocean Boulevard*
Release: July 1974

Studio: Criteria Studios, Miami, FL

Personnel: Eric Clapton (vocals, guitar), Dick Sims (keyboards), George Terry (guitar), Carl Radle (bass guitar), Al Jackson Jr. (drums), Albhy Galuten (synthesizer)

Writer: Eric Clapton

Producer: Tom Dowd

Label: RSO

Highest Chart Position: As the B-side of "I Shot the Sheriff" – 1 (US), 9 (UK)

Other Significant Recordings: Prof. Harold Boggs (1976)

Also by Eric Clapton: "In the Presence of the Lord" (1969), "We've Been Told (Jesus Coming Soon)" (1975), "Swing Low Sweet Chariot" (1975)

53

WORD ON A WING

DAVID BOWIE

1976

B y 1975, David Bowie was professionally and artistically successful, but, in his own words, "in a lot of spiritual and emotional trouble." When not on location filming *The Man Who Fell to Earth* with director Nicolas Roeg, he was locked away behind permanently drawn curtains and surrounded by black candles in a rented house on Doheny Drive in LA, sinking deeper into a cocaine habit.

He was also studying occult theories to find answers to his pressing questions about the human condition and the purpose of life. He read books on everything from theosophy and numerology to the kabbalah and the Arthurian myth of the Holy Grail.

Cocaine made him paranoid. He became fixated with spurious conspiracy theories, had his house purged by an exorcist, and believed that jealous witches and Satanists were targeting him. The more theories he investigated, the less certain he became that there was any absolute truth against which they could be tested.

It was in this state of anxiety that he wrote "Word on a Wing," a song he would later describe as "a hymn." Distinctively Christian in nature, rather than vaguely and fashionably spiritual, it was more a prayer for what he hoped might be true (and therefore protect him from outside attack and internal disintegration) than it was a statement of faith.

"There were days of such psychological terror when making the [Nicolas] Roeg film [*The Man Who Fell to Earth*] that I nearly started to approach my reborn, born again thing," he later said. "It was the first time I'd really seriously thought about Christ and God in any depth, and 'Word on a Wing' was a protection. It did come as a complete revolt against elements that I found in the film. The passion in the song was genuine . . . something I needed to produce from within myself to safeguard myself against some of the situations that I felt were happening on the film set."[83]

It's written in the form of a personal prayer to God. It may even be specifically to Jesus, as he refers to his "sweet name" (John Newton, author of "Amazing Grace," wrote the popular hymn "Jesus Is the Sweetest Name I Know" in the eighteenth century) and alludes to the idea of being "born once again."

He admits that he is living in "illusion" but that God "walked into" his life. He implies that he's a somewhat reluctant convert who doesn't want to relinquish his mission to "question everything in heaven or hell," and yet confesses that it's better to be with this "Lord," whom he's now kneeling before, than to be in "a strange land."

The strange land references the Egyptian captivity of the Israelites: "Love ye therefore the stranger: for ye were strangers in the land of Egypt" (Deuteronomy 10:19). At other times they were referred to as sojourners, aliens, or foreigners. Alienation was a significant theme in Bowie's work. He admired Robert A. Heinlein's 1961 sci-fi novel *Stranger in a Strange Land*, the title of which was taken from a saying of Moses: "I have been a stranger in a strange land" (Exodus 2:22).

In Heinlein's novel, Valentine Michael Smith, a human raised on Mars after being born on a US rocket mission, comes to earth and challenges its beliefs and behavior. The original title was "The Heretic." *The Man Who Fell to Earth*, a novel written two years later by Walter Tevis, explored similar territory, although his protagonist (eventually played by Bowie) was a humanoid alien. The "strange land" in Bowie's lyrics may also be directed at the film, which he believed had taken him to a dark place.

His experience of Christianity didn't stick, although he remained curious. Asked in 1979 whether he was still involved in the Buddhism that interested him in the 1960s, Bowie said, "When push came to shove I realized that there must be something in the West that I could adhere to, rather than something in the East—that surely we must have some kind of spiritual backbone in the West. Everything [I've done] since has been some kind of search for it."[84]

Song: "Word on a Wing"

Artist: David Bowie

Album: *Station to Station*

Release: January 23, 1976

Studio: Cherokee Studios, Hollywood, CA

Personnel: David Bowie (vocals), Earl Slick (lead guitar), Carlos Alomar (rhythm guitar), George Murray (bass guitar), Roy Bittan (piano, organ), Warren Peace (percussion, backing vocals) Dennis Davis (drums), Harry Maslin (synthesizers, vibraphone)

Writer: David Bowie

Producers: David Bowie, Harry Maslin

Label: RCA Records

Also by David Bowie: "Loving the Alien," (1984), "Sunday," (2002), "Lazarus" (2015)

54

ANARCHY IN THE U.K.

THE SEX PISTOLS

1976

The opening lines to "Anarchy in the U.K."—"Right now, ha, ha, ha, ha, ha / I am an antichrist / I am an anarchist"—were some of the most explosive and deliberately provocative on a single since those of "Fire" by the Crazy World of Arthur Brown in 1968—"I am the god of hellfire and I bring you / Fire, I'll take you to burn."

John Lydon (a.k.a. "Johnny Rotten") was using the title "antichrist" to stir controversy. He was a disgruntled youth with genuine grievances against British society. What could be more offensive to that society than to apparently align oneself with the biggest threats to its church (antichrist) and its state apparatus (anarchy)?

The "antichrist" bit of the lyric was deliberate, but the "anarchist" (memorably pronounced by Rotten as "anar-kyst" to parallel "antichrist") was a forced rhyme created on the spot in the rehearsal studio (to the annoyance of fellow Pistol Glen Matlock). Years later he admitted that although he was opposed to organized religion and didn't trust political parties, he did it "for shock value."

Angry is a complete energy. And it's wonderful. I recommend
it. But don't let it turn to violence. Find an outlet for it and
it can be amazingly rewarding. It's a very useful tool. I don't
know if it's the driving force in me. I would say completely
not. There are many tools out there: all the human emotions.
I get angry when I see people oppressed, the disenfranchised.
I'm constantly churning up emotions for that. My enemy
will always be all political systems. All of them. I support no
government or politician anywhere, ever.[85]

His antipathy toward religion came from being raised in working-class
London-Irish Catholic home and being educated by nuns. He claimed that at
school he was made to believe that his natural left-handedness was an indication of devilishness. There may be some truth in this because the medieval
church did regard left-handedness with suspicion. In the Bible, the left is
often identified as being inferior to the right. After the risen Jesus's ascent
to heaven, he was at "the right hand of God" (Mark 16:19; Acts 7:55–56;
Romans 8:34; Colossians 3:1). At the final judgment, all the nations will be
gathered before God, "And he will separate the people one from another as
a shepherd separates the sheep from the goats. He will put the sheep on his
right and the goats on his left" (Matthew 25:32–33 NIV). Catholic schools had
a reputation for forcing pupils to write with their right hands, often using
punishments to correct them.

The term *antichrist* only appears five times in the New Testament—all of
them in the epistles of John. In four of the instances, the mentions are singu-
lar. In one it is plural. Some theologians believe a particular individual is being
described, whereas others suggest that it's a general spirit of opposition. There
is debate as to whether "the antichrist" is also the great beast and false prophet
mentioned in the book of Revelation, a false Christ as spoken of by Jesus, and
the lawless one predicted by Paul in his second letter to the Thessalonians.

It may be no coincidence that the movie *The Omen* had been released in
the UK in June 1976, which told the story of the child Damien, who is the
antichrist (and also the beast 666). "Anarchy in the U.K." was first rehearsed
in July 1976.

The antichrist line irritated the people he meant to offend. When the band's first tour arrived in Caerphilly, Wales, local church members sang hymns outside the venue. "[It] just compounded my attitude towards religion. And the fact we were doing something right," Lydon later said. "Religion is a form of control, asking you to accept the obviously stupid over reality."[86]

Song: "Anarchy in the U.K."

Artist: Sex Pistols

Single: A-side: "Anarchy in the U.K." / B-side: "I Wanna Be Me"

Release: November 26, 1976

Studio: Wessex Studios, London

Personnel: John Lydon, a.k.a. "Johnny Rotten" (vocals), Glen Matlock (bass guitar), Steve Jones (lead guitar), Paul Cook (drums)

Writers: John Lydon, Glen Matlock, Steve Jones, Paul Cook

Producers: Chris Thomas, Bill Price, Dave Goodman

Label: EMI

Highest Chart Position: 38 (UK)

Other Significant Recordings: Megadeath (1988), Mötley Crüe (1991), Green Jelly (1993)

Also by the Sex Pistols: "God Save the Queen" (1977)

55

EXODUS

BOB MARLEY AND THE WAILERS

1977

Rastafari is a small (less than a million devotees) and relatively new religious movement (1930s) centered in the Caribbean islands. During the 1970s, Bob Marley became its public voice, and by incorporating Rasta views into his reggae songs he spread the message around the world so that millions of music lovers gained at least a rudimentary knowledge of the religion.

Because Rastafari (also called Rastafarianism) has no central organization, systematic theology, or catechism, it's difficult to be precise about its beliefs. Rastas feel free to disagree with each other over interpretation, and it's primarily a religion of feeling rather than doctrine.

Rasta contains a mixture of fundamentalist Christianity, post-colonial politics, drug mysticism, and residual West African ritual. Rastas believe in one God—*Jah* (a contraction of Jehovah)—who indwells all people. Many of them believe that the Ethiopian emperor Haile Selassie (1892–1975) was the incarnation of the Second Coming of Christ. It is from him that the term *Rastafari* derives; he was *Ras* (Prince) Tafari Makonnen—although, as a Christian, he didn't accept their view of him. They also believe that the drug ganja (cannabis) is a divine gift predicted in such verses as Genesis 1:29, Psalm 18:8, and Revelation 22:2.

Central to their beliefs—and central to Marley's song—is the idea that they, like the ancient Israelites, were taken captive from Africa and are now in bondage in Babylon. They yearn to be set free and restored to their homeland in Africa—preferably Ethiopia.

"Exodus" conflates two of Israel's experiences and one of the church at the end of time into a single incident. The song's title refers to the time when the Israelites were led out of Egypt—hence the call for "another brother Moses" and mention of the Red Sea. Then it says, "We're leaving Babylon / We're going to our fatherland"—a reference to the time when Judah and Jerusalem were conquered by Nebuchadnezzar and many Jews were deported to Babylon (2 Kings 24–25). They returned seventy years later, when the Persians defeated the Babylonians. The "great tribulation" refers to the persecution of "a great multitude, which no man could number, out of every nation and of all tribes and peoples and tongues" that stand before God's throne at the end of time (Revelation 7:9–17 ASV).

Marley's descriptions of *Jah* in the final rallying call are taken from throughout the Bible. The breaking of oppression could come from Psalm 9:9: "Jehovah also will be a high tower for the oppressed, a high tower in times of trouble" (ASV). The "wipe away transgressions" comes from the prophet Isaiah: "I am he that blotteth out thy transgressions for mine own sake" (Isaiah 43:25). "Set the captives free" also comes from Isaiah: "The spirit of the Lord GOD is upon me; because the LORD hath anointed me to preach good tidings unto the meek; he hath sent me to bind up the brokenhearted, to proclaim liberty to the captives, and the opening of the prison to them that are bound" (61:1). Jesus at the synagogue in Nazareth read this passage when he started his ministry, and he closed the reading by announcing, "To-day hath this scripture been fulfilled in your ears" (Luke 4:21 ASV).

After Marley's death in May 1981, he was laid in an open casket at the National Heroes Arena in Kingston, Jamaica. In one of his hands was placed a Gibson Les Paul guitar. In the other was a King James Version of the Bible.

Song: "Exodus"
Artist: Bob Marley and the Wailers
Album: *Exodus*

Single: A-side: "Exodus" / B-side: "Exodus" (instrumental version)

Release: June 25, 1977

Studio: Harry J. Studios, Kingston, Jamaica; Island Studios, London

Personnel: Bob Marley (vocals, rhythm guitar), Aston Barrett (bass guitar), Carlton Barrett (drums), Tyrone Downie (keyboards), Junior Marvin (lead guitar), Alvin Patterson (percussion), Rita Marley (backing vocals), Marcia Griffiths (backing vocals), Judy Mowatt (backing vocals)

Writer: Bob Marley

Producers: Bob Marley and the Wailers

Label: Island Records

Highest Chart Position: 14 (UK)

Other Significant Recordings: The Gladiators (1979), U2 (2008), Santana (2010)

Also by Bob Marley: "So Many Things to Say" (1977), "Babylon System" (1979), "Redemption Song" (1980)

56

WAITING FOR THE END OF THE WORLD
ELVIS COSTELLO

....

1977

D id the Bible inspire this track? Not that we are claiming that Elvis Costello got his initial idea out of the book of Revelation or that he wrote with a Bible at his side to ensure theological accuracy. Yet the song wouldn't have taken the direction it did without his biblical knowledge, gleaned from a childhood in the Catholic church and at Catholic schools in Liverpool and London.

The "end of the world" in this song isn't just any old apocalyptic scenario with falling bombs or ecological disaster, but the return of Jesus and final judgment—"Dear Lord, I sincerely hope you're coming."

Although the Bible doesn't envisage life in its present state going on indefinitely, the phrase "end of the world" is used sparingly, and even then can be translated as "consummation of the age." The best known examples are in the words of Jesus spoken to his disciples after having told them the parable of the wheat and tares, in which both plants grow side by side and can appear indistinguishable. When they are harvested, though, the tares (weeds) are burnt and the wheat is taken to the barn. Jesus explained that "the good seed" represented "the children of the kingdom" and the tares "the children of the wicked one." He continued:

> The enemy that sowed them is the devil; the harvest is the end of the world; and the reapers are the angels. As therefore the tares are gathered and burned in the fire; so shall it be in the end of this world. The Son of man shall send forth his angels, and they shall gather out of his kingdom all things that offend, and them which do iniquity; And shall cast them into a furnace of fire: there shall be wailing and gnashing of teeth. (Matthew 13:39–42)

In his autobiography, *Unfaithful Music & Disappearing Ink*, Costello said the song "turned a simple homeward journey on the [London] Underground into a claustrophobic travelogue, pulling the hysteria out of newspaper headlines into the everyday boredom of the commuter."[87]

He got stuck in a tunnel between stations due to a power failure, and in the dark and cramped conditions began to contemplate final things. This could have been (seriously) because his fears were heightened and led him to think of death or (jokingly) because at least the second coming of Jesus would get him out of the tunnel sooner or later, even if London Transport couldn't fix the problem.

Theology has never been a dominant motif in Costello's work to the extent that it has been for a band like U2 or a singer like Leonard Cohen, but in describing the battle between good and evil he often resorts to church liturgy or the Bible for the most convenient language of exploration. He has said that his experience of Catholicism was benevolent, although he's no longer a believer its key doctrines. "I'm suspicious of people who think they know what God knows," he said. "I actually think that's blasphemy."[88]

Song: "Waiting for the End of the World"
Artist: Elvis Costello
Album: *My Aim Is True*

Release: July 22, 1977

Studio: Pathway Studios, London

Personnel: Elvis Costello (guitar, vocals), John McFee (lead guitar), Sean Hopper (piano, organ), Johnny Ciambotti (bass guitar), Mickey Shine (drums)

Writer: Elvis Costello

Producer: Nick Lowe

Label: Stiff Records

Highest Chart Position: 14 (UK)

Also by Elvis Costello: "Blame It on Cain" (1977), "The Sharpest Thorn" (2006), "Pardon Me Madam" (2008)

57

ADAM RAISED A CAIN

BRUCE SPRINGSTEEN

1978

O n *Darkness on the Edge of Town,* Bruce Springsteen united great themes from rock 'n' roll such as frustration, conflict, and escape with biblical language such as sin, faith, prayer, and salvation. He found a way of reviewing his adolescent passions that was true to both his musical heritage and his Catholic background.

The landscape of *Darkness on the Edge of Town* is bleak, colorless, and corrosive of the soul. The people he sees either capitulate to the way things are or believe they "deserve much more than this" ("Prove It All Night"). The latter group seeks its redemption through passionate and potentially dangerous acts that remind them that they're bigger than what they've been made to feel. These are the people he identifies with and whose case he states.

For Springsteen, the car has to suffice as a symbol of release from the world of backbreaking toil, frustrated expectations, and diminished dreams. Those who want to grab the heart and soul go racing in the street or drive out into the darkness at the edge of town because they believe it's through such existential acts that they stand some hope of attaining glory.

Across the album, he expresses the search for transcendence in religious words. In "Badlands," he believes in "the faith that can save me" and prays that "someday it may raise me." At the conclusion of "Racing in the Street," he says that he and his girl are going to "ride to the sea / and wash these sins off our hands." In "The Promised Land," he affirms, "I believe in the promised land."

His "badland" is the world outside of paradise. In the present age there is a disconnection between our natural longings and life as we find it. Echoing St. Augustine's fourth-century observation, "Thou has made us for thyself, O Lord, and our heart is restless until it finds its rest in thee," Springsteen sings, "Everybody's got a hunger, a hunger they can't resist" ("Prove It All Night").

In "Adam Raised a Cain," he makes explicit reference to the doctrine of original sin. As Springsteen puts it, "You're born into this life paying for the sins of somebody else's past." Given the biblical framework he's chosen to use, he could mean that we all now suffer the consequences of Adam's revolt—"through one man sin entered into the world, and death through sin; and so death passed unto all men, for that all sinned" (Romans 5:12 ASV)—or he could have in mind, "The LORD is longsuffering, and of great mercy, forgiving iniquity and transgression, and by no means clearing the guilty, visiting the iniquity of the fathers upon the children unto the third and fourth generation" (Numbers 14:18).

The story he uses is that of Adam and Eve's eldest child, Cain, killing his brother, Abel. God condemned him to be "a fugitive and a wanderer" (Genesis 4:12 ASV). For the rest of his life he bore what has become known as "the mark of Cain," a curse that identified him to others as someone to avoid. The song says that "East of Eden he was cast," but Genesis doesn't say that he was ejected, simply that "Cain went out from the presence of the LORD, and dwelt in the land of Nod, on the east of Eden" (Genesis 4:16).

The song also worked on a more personal level. Springsteen felt damaged by his father's shortcomings. In his 2016 autobiography, *Born to Run*, he revealed that Springsteen Sr. was harsh, unloving, and disappointed that his son pursued such "soft" things as music, poetry, books, and fashion rather than being tough and unsentimental like he was.[89]

The truth, though, was more complex. In Springsteen's adult judgment, his father's toughness was a false projection, and what upset him about his son's choices was that he saw himself in them. Unable to attack himself for what he perceived as a weakness, he turned on Bruce.

It was in this way that Springsteen felt that he bore the sins of his father and in turn paid the consequences of bearing them. As he put it in "Adam Raised a Cain"—"But you inherit the sins, you inherit the flames."

Song: "Adam Raised a Cain"

Artist: Bruce Springsteen

Album: *Darkness on the Edge of Town*

Release: June 2, 1978

Studio: The Record Plant, New York, NY

Personnel: Bruce Springsteen (lead guitar, vocals), Clarence Clemons (saxophone, percussion), Danny Federici (organ), Roy Bittan (piano), Garry Tallent (bass guitar), Steve Van Zandt (guitar), Max Weinberg (drums)

Writer: Bruce Springsteen

Producers: Bruce Springsteen, Jon Landau

Label: Columbia

Other Significant Recordings: Sandra Stephens (2001), Alabama Shakes (2014), Murder by Death (2015)

Also by Bruce Springsteen: "It's Hard to Be a Saint in the City" (1973), "Hungry Heart" (1980), "My Father's House" (1982)

58

PRIVILEGE (SET ME FREE)
THE PATTI SMITH GROUP

1978

W ritten for the 1967 film *Privilege* by British songwriters Mark London (lyrics) and Mike Leander (music), this song was performed by former Manfred Mann vocalist Paul Jones under the title "Free Me." Although Patti Smith kept the music and stuck to the theme of the original song, she radically altered the lyrics and interpolated them with two readings from Psalm 23.

In the movie, Paul Jones plays the role of a manufactured and controlled pop star, Steven Shorter, whose management leases him to the church and state to tame rebellious youth. A former teen criminal who uses his story to give his fans the impression they are walking on the wild side by even listening to his music, his controllers make him a Christian convert who then preaches a message of repentance and conformity.

The "Free Me" song is part of a dramatic stage act that Shorter performs in a heavily spotlighted cage. Truncheon-toting actors posing as prison guards patrol the exterior while a handcuffed Shorter rattles the bars and cries out for release. It's an incident from his past life but is used in the movie as a metaphor for his condition as a pop star enslaved by PR, business, and the expectations of fans. When he "converts," his resident songwriter revises the lyrics to make it a sentimental hymn.

Patti Smith, raised in the Jehovah Witness faith by her mother and encouraged by her agnostic father to read and explore, had long been fascinated by rebellious rock 'n' roll and the power of religion. As a child, she wanted to become a missionary, but rejected her Jehovah Witnesses background at the age of twelve and instead worshiped at the shrine of the Rolling Stones, Bob Dylan, the Beat Generation authors, French symbolist poets, and William Blake.

She came to view artists as missionaries of a sort. The best of them ventured deep into their consciousnesses and returned with enlightenment and inspiration to gift to their followers. That was the sort of art she determined to create.

The messianic nature of Steven Shorter in *Privilege*—the idea of a rock star as a spiritual leader—naturally intrigued her. In the sleeve notes of the *Easter* album, she wrote that it was "a movie that merged the rock martyr with all the sacristal [*sic*] images of the sixties—the cross . . . the Christ . . . the whip."

Whereas Shorter's song tempts his followers to believe that they have the power to release him, Smith's version is a prayer of petition to God. She feels drained by her job and begs for the gift of something to pass on to her listeners rather than for physical freedom. She's an artist beseeching her creator for something to say that will be worth saying.

In the middle of her request, she recites the comforting words of the psalmist:

> The LORD is my shepherd; I shall not want. He maketh me
> to lie down in green pastures: he leadeth me beside the still
> waters. He restoreth my soul: he leadeth me in the paths of
> righteousness for his name's sake. Yea, though I walk through
> the valley of the shadow of death, I will fear no evil: for thou
> art with me. (Psalm 23:1–4)

The song ends with the rest of the psalm, and then some repeated blasphemies that guaranteed that the single got little radio play. These seem designed not to malign God but to spur him to action, because when they have finished she says simply, "Here I am," an allusion to the obedience of

Mary: "Then Mary said, 'Here am I, the servant of the Lord; let it be with me according to your word'" (Luke 1:38 NRSV). At the end of the album credits, she wrote, "I have fought a good fight, I have finished my course" (2 Timothy 4:7).

Song: "Privilege (Set Me Free)"

Artist: Patti Smith Group

Extended Play: "Set Free" A-side: "Privilege (Set Me Free)" | "Ask the Angels" / B-side: "25th Floor (Live Version)" | "Babelfield"

Album: *Easter*

Release: August 4, 1978

Studio: The Record Plant, New York, NY; House of Music, West Orange, NJ

Personnel: Patti Smith (vocals, guitar), Lenny Kaye (vocals, guitar), Jay Dee Daugherty (drums), Ivan Král (guitar), Bruce Brody (keyboards, synthesizer), John Paul Fetta (bass guitar)

Writers: Mark London, Mike Leander

Producer: Jimmy Iovine

Label: Arista

Highest Chart Position: 72 (UK)

Other Significant Recordings: Paul Jones (1967), Lucy Cotter (1997)

Also by Patti Smith: "Easter" (1978), "Hymn" (1979), "People Have the Power" (1988)

59

RIVERS OF BABYLON

BONEY M.

1978

The Jamaican rocksteady band the Melodians recorded "Rivers of Babylon" in 1970, and it was used on the soundtrack of the reggae movie *The Harder They Come* starring Jimmy Cliff as a country boy in search of work in Kingston, Jamaica. Two band members, Brent Dowe and Trevor McNaughton, wrote it.

The words are taken from two psalms. Three verses are from Psalm 137: "By the rivers of Babylon, there we sat down, yea, we wept, when we remembered Zion" (v. 1); "For there they that carried us away captive required of us a song" (v. 3); "How shall we sing the LORD's song in a strange land?" (v. 4). One verse is from Psalm 19: "Let the words of my mouth, and the meditation of my heart, be acceptable in thy sight, O LORD, my strength, and my redeemer" (v. 14).

Psalm 137 was written when the Jews were in Babylonian captivity and yearned to be released. Their thoughts were in Jerusalem ("Zion"), and they asked how it was possible for them to sing to God when surrounded by a hostile culture. To Rastafarians, Babylon was any repressive culture.

Lyricist Brent Dowe wanted the song to be an anthem for Rastafari that would spread its beliefs internationally. The two significant alterations he made to the biblical text were to replace "The LORD's song" with "King Alpha's song" ("King Alpha" being one of the titles accorded to Emperor Haile Selassie of Ethiopia), and to introduce the name Far-I.

Although the recording by the Melodians reached a lot of people, particularly through the soundtrack album of *The Harder They Come*, it was the recording by the disco group Boney M. eight years later that brought it to the world.

Boney M. was initially a studio project by German record producer Frank Farian, who sang all the male parts, played the instruments, and hired in female backing vocalists. After having chart success in Germany, requests came in for the "group" to tour and appear on TV. To satisfy such demands, Farian had to create a vocal dancing group to perform his material live—Jamaicans Liz Mitchell and Marcia Barrett, Maizie Williams from Montserrat, and Bobby Farrell from Aruba.

Mitchell and Barrett were used on the recording of "Rivers of Babylon" with Farian contributing the male vocals. The song had the specific Rastafarian mentions removed—"King Alpha's son" was restored to the biblical "LORD's song" and "O Far-I" became "here tonight." The resulting single combined the exuberance of Caribbean rocksteady with the throbbing beat of European disco.

It became one of the biggest international hits of all time. It made the number one spot in thirteen countries, remained forty weeks on the UK charts, and sold over 4.5 million copies. Later that year Boney M. became the first Western pop group officially invited to perform in the USSR. "It was so momentous," said Liz Mitchell. "It was the beginning of the big changes in Russia and Russians never let me forget that. 'Rivers of Babylon' played a large part. It was a song that that meant so much to many Russian Jews."[90]

Song: "Rivers of Babylon"

Artist: Boney M.

Album: *Nightflight to Venus*

Single: A-side: "Rivers of Babylon" / B-side: "Brown Girl in the Ring"

Release: April 3, 1978

Studio: Union Studios, Munich, Germany

Personnel: Liz Mitchell (vocals), Marcia Barrett (vocals), Frank Farian (vocals)

Writers: Brent Dowe, Trevor McNaughton, Frank Farian, Hans-Jörg Mayer

Producer: Frank Farian

Label: Sire (US), Hansa (Germany)

Highest Chart Position: 1 (UK), 30 (US)

Other Significant Recordings: The Melodians (1970), Steve Earle (1995), the Neville Brothers (2004)

Also by Boney M.: "I'm Born Again" (1979), "Mary's Boy Child / Oh My Lord" (1981), "Zion's Daughter" (1982)

60

PRECIOUS ANGEL

BOB DYLAN

. . . .

1979

B ob Dylan had always written songs reflecting his interest in the Bible, but when he released the album *Slow Train Coming* in 1979 with its overtly Christian lyrics, it was one of the biggest turnarounds since Little Richard announced that he was abandoning rock 'n' roll for the pulpit in October 1957 and threw his jewelry into the waters beneath Sydney Harbour Bridge.

Dylan was regarded as a leader of a counterculture critical of traditional values, especially those derived from the Christian religion. It was one thing to employ biblical symbolism or even to sing spirituals, but quite another to embrace Christianity in a personal way.

Fans who had followed Dylan devotedly over almost two decades felt betrayed. They thought he articulated their values, but now he criticized them. Between songs in concert, he was evangelizing and warning about the final judgment. Some critics thought maybe he was just exploring the gospel in the way that he had explored folk, blues, rock, and country in the past.

But something had happened to Bob Dylan. He had converted, attended a Los Angeles church called the Vineyard Christian Fellowship, and was enrolled part time in its Bible school.[91] His new songs didn't just allude to

Christian doctrine; they were saturated in it. It was if he were directly converting his notes from Bible class into lyrics.

He displayed zeal and impetuousness, as if he was afraid that Jesus could return before he'd successfully gotten the message out. He knew that his audience placed value on his observations and insights, and now he believed he had something substantial to deliver.

In 1980, he told music critic Robert Hilburn of the *Los Angeles Times*, "I truly had a born-again experience, if you want to call it that. It's an overused term, but it's something that people can relate to. It happened in 1978. I always knew there was a God or a creator of the universe and a creator of the mountains and the sea and all that kind of thing, but I wasn't conscious of Jesus and what that had to do with the Supreme Creator."[92]

"Precious Angel" was the background to that experience, and the angel in question is African American actress Mary Alice Artes, the woman who introduced him to two young pastors from the Vineyard Christian Fellowship, who answered his questions and took him under their wing. No other pop or rock song had drawn so extensively from the Bible. There are at least a dozen references from Genesis to Revelation.

Artes is his "angel" because an angel is "a messenger from God." She has shown him that he was "blinded" ("The god of this world hath blinded the minds of the unbelieving" [2 Corinthians 4:4 ASV]) and that the foundations of his life were "weak" ("Every one that heareth these words of mine, and doeth them not, shall be likened unto a foolish man, who built his house upon the sand" [Matthew 7:26 ASV]).

He describes "spiritual warfare" and "flesh and blood" breaking down ("For our wrestling is not against flesh and blood, but against the principalities, against the powers, against the world-rulers of this darkness, against the spiritual hosts of wickedness in the heavenly places" [Ephesians 6:12 ASV]). "The enemy" he speaks of is Satan, whom he says is "subtle" ("Now the serpent was more subtle than any beast of the field" [Genesis 3:1 ASV]) and out to deceive ("When he [the devil] speaketh a lie, he speaketh of his own: for he is a liar, and the father thereof" [John 8:44 ASV]).

His "so-called friends" who don't share his Christian views are targeted. He quotes them as saying, "All is well" ("When they are saying, Peace and safety, then sudden destruction cometh upon them" [1 Thessalonians 5:3 ASV]), and warns that one day they'll "beg God to kill them" ("And in those days men shall seek death, and shall in no wise find it; and they shall desire to die, and death fleeth from them" [Revelation 9:6 ASV]).

When he says, "We are covered in blood, girl," he could mean that they're both members of racial groups who've suffered persecution and slavery or that they're both saved by the blood of Jesus ("But if we walk in the light, as he is in the light, we have fellowship one with another, and the blood of Jesus his Son cleanseth us from all sin" [1 John 1:7 ASV]).

Slow Train Coming was a deliberately confrontational album, and its follow-up, *Saved*, even more so. The biggest surprise was that he forsook the oblique poetic approach that had always characterized his work and was writing songs that were direct and unambiguous: "Ya either got faith or ya got unbelief / and there ain't no neutral ground" ("Precious Angel").

Song: "Precious Angel"

Artist: Bob Dylan

Single: A-side: "Precious Angel" / B-side: "Trouble In Mind" (UK)

Release: June 22, 1979 (UK)

Album: *Slow Train Coming*

Studio: Muscle Shoals Sound Studios, Muscle Shoals, AL

Personnel: Bob Dylan (guitar, vocals), Mark Knopfler (lead guitar), Tim Drummond (bass guitar), Pick Withers (drums), Mickey Buckins (percussion), Carolyn Dennis (backing vocals), Helena Springs (backing vocals), Regina Havis (backing vocals)

Writer: Bob Dylan

Producers: Jerry Wexler, Barry Beckett

Label: Columbia

Other Significant Recordings: World Wide Message Tribe (1998), Valdemar (2007)

Also by Bob Dylan: "You Gotta Serve Somebody" (1979), "In the Garden" (1980), "Saving Grace" (1980)

61

POWER OF LOVE

T BONE BURNETT

· ·

1980

F or his mid-1970s *Rolling Thunder Revue* concert tour, Bob Dylan gathered around him a group of performers including Joan Baez, Rambling
Jack Elliot, Roger McGuinn, painter and musician Bobby Neuwirth,
poet Allen Ginsberg, and David Bowie's guitarist, Mick Ronson. While touring America with them, he was also improvising a four-hour movie, *Renaldo
& Clara.*

Although not prompted by anything specific on the tour, within two years
of its completion, five of its participants—Roger McGuinn, David Mansfield,
Steven Soles, Bob Dylan, and T Bone Burnett—had become Christians. Soles,
Mansfield, and Burnett formed a group, the Alpha Band, and were signed by
Arista Records. In 1980, Burnett began recording under his own name.

When it came to writing songs expressing his newfound faith, Burnett
took a very different approach from his old boss. Where Dylan was com-
bative, direct, and overtly religious, Burnett developed an apologetic that
stealthily poked at flaws in the secular worldview rather than selling Jesus. At
the time he said his aim was to make unbelievers doubt their unbelief.

A fan of British authors G. K. Chesterton (*Orthodoxy*) and C. S. Lewis
(*Mere Christianity*), he was fond of quoting Lewis's claim that "I believe in

Christianity as I believe that the sun has risen: not only because I see it, but because by it I see everything else."[93] He argued that just as it was possible to make art about the sun (in the manner of Dylan), it was also possible to make art about what the sun made visible.

It was a tough challenge. There were few role models. Most artists who became Christians felt that their art should become evangelistic. He found sustenance and encouragement in Russian novelists like Dostoevsky, Tolstoy, and Solzhenitsyn, short-story writer Flannery O'Connor (*Wise Blood*), and Catholic convert Walker Percy (*The Moviegoer*).

Burnett was naturally oblique, literary, and impressionistic. His songs were open invitations to engage rather than creeds that had to either be agreed with or argued against. Even though he was born and raised in Texas, he was from the Episcopal rather than hot gospel tradition. Always open about his commitment to the historical Christian faith, he didn't see himself as an ad man for Jesus.

"Power of Love" was the closest he got to a gospel song. It was a subtle piece of work that used inference rather than statement and relied to a great extent on the cultural memory of the audience and its ability to join dots.

"The power of love," he says, "can make a blind man see." At first it sounds like any other song about the transformative properties of love. It "can bring a man to his knees . . . can make a skeptic believe." It could still be about human love, but then in the second verse he sings, "The power of love is the name of names / And burns away all the pain." He is referencing Paul's claim about Jesus: "Wherefore God also hath highly exalted him, and given him a name which is above every name" (Philippians 2:9). It's Jesus who makes the blind see, brings people to their knees, and causes skeptics to believe.

The other types of people that he says can be changed include gangsters, losers, strong men, bigots, cowards, heroes, and misers. In each case they discover the qualities they lacked—the gangsters learn to cry, cowards become brave, and misers develop generosity.

The final line is, "The power love can make a miser give / Can make a dead man live." He could have been thinking of the wealthy tax collector, Zacchaeus, who was so changed by meeting Jesus that he redistributed his money—"Behold, Lord, half of my possessions I will give to the poor, and if I have defrauded anyone of anything, I will give back four times as much" (Luke 19:8 NASB)—and also of Lazarus, the brother of Jesus's friends Mary and Martha, whom Jesus resurrected—"When He had said these things, He cried out with a loud voice, 'Lazarus, come forth.' The man who had died came forth, bound hand and foot with wrappings, and his face was wrapped around with a cloth. Jesus said to them, 'Unbind him, and let him go'" (John 11:43–44 NASB).

"In all lyrics some view of the word is being presented," he told *LA Weekly*. "Nobody speaks in a vacuum. I don't think there's any view that knows a man better than Christianity."[94]

Song: "Power of Love"

Artist: T Bone Burnett

Album: *Truth Decay*

Release: July 1980

Studio: Reggie Fisher Studio, Los Angeles, CA

Personnel: T Bone Burnett (guitar, vocals), Steven Soles (guitar, vocals), Stephen Bruton (guitar), David Mansfield (guitar), Jerry McGee (guitar), David Miner (bass guitar), David Kemper (drums)

Writer: T Bone Burnett

Producer: Reggie Fisher

Label: Takoma

Other Significant Recordings: Arlo Guthrie (1981)

Also by T Bone Burnett: "Spark in the Dark" (1977), "Shut It Tight" (1983), "Every Time I Feel the Shift" (2006)

THE JEZEBEL SPIRIT

62 DAVID BYRNE AND BRIAN ENO

1981

My *Life in the Bush of Ghosts* was a groundbreaking album by David Byrne of Talking Heads and former Roxy Music keyboard player Brian Eno that put dance beats and Afro rhythms beneath the sounds of passionate voices found on American radio and on records from the Middle East. Seven out of ten tracks featured the voices of preachers or religious singers, four of them Christian.

It was an exercise in isolating voices at their most ecstatic to capture some of the excitement that early rock 'n' roll had produced. It was also a way of producing tracks that didn't require them to write lyrics or sing. They were the manipulators of found sounds. Their techniques would become very influential on future rap, ambient, house, and electronica records.

What they liked about radio preachers was their passionate commitment and the range of inflections used. Said Brian Eno:

> To hear people talking with conviction on radio and TV is such
> an amazingly rare thing in America that when it does happen
> it's quite startling. Part of the effect of recontextualizing
> is saying, look, there is something really happening here.

200

Everyone dismisses it. They say, oh, religion? We don't listen to that. It's seen as being some aberrant part of society in the way that graffiti used to be seen.[95]

"The Jezebel Spirit" recorded an exorcism on a New York radio station. The unidentified preacher prays for a woman who can be heard hyperventilating. She must have told him that she was oppressed and that voices are tormenting her. The preacher tells her that she has a "Jezebel spirit" in her: "You have a spirit of grief. You have a spirit of destruction." "The Jezebel spirit" is Pentecostal shorthand for someone who seduces Christians away from God to worship idols and false gods: "Thou sufferest that woman Jezebel, which calleth herself a prophetess, to teach and to seduce my servants to commit fornication, and to eat things sacrificed unto idols" (Revelation 2:20).

After asking the woman if she's "ready to be delivered," the preacher speaks to the spirit directly: "Jezebel, spirit of destruction, spirit of grief, I bind you with chains of iron"—"Verily I say unto you, Whatsoever ye shall bind on earth shall be bound in heaven: and whatsoever ye shall loose on earth shall be loosed in heaven" (Matthew 18:18)—and says he is doing it "in the name of Jesus"—"If ye shall ask any thing in my name, I will do it" (John 14:14).

The preacher then becomes more dramatic as he commands the spirit to leave: "Loosen your hold and come out of her now . . . out, out, Jezebel. Come out now . . . out in the name of Jesus. Come out destruction, come out destruction. Come out grief. Jezebel, you are going to listen to me. Go ahead sister, keep going, Jezebel will abandon you."

Byrne and Eno were attracted by language fashioned in the intensity of the moment. The preacher had no thought of posterity. The musical funk with which they underpinned it transformed the ritual into a dance track and subverted the original meaning.

As Marcus Boon wrote in his essay "On Appropriation":

The swirling gamelan funk that Byrne and Eno create
appropriates in one direction, while the voice of
the unidentified New York exorcist enacts the literal

reappropriation of the mind of the woman possessed by "The Jezebel Spirit" in another direction. The funk on "The Jezebel Spirit" intensifies into a swirling loop as the exorcism proceeds mimicking the struggling forces, and yet it does not resolve itself at the end of the track. We are caught between different modes of appropriation—as perhaps we always are.[96]

Accused of trivializing the religious moment, Brian Eno defended himself. "It certainly changes the nature of the communication," he agreed. "You create a different meaning by moving something into a different context. However, there were certain aspects I wanted to keep like that there were spiritual matters being dealt with. But there were also aspects I wanted to lose and one of those was its minority quality."[97]

Song: "The Jezebel Spirit"

Artists: David Byrne and Brian Eno

Album: *My Life in the Bush of Ghosts*

Release: February 1, 1981

Studio: Various

Personnel: "Prairie" Prince (bass drums), Mingo Lewis (bata, percussion), David Byrne (guitar), Brian Eno (synthesizer)

Writers: David Byrne, Brian Eno

Producers: David Byrne, Brian Eno

Label: Sire

Also by David Byrne and Brian Eno: "Help Me Somebody" (1981), "Come with Us" (1981), "One Fine Day" (2008)

DWELLER BY A DARK STREAM

63 BRUCE COCKBURN

1981

R ecorded for 1976's *In the Falling Dark* but not released until 1981 on the compilation album *Mummy's Dust*, this song is representative of what the Canadian songwriter Bruce Cockburn regarded as "a refinement of Christian lyrical content"[98] that had started with his 1974 recording *Salt, Sun, and Time*. It's a song expressing gratefulness for salvation, but also an admission of his own complicity in human sinfulness and his natural antipathy to God.

He sets the scene by saying that "it could have been me put the thorns in your crown," referring to the way in which the Roman soldiers scarred the head of Jesus and mockingly dressed him as royalty. Three Gospels—Matthew, Mark, and John—mention this, but it is from John's account that Cockburn took the image of the crown: "Then came Jesus forth, wearing the crown of thorns, and the purple robe. And Pilate saith unto them, Behold the man!" (John 19:5).

The song's main thesis that he is in debt to evil until rescued by the love of Jesus—"And you showed me what you've done"—is consistent with New Testament teaching, but his specific images of being planted "in a violent ground," of dwelling "by a dark stream," and being "hooked on a dark dream" are his own.

Twice he uses the image of imprisonment—having a "convict soul" and walking through a "prison camp world"—which again don't appear in the New Testament but are close to images of slavery, servitude, and bondage used by Jesus (and Paul): "Verily, verily, I say unto you. Whosoever committeth sin is the servant of sin. And the servant abideth not in the house for ever: but the Son abideth for ever. If the Son therefore shall make you free, ye shall be free indeed" (John 8:34–36).

Of Jesus, he says, "You offered up your flesh and death was overthrown." This phrase is taken from two biblical sources, the first part from "who needeth not daily, as those high priests, to offer up sacrifice, first for his own sins, and then for the people's: for this he did once, when he offered up himself" (Hebrews 7:27), and the second part from "the last enemy that shall be destroyed is death" (1 Corinthians 15:26).

He closes the song with the hope of seeing the world "like in the vision John saw," referring to the account written by John about his experience on the Greek island of Patmos "in the Spirit on the Lord's day" (Revelation 1:10) when he saw and heard events, "which must shortly come to pass" (v. 1).

In particular, Cockburn is eager to get a "glimpse of the new life unfurled," a specific reference to the "new heaven and a new earth" witnessed by John where he saw "the holy city, new Jerusalem, coming down from God out of heaven" and heard a voice saying,

> Behold, the tabernacle of God is with men, and he will dwell with them, and they shall be his people, and God himself shall be with them, and be their God. And God shall wipe away all tears from their eyes; and there shall be no more death, neither sorrow, nor crying, neither shall there be any more pain: for the former things are passed away. And he that sat upon the throne said, Behold I make all things new. (Revelation 21:1–5)

Song: "Dweller by a Dark Stream"

Artist: Bruce Cockburn

Album: *Mummy Dust*

Release: April 1981

Studio: Eastern Sound, Toronto, ON, Canada

Personnel: Bruce Cockburn (guitar, vocals), Dennis Pendrith (bass), Jørn Andersen (drums)

Writer: Bruce Cockburn

Producer: Eugene Martynec

Label: True North Records

Also by Bruce Cockburn: "Christmas Song" (1974), "What about the Bond" (1980), "Cry of a Tiny Babe" (1991)

EVERY GRAIN OF SAND

64

BOB DYLAN

....

1981

y any measure, "Every Grain of Sand" is one of Bob Dylan's greatest creations. He said of it, "That was an inspired song that came to me. I felt like I was just putting down words that were coming from somewhere else, and I just stuck it out."[99]

It was recorded for *Shot of Love*, an album now seen as the last of his "born again trilogy." Of the three, the previous release *Saved* was the most pugnacious and this was the most peaceable, but he was still committed to the same overall message. The sleeve notes opened with, "I thank thee, O Father, Lord of heaven and earth, because thou hast hidden these things from the wise and prudent, and hast revealed them unto babes" (Matthew 11:25), revealing how he was now willing to observe from a Christian viewpoint rather than feeling compelled to evangelize.

"Trouble," for example, says no more than there's trouble in the world. "Lenny Bruce" reflects on the late comic's life and work and commends him because he "told the truth" and "shined a light." Bruce was no friend of religion, but there was something prophetic about his work that Dylan could admire. "The Groom's Still Waiting at the Altar" could have been about a relationship, but also worked as the biblical image of Jesus as the groom awaiting the resurrection of his church, the bride.

Many critics hoped that his evangelical fervor had cooled and that normal service would be resumed. Dylan saw it as progress. He'd come to terms with his back catalogue, felt he'd delivered a comprehensive set of explicit gospel songs and wanted to move on. "They [my songs] have evolved," he told Robert Hilburn of the *Los Angeles Times*. "I've made my statement, and I don't think I could make it any better than in some of those songs. Once I've said what I need to say in a song, that's it. I don't want to repeat myself."[100]

He had finished his three-month Bible course and was no longer as connected with the Vineyard Christian Fellowship. His relationship with Mary Alice Artes, his "precious angel," had also ended. Maybe he was clearing his head and trying to fathom how much of his religious enthusiasm had been ignited by romance and how much was a deep and enduring change of belief.

Like T Bone Burnett, he may also have been realizing that he could write about what he saw because of the light as well as writing about the light itself; he could write songs shaped by a Christian worldview just as Blake, Donne, Eliot, Auden, and others had done so with their poems. "Heart of Mine" is a love song about impetuousness but is also a frank Christian assessment of the human condition. Dylan's observation that his heart is "so full of guile" echoes "The heart is deceitful above all things and beyond cure. Who can understand it?" (Jeremiah 17:9 NIV). "Watered-Down Love" reflects on Paul's love poem: "Love bears all things, believes all things, hopes all things, endures all things" (1 Corinthians 13:7 ESV).

The greatest realization of this approach comes in "Every Grain of Sand," where he touches on issues of temptation, sin, spiritual death, repentance, and redemption, but knits them into a poem rather than a sermon. He doesn't mention God by name, yet no one can hear this song and not realize that every line is infused with appreciation of the divine.

In the first verse, he describes his conversion without resorting to clichés or condemnation. He's humble rather than arrogant or proud. There's a "newborn seed," but it isn't zeal that waters it, but the tears of his confession. It's a memorable image of humility. The "dyin' voice" within him toils in what he calls "the morals of despair." He implies that trying to achieve redemption through morality is in itself a desperate state (the album's title track makes a similar claim).

When he writes of seeing "the Master's hand" in every leaf and "every grain of sand," he is referencing William Blake, who wrote in "Auguries of Innocence":

> To see a World in a Grain of Sand
> And a Heaven in a Wild Flower,
> Hold Infinity in the palm of your hand
> And Eternity in an hour.

And he is also referencing God's promise to Abraham: "I will greatly bless you, and I will greatly multiply your seed as the stars of the heavens and as the sand which is on the seashore" (Genesis 22:17 NASB).

The grains of sand are mentioned twice more, and both times it is to assert his significance in the eyes of God. The Bible uses the metaphor of sand grains to mean both numerous and individually unique. Dylan couples the grains first with "every hair" (which he says are similarly unique and numbered) and "every sparrow falling." These also are biblical images taken from the words of Jesus: "Are not five sparrows sold for two farthings, and not one of them is forgotten before God. But even the very hairs of your head are all numbered. Fear not therefore: ye are of more value than many sparrows" (Luke 12:6–7).

The song moves from repentance and the errors of his past to an admission that he's still vulnerable to spiritual attack. He stares into the doorway of "temptation's angry flame" and says that whenever he does so, "I always hear my name." It could be a brothel with the beckoning call of a prostitute, but equally it could be the temptation to disbelieve in God or to submit to pride. The significant thing is that the invitation is personal.

This note of vulnerability didn't appear in the earlier "born again" songs. Now he hears the "ancient footsteps" (Daniel referred three times to God as "the Ancient of Days"), but sometimes when he turns, "there's someone there, other times it's only me." This is a modest admission that he may not always get it right; that sometimes he may think God is addressing him when it's only his inner voice: "Thy way was in the sea, and thy paths in the great waters, and thy footsteps were not known" (Psalm 77:19 ASV).

Song: "Every Grain of Sand"

Artist: Bob Dylan

Album: *Shot of Love*

Release: August 10, 1981

Studio: Clover Recording Studios, Hollywood, CA

Personnel: Bob Dylan (vocals, harmonica), Clydie King (vocals), Carl Pickhardt (piano), Tim Drummond (bass guitar), Jim Keltner (drums), Benmont Tench (organ), Steve Douglas (alto sax), Madelyn Quebec (backing vocals), Carolyn Dennis (backing vocals), Regina McCrary (backing vocals)

Writer: Bob Dylan

Producers: Chuck Plotkin, Bob Dylan

Label: Columbia

Other Significant Recordings: Emmylou Harris (1995), Julie Felix (2002), Luka Bloom (2014)

Also by Bob Dylan: "Heart of Mine" (1981), "Property of Jesus" (1981) , "God Knows" (1990)

THE NUMBER OF THE BEAST

65

IRON MAIDEN

1982

ascinated with danger, destruction, demons, doom, and death, it was perhaps inevitable that heavy metal music would turn to the dark arts for resource material. Even though the musicians may not have been particularly interested in the occult, they found that tales of sorcery and Satanism added to their mystique and increased their status as rebels.

"The Number of the Beast" was written by Iron Maiden's bass player, Steve Harris, and became not only one of the group's most popular songs but also one of the Top Ten heavy metal tracks of all time. The guitar solos by Dave Murray and Adrian Smith, the curdling scream of singer Bruce Dickinson, the thundering bass patterns of Steve Harris, and the lyrical preoccupation with evil, hellfire, sacrifice, possession, and Satan ticked all the right boxes to make this a heavy metal classic.

The song begins with actor Barry Clayton's somber recitation of two verses from the book of Revelation recounting the visions experienced by John while on the Greek island of Patmos in the first century. The first tells of a battle in the heavens between Michael and his angels and the ultimate embodiment of evil: "the great dragon," "the old serpent," "the beast," "the Devil" and "Satan"—"Woe to you, oh Earth and Sea, for the Devil sends the beast with wrath because he knows his time is short" (referencing Revelation 12:12). The second identifies this character as working through a human agency: "Let him who hath understanding reckon the number of the beast for it is a human number. Its number is six hundred and sixty-six" (referencing Revelation 13:18).

Christian groups who protested and burned albums during Iron Maiden's 1982 tour of America assumed that by singing about "the beast" the group was somehow endorsing or promoting the devil. However, the song arose from a nightmare that Harris experienced after watching the 1978 horror movie *Damien: Omen II* in which an adopted boy (played by Jonathan Scott-Taylor) discovers that he is the son of Satan.

This provided material for the opening verse. The rest of the action—a satanic ritual involving blazing torches, chanting, fires, sacrifice—were suggested by "Tam o' Shanter," a poem by Scottish poet Robert Burns.

Burns wrote the poem in 1790 after seeing an etching of the ruined church known as Alloway Kirk. He'd heard a story about a drunkard who encounters the ruin while riding home one night and sees warlocks and witches dancing around the devil. When they notice him looking, they give chase and he gallops away toward the river because legend has it that the devil can't cross rivers. As he enters the waters, a witch makes a grab and pulls half the horse's tail off, but Tam o' Shanter makes it safely to the other side. Whenever he looks at the tail of his horse, he remembers that terrifying night and resolves never to get drunk again or mess with the devil.[101]

"The Number of the Beast" doesn't conclude with such a moral but with the beast's warning that he will come back to "possess" the narrator for no other reason than because he has the power "to make my evil take its course."

Song: "The Number of the Beast"

Artist: Iron Maiden

Single: A-side: "The Number of the Beast" / B-side: "Remember Tomorrow" (live)

Release: April 25, 1982 (UK)

Album: *The Number of the Beast*

Studio: Battery Studios, London

Personnel: Bruce Dickinson (lead vocals), Dave Murray (guitar), Adrian Smith (guitar), Steve Harris (bass guitar), Clive Burr (drums)

Writer: Steve Harris

Producer: Martin Birch

Label: EMI (UK), Harvest (US)

Highest Chart Position: 18 (UK)

Other Significant Recordings: Sinergy (1999), Powderfinger (2001), Iced Earth (2001), Avulsed (2001)

Also by Iron Maiden: "Purgatory" (1981), "Hallowed Be Thy Name" (1982), "Revelations" (1983)

YAH MO BE THERE

JAMES INGRAM AND MICHAEL MCDONALD

66

1983

roducer Quincy Jones discovered James Ingram when he heard a demo disc of a song by Barry Mann and Cynthia Weil for which Ingram had been the hired vocalist. He had been paid $50 for the session. Jones immediately invited him to audition the song and subsequently signed him to his label, Qwest.

For Ingram's first album, *It's Your Night*, he planned a duet with Michael McDonald. It began as a song called "I'm Gonna Be There," became "I Will Be There," and finally arrived as "Ah Mo Be There" ("Ah mo be" being street slang for "I'm gonna be"). Ingram, who grew up in a strong Christian family (his father was a church deacon and Sunday school teacher), asked Jones if he could possibly add a *Y* at the front of the first word to make it "Yah Mo Be There" (registered as "Yah Mo B There")—*Yah* referring to Yahweh, the ancient Hebrew name for God (YHWH). Said McDonald, "We were talking about how to say 'G-d will be there' without scaring most of the audience away."[102]

This adjustment, made during the session, turned it from a straightforward love song along the lines of "(Reach Out) I'll Be There" by the Four

Tops into a contemporary gospel song. It was now a song addressed to the "heavenly father" watching over us, and the calling of the name referred to the biblical language of "For whosoever shall call upon the name of the Lord shall be saved" (Romans 10:13) or "Call upon me in the day of trouble: I will deliver thee" (Psalm 50:15).

In a song that advocates calling on God, Ingram naturally reached for the Bible verses that were embedded in his imagination. When he sings, "Don't let your heart grow cold," he's thinking of the words of Jesus: "Because of the increase of lawlessness, the love of many will grow cold" (Matthew 24:12 NRSV). His images of light and dark could also come from Jesus, who said, "I am the light of the world. Whoever follows me will never walk in darkness but will have the light of life" (John 8:12 NRSV).

Song: "Yah Mo Be There"

Artists: James Ingram with Michael McDonald

Single: A-side: "Yah Mo Be There" / B-side: "Come a da Machine (To Take a My Place)"

Release: December 9, 1983

Studio: Oceanway Studios, Los Angeles, CA

Personnel: James Ingram (vocals), Michael McDonald (vocals), Michael Boddicker (synthesizer), Rod Temperton (synthesizer), Paulinho Da Costa (percussion), John Robinson (drums), Quincy Jones (vocal arranger)

Writers: James Ingram, Michael McDonald, Rod Temperton, Quincy Jones

Producer: Quincy Jones

Label: Qwest

Highest Chart Position: 5 (US), 12 (UK)

Other Significant Recordings: Jon Gibson (1988), Louise Seville (1996), Steve Brookstein (2005)

Also by James Ingram: "Some Day We'll All Be Free" (1989), "Stand (In the Light)" (2008), "Mercy" (2008)

Also by Michael McDonald: "East of Eden" (1993), "Blink of an Eye" (1993), "To Make a Miracle" (2001)

67

40

U2

. . . .

1983

U 2 appeared to be a rock 'n' roll anomaly—a band that was inspired by punk yet guided by the words of King David, Jeremiah, Paul, and Jesus—but they would, over time, realize that they were the latest contestants in the battle between spiritual calling and earthly desire. They were the heirs of Sister Rosetta Tharpe, Little Richard, Johnny Cash, Van Morrison, Marvin Gaye, Patti Smith, and many others.

Bono [Paul David Hewson], Edge [David Howell Evans], and Larry Mullen had been introduced to an informal charismatic Christian church by a teacher at their school in Dublin and were excited by what they discovered. They were also enlivened by rock 'n' roll—particularly by the then-recent music of the Ramones, Clash, and Sex Pistols that was vigorous, noisy, and challenging. They saw no conflict between faith and music. The views in the Bible, if set to music, would range from consoling folk to coruscating punk. "I would like to think that in U2, we are a very aggressive band, we are an emotional band, we are a live band. I think that's good, I think it's good in the Lord, because . . . John the Baptist and Jeremiah were very loud and quite aggressive, and yet glory-full," Bono told a small conference of Christian musicians in January 1981. "I think we have a love, an emotion, without the sort of flowers in our hair. And I think we have this sort of aggression without the safety pins in our noses."[103]

Some elders of the Shalom Christian Fellowship, to which they belonged, warned them of the dangers of getting too entrenched in "the world." They believed that despite the band's intention to stay true to their faith and explore whatever contradictions they encountered through their music, it was inevitable that they'd be forced to compromise somewhere along the line.

They didn't just shrug off these concerns. Bono wrestled with the apparent contrast between the sacrificial life commanded by Jesus and the death of self as described by Paul with the demands of rock 'n' roll to elicit praise and attention. Was it possible to be humble while in the spotlight? Was it possible to receive adulation while esteeming others better than yourself (Philippians 2:3)?

U2 contemplated ending the group if that was what faithfulness demanded, but they finally decided that rather than walking away from the apparent contradictions they would learn to embrace them.

When recording their third studio album, *War*, they were still working out how to reconcile the calling of art and the calling of faith. The inner debate can be heard in songs like "Two Hearts Beat as One," "Red Light," and "Like a Song." "If I wanna live," Bono sings in "Surrender," "I gotta die to myself someday." This echoed not only his favorite Christian author of the time, Chinese mystic Watchman Nee, but also Paul, who wrote, "Lay aside the old self, which is being corrupted in accordance with the lusts of deceit, and . . . be renewed in the spirit of your mind, and put on the new self, which in the likeness of God has been created in righteousness and holiness of the truth" (Ephesians 4:22–24 NASB).

"40" was the final song recorded for *War* and (according to Bono) was composed and recorded within an hour. Adam Clayton, the one group member who was not a Christian at the time, had already left the studio for the day, and so Edge filled in by playing bass.

It was a rephrasing of a psalm that was special to the group. King David, the credited author of the psalm, was Bono's favorite biblical character. He identified with this flawed individual who was said to be "a man after [God's] own heart" (1 Samuel 13:14; see also Acts 13:22), this shepherd who became a king, this warrior who was also a poet and a musician. "At age 12, I was a fan of David," Bono would later write in his introduction to Canongate's *The Book of Psalms*. "He felt familiar . . . like a pop star could feel familiar. The words of the psalms were as poetic as they were religious and he was a star."[104]

Although they remixed David's words, almost everything in the song can be found in the first three verses of Psalm 40: "I waited patiently for the LORD; and he inclined unto me, and heard my cry. He brought me up also out of an horrible pit, out of the miry clay, and set my feet upon a rock, and established my goings. And he hath put a new song in my mouth, even praise unto our God: many shall see it, and fear, and shall trust in the LORD."

The only words not found in Psalm 40 are the repetitions of "How long" that they took from "My soul is also sore vexed: but thou, O LORD, how long?" (Psalm 6:3). "I thought of it as a nagging question—pulling at the hem of an invisible deity whose presence we glimpse only when we act in love," said Bono. "How long . . . hunger? How long . . . hatred? How long until creation grows up and the chaos of its precocious, hell-bent adolescence has been discarded? I thought it odd that the vocalizing of such questions could bring such comfort [to thousands of fans]; to me too."[105]

Song: "40"

Artist: U2

Album: *War*

Release: February 28, 1983

Studio: Windmill Lane Studios, Dublin, Ireland

Personnel: Bono (lead vocals), Edge (lead guitar, bass guitar), Larry Mullen (drums)

Writers: U2

Producer: Steve Lillywhite

Label: Island

Other Significant Recordings: DC Talk (2001), Michael W. Smith (2002), the Frames (2005)

Also by U2: "I Will Follow" (1980), "Gloria" (1981), "Rejoice" (1981)

68

JESUS WALKING ON THE WATER

VIOLENT FEMMES

1984

Violent Femmes was an unusual group that combined punk-folk directness, avant-garde experimentation, dark tales of violence, and down-home, old-time gospel. A lot of fans assumed that the gospel was intended ironically, but it wasn't. Lead vocalist and composer Gordon Gano was a Christian, and these songs expressed his beliefs (although not those of the two other group members).

Formed in Milwaukee, Wisconsin, in 1980, they had success with their debut album and picked up fans like Talking Heads, U2, and the Pretenders. They benefitted from the post-punk attitude that generously embraced oddballs, eccentrics, and fundamentalists of all kinds.

"Jesus Walking on the Water," recorded for their second album, *Hallowed Ground*, was played on acoustic guitars and a violin, and sounded like a hillbilly hymn. The lyrics were sparse and direct. There was no attempt to wrap the faith in symbolism or to hide the words behind deafening feedback.

It was a straightforward retelling of the famous New Testament miracle of Jesus walking on the Sea of Galilee immediately after the feeding of the five thousand.

> And straightway Jesus constrained his disciples to get into a ship, and to go before him unto the other side, while he sent the multitudes away. And when he had sent the multitudes away, he went up into a mountain apart to pray: and when the evening was come, he was there alone. But the ship was now in the midst of the sea, tossed with waves: for the wind was contrary. And in the fourth watch of the night Jesus went unto them, walking on the sea. And when the disciples saw him walking on the sea, they were troubled, saying, It is a spirit; and they cried out for fear. But straightway Jesus spake unto them, saying, Be of good cheer; it is I; be not afraid. And Peter answered him and said, Lord, if it be thou, bid me come unto thee on the water. And he said, Come. And when Peter was come down out of the ship, he walked on the water, to go to Jesus. But when he saw the wind boisterous, he was afraid; and beginning to sink, he cried, saying, Lord, save me. And immediately Jesus stretched forth his hand, and caught him, and said unto him, O thou of little faith, wherefore didst thou doubt? And when they were come into the ship, the wind ceased. Then they that were in the ship came and worshipped him, saying, Of a truth thou art the Son of God. (Matthew 14:22–34; see also Mark 6:45–53 and John 6:16–21)

It's a song you can imagine being played on a gospel radio station in Arkansas during the 1930s. It even closes with a promise to be faithful. Will the writer stay faithful? Will he give everything to his Savior? "Oh yes sir, yes sir, yes sir, I come when you call," he responds. "And yes sir, yes sir, yes sir, sweet Jesus my all-in-all."

"It does come in a very unexpected context," Gordon Gano admitted to me in 1986. "'Jesus Walking on the Water' turned out to be a good one because it raised the question, 'What if it was true?' Some people think it's being sarcastic—especially in Britain. Journalists in London were congratulating us and saying, 'Wonderful tongue-in-cheek sarcasm,' and I was having to tell them that I was sincere."

Song: "Jesus Walking on the Water"

Artist: Violent Femmes

Album: *Hallowed Ground*

Release: May 14, 1984

Studio: Secret Sound Studios, New York, NY

Personnel: Gordon Gano (lead vocals, electric guitar, violin), Brian Ritchie (vocals, bass guitar), Victor DeLorenzo (drums), Christina Houghton (autoharp), Peter Balestrieri (vocals), Cynthia Gano Lewis (vocals)

Writer: Gordon Gano

Producer: Mark Van Hecke

Label: Slash

Other Significant Recordings: Asylum Street Spankers (2009)

Also by Violent Femmes: "Hallowed Ground" (1984), "Faith" (1986), "Jesus of Rio" (1994)

HALLELUJAH

69 LEONARD COHEN

. . . .

1985

L eonard Cohen, one of the most biblically literate songwriters of the rock era, loved the language and symbolism of both the Hebrew Bible and the New Testament. He could claim in an interview not to be particularly religious, and yet when introducing "Hallelujah" at the Sala Kongresowa in Warsaw, Poland, in March 1985 could say, "I know there is an eye that watches all of us. There is a judgment that weighs everything we do. And before this great force, which is greater than any government, I stand in awe and I kneel in respect."[106]

He grew up in a religiously Jewish household in Montreal, Canada, attended his local synagogue regularly, and observed the rituals of the faith. One of his great-grandfathers was a rabbinical scholar; one of his grandfathers was a rabbi. "I was touched as a child by the music and the kind of charged speech I heard in the synagogue, where everything was important."[107]

Even when he abandoned the regular observance, he still clung to some of the routines, and his work right up to the end of his life was characterized by the pursuit of meaning through a religious view of the world. There are few pop songs as biblical as "You Want It Darker," the title track of his final album, *You Want It Darker.*

Magnified, sanctified, be thy holy name
Vilified, crucified, in the human frame
A million candles burning for the help that never came
You want it darker
Hineni, hineni ["Here I am, here I am" in Hebrew]
I'm ready, my Lord.

What became his best-known and most widely covered song was recorded for *Various Positions*, an album recorded during a low point in his career. Like all of his songs, it was the result of much contemplation, revision, and hard labor. He said it was completed sitting on the floor of the Royalton Hotel while he was in New York recording the album. At times he became so absorbed that he banged his head on the floor in frustration when the lines didn't seem right. The finished version ran over forty verses. By the time he cut the track, it had been reduced to four (three of the discarded verses were included in his poetry collection *Stranger Music*). He told Bob Dylan that it took him two years to write, but later he admitted that it actually took longer.

He was conscious that "Hallelujah" was a prayer. "In our time certain spiritual mechanisms that were very useful have been abandoned and forgot," he told an interviewer. "Redemption, repentance, resurrection. All those ideas are thrown out with the bathwater. People became suspicious of religion plus all these redemptive mechanisms that are very useful."[108]

The word *hallelujah* is used twenty-four times in the Psalms. At its most basic it means "praise God," and frequently in the Psalms "joyous praise in song" (*hallel*) to God (Yah, i.e., YHWH). It is also used four times in Revelation 19, where it is the song of triumph sung to God (the inspiration for Handel's "Hallelujah" chorus from his *Messiah*).

Cohen connects his song to the life of the psalmist David. He tantalizes by saying that it's rumored that David had "a secret chord" that he knew "pleased the Lord." This is not stated in the Bible, but Cohen must have been taking poetic license with the story of David calming his predecessor, King Saul, when an evil spirit tormented him.

Saul ordered his assistants to find the best musician to soothe him, and they discovered David, the son of Jesse, who they said was a "cunning" player on the harp: "And Saul sent to Jesse, saying, let David, I pray thee, stand before me; for he hath found favour in my sight. And it came to pass, when the evil spirit from God was upon Saul, that David took an harp, and played with his hand: so Saul was refreshed, and was well, and the evil spirit departed from him" (1 Samuel 16:22–23).

In the second verse, Cohen is still with David, who sees the married woman Bathsheba "bathing on the roof" and has an affair with her (2 Samuel 11), but then Cohen segues into an unrelated story (Judges 16) of Delilah, who tricks Samson into revealing the source of his strength (which is his long hair) and promptly cuts off his locks, therefore weakening him. With the line, "She broke your throne and she cut your hair," Cohen neatly mashes up the two stories with references to David's throne and Samson's hair.

The conclusion of the song is open-ended. He distinguishes between the "holy" and the "broken" hallelujah but doesn't make it clear whether he defines a broken hallelujah as a genuine hallelujah uttered during a time of brokenness (as David must have done after his adultery with Bathsheba, according to Psalm 51), a hallelujah to a false God, or a hallelujah to no God at all.

It may be that he thinks it doesn't matter. When he says, "You say I took the name in vain," he refers to the third commandment: "Thou shalt not take the name of the LORD thy God in vain, for the LORD will not hold him guiltless that taketh his name in vain" (Exodus 20:7). But he then appears to argue that the word contains its own power regardless of the intention or spiritual condition of the one who utters it—"There's a blaze of light in every word."

Hebrew scholar Agata Paluch said, "In Jewish mystical tradition, any name and its designated object are directly linked, so that the name reflects the nature of its object. Each and every entity possesses a linguistic equivalent—a name—and God is no exception."[109]

When I questioned him about the song in 1987 he told me, "I say it doesn't matter which Hallelujah you utter—the profane or the sacred one. It doesn't matter. It's just saying Amen to what is."

Song: "Hallelujah"

Artist: Leonard Cohen

Album: *Various Positions*

Release: December 1984 (Canada), February 1985 (US, UK)

Studio: Quadrosonic Sound, New York, NY

Personnel: Leonard Cohen (guitar, vocals), Jennifer Warnes (vocals), John Lissauer (piano), John Crowder (bass guitar), Sid McGinnis (guitar), Richard Crooks (drums), Anjani Thomas, Crissie Faith, Erin Dickins, Lani Groves, Merle Miller, Ron Getman, Yvonne Lewis (backing vocals)

Writer: Leonard Cohen

Producer: John Lissauer

Label: Columbia

Highest Chart Position: 36 (UK), 59 (USA)

Other Significant Recordings: John Cale (1991), Jeff Buckley (1994), Rufus Wainwright (2001), Alexandra Burke (2008)

Also by Leonard Cohen: "Story of Isaac" (1969), "If It Be Your Will" (1985), "Amen" (2012)

PIE JESU

70

SARAH BRIGHTMAN AND PAUL MILES·KINGSTON

....

1985

B y 1985, composer Andrew Lloyd Webber was the most successful post-war composer of musicals, having already written the music for (among others) *Jesus Christ Superstar, Joseph and the Amazing Technicolor Dreamcoat, Evita, Cats*, and *Starlight Express*. He now wanted to compose a classical piece of music to prove his talent wasn't limited to the pop style.

Requiem, his take on the traditional requiem mass for the "repose of the souls of the dead"—*requiem* means "rest"—was inspired by two things: the memory of his father, William Lloyd Webber, a church organist and composer of sacred music who died in 1982, and a harrowing news story he read in the *New York Times* about a Cambodian boy captured by the Khmer Rouge who was given the ultimatum of either killing himself or killing his already muti- lated sister. It was scored for three soloists, a chorus, and a large orchestra.

Lloyd Webber's *"Pie Jesu"* combined two parts of the traditional lit- urgy—the *"Agnus Dei"* ("Lamb of God"), usually chanted or sung as the host is being taken during mass, and the *"Pie Jesu"* ("Merciful Jesus"), part of the *"Dies irae"* ("Day of wrath"), a thirteenth-century hymn sung during a requiem mass that describes the day of judgment.

Lloyd Webber started with a form of the final couplet from the Latin hymn *"Dies irae"*—"Merciful Jesus who takes away the sins of the world / Grant them rest"—and then segues into the liturgical chant *"Agnus Dei"*— "Lamb of God who takes away the sins of the world / Grant them rest everlasting / Everlasting, eternal rest."

The promise of rest comes directly from the words of Jesus ("Come unto me, all ye that labour and are heavy laden, and I will give you rest" [Matthew 11:28]), as does the promise of eternal life to all who believe ("For God so loved the world that he gave his only begotten Son, that whosoever believeth in him should not perish, but have everlasting life" [John 3:16]).

Linking *"Pie Jesu"* to the *"Agnus Dei"* is the story of John the Baptist's encounter with Jesus at the beginning of his ministry: "The next day John seeth Jesus coming unto him, and saith, Behold the Lamb of God, which taketh away the sin of the world" (John 1:29).

Requiem was premiered at Saint Thomas Church in New York on February 24, 1985. *"Pie Jesu"* was sung by Lloyd Webber's then-wife, Sarah Brightman, accompanied by twelve-year-old chorister Paul Miles-Kingston from the choir of Winchester Cathedral in England. Their recording of the piece had been released as a single in the UK the day before and would become a Top Ten hit. *Requiem* won Lloyd Webber a Grammy and topped the Billboard album charts.

Song: *"Pie Jesu"*

Artists: Sarah Brightman and Paul Miles-Kingston

Single: A-side: *"Pie Jesu"* / B-side: *"Recordare"* (Sarah Brightman)

Release: March 1, 1985

Album: *Requiem*

Studio: EMI Studios, Abbey Road, London

Personnel: Sarah Brightman (soprano vocal), Paul Miles-Kingston (treble vocal), James Lancelot (organ), Winchester Cathedral Choir, Martin Neary (choral director), English Chamber Orchestra, Lorin Maazel (conductor)

Writer: Andrew Lloyd Webber

Producer: David R. Murray

Label: EMI

Highest Chart Position: 3 (UK)

Other Significant Recordings: Charlotte Church (1998), Celtic Woman (2008)

Also by Sarah Brightman: "How Can Heaven Love Me" (1995), "Alleluja" (1997), "Ave Maria" (2001)

THE CROSS

71 PRINCE

1987

Prince's religious roots were in the Seventh Day Adventist Church, and during his career he tried to reconcile the demands of Christian obedience he'd been taught as a child with the abandonment to instinct that was emphasized in rock 'n' roll.

The album title *Sign o' the Times* comes from a question the disciples asked Jesus on Jerusalem's Mount of Olives: "Tell us, when will these things be, and what will be the sign of your coming and of the end of the age?" (Matthew 24:3 ESV). Jesus said the signs will be wars, famines, earthquakes, false prophets, persecution, and lawlessness. Prince thinks they are AIDS, addictions, hurricanes, poverty, gang warfare, and violence.

"The Cross" is a conventional evangelistic warning—"He [Jesus] is coming"—followed by an equally conventional appeal—"Don't die without knowing the cross." In Christian teaching, "the cross" doesn't merely refer to the means used to kill Jesus but is shorthand for the core gospel message that "while we were yet sinners, Christ died for us" (Romans 5:8). Prince may have had in mind a comment made by Paul to the church in Corinth: "For I determined to know nothing among you except Jesus Christ, and Him crucified" (1 Corinthians 2:2 NASB).

Many protestant hymns have celebrated the cross, the best known perhaps being "The Old Rugged Cross" (1912) by the American evangelist George Bennard. In another such hymn, written in the eighteenth century, "Rock of Ages," Augustus Toplady wrote:

Nothing in my hand I bring,
Simply to Thy cross I cling;
Naked, come to Thee for dress;
Helpless, look to Thee for grace;
Foul, I to the fountain fly;
Wash me, Savior, or I die.

In the second verse of "The Cross," Prince wrote of "bearing" the cross, a reference to the Roman practice of forcing condemned criminals to drag to the execution spot the wooden structure they were about to be nailed on. In his ministry, Jesus used the image of cross carrying to warn of the shame and strain of true discipleship: "And he said to them all, If any man will come after me, let him deny himself, and take up his cross daily, and follow me" (Luke 9:23).

Like a good evangelist, Prince warns of the consequences of ignoring the cross. First, Jesus could return and catch us unawares "for he is coming": "Therefore keep watch because you do not know when the owner of the house will come back—whether in the evening, or at midnight, or when the rooster crows, or at dawn. If he comes suddenly, do not let him find you sleeping. What I say to you, I say to everyone: 'Watch!'" (Mark 13:35–37 NIV). Second, we could die unexpectedly—"Don't die without knowing the cross."

Prince declares that all our troubles can find a resolution in the cross— "Soon all of our problems, y'all / Will be taken by the cross"—but his focus in the song is more about lack of love and hope, and such social ills as food shortages and poor housing, than it is about freedom from the power and penalty of individual sin. His vision is close to that glimpsed in John's revelation of the multitude clothed in white robes who "will hunger no longer, nor thirst anymore; nor will the sun beat down on them, nor any heat; for the Lamb in the center of the throne will be their shepherd, and will guide them to springs of the water of life; and God will wipe every tear from their eyes" (Revelation 7:16–17 NASB).

In the 1990s, Prince switched his allegiance to the Jehovah Witnesses after long conversations with bass player Larry Graham from Sly and the Family Stone. Discovering that the denomination's teaching was that Jesus was executed on a stake rather than an upright with a crossbeam, he replaced the word *cross* with "Christ" in the song when performing it in concert. At the 1998 Essence Awards, he introduced the song by saying, "*Stauros*. By definition a wooden stake driven in the ground used to cause torture or death. *Stauros*. Perhaps someone lied about the way that someone died."

Song: "The Cross"

Artist: Prince

Album: *Sign o' the Times*

Release: March 1987

Studio: Sunset Sound, Hollywood, CA

Personnel: Prince (vocals and all instruments)

Writer: Prince

Producer: Prince

Label: Paisley Park Records / Warner Brothers

Highest Chart Position: 6 (US)

Other Significant Recordings: Laibach (1996), the Blind Boys of Alabama (2002), Audrey Horne (2008)

Also by Prince: "Controversy" (1981), "God" (1984), "The Holy River" (1996)

72

I STILL HAVEN'T FOUND WHAT I'M LOOKING FOR

U2

1987

aving established their Christian commitment, U2 released a single that appeared to throw doubt on it. "I Still Haven't Found What I'm Looking For" suggested that far from having arrived at a solution, they were still engaged in search for whatever it was everyone was looking for.

The song itself, however, was drenched in specifically biblical language. There were loosed chains, broken bonds, and a cross of shame. Whatever uncertainties they were experiencing came from within the tradition they had voluntarily entered.

Bono would later explain that the song wasn't a complaint that Christianity was insufficient or unsatisfying, but a recognition that faith wasn't a plateau. "People expect you, as a believer, to have all the answers, when really all you get is a whole new set of questions," said Bono. "I think that if 'I Still Haven't Found What I'm Looking For' is successful it will be because it's not affirmative in the ordinary way of a gospel song. It's restless, yet there's a pure joy in it somewhere."[110]

The music emerged from a studio jam and the lyrics out of a single line that Edge had stored as a potential future title—"I still haven't found what I'm looking for." It came, he later remembered, from a line from Bob Dylan's "Idiot Wind"—"You'll find out when you reach the top / You're on the bottom."

Bono, who improvised the lyrics at the microphone, took Edge's phrase in a spiritual direction. He kicked off with a poetic description of his union with God— "only to be with you." The relationship is described in passionate physical terms. He "climbs," "runs," "crawls," and "scales" in his efforts. It's not a comfy-seat religion.

The second verse confronts temptation and sin. The "tongue of angels" refers to Paul's warning that it's possible to perform good and even religious acts and yet be devoid of God's love: "Though I speak with the tongues of men and of angels, and have not charity, I am become as sounding brass, or a tinkling cymbal" (1 Corinthians 13:1).

Just as it's possible to do good without love, it's possible to do love without good. The "honey lips" are the lips of loveless seduction or unfaithfulness: "For the lips of a strange woman drop as an honeycomb, and her mouth is smoother than oil" (Proverbs 5:3). This type of liaison has the power to burn "like fire." He could be thinking of the traditional image of passion as "smoldering" or being "hot" (as in Johnny Cash's "Ring of Fire"), but more likely it's the incendiary effect of "playing with fire" expressed elsewhere in Proverbs: "Can a man take fire in his bosom, and his clothes not be burned?" (6:27).

He reasserts what he's sure of. He believes in the "Kingdom Come" (taken from Jesus's prayer in Matthew 6:10 and Luke 11:2), when all struggles, conflicts, and doubts will be resolved. He believes that God "broke the bonds" ("He brought them out of darkness and the shadow of death, and brake their bands in sunder" [Psalm 107:14]), "loosed the chains" ("And, behold, the angel of the Lord came upon him, and a light shined in the prison: and he smote Peter on the side, and raised him up, saying, Arise up quickly. And his chains fell off from his hands" [Acts 12:7]), and that Jesus "carried the cross of my shame" ("Let us lay aside every weight, and the sin that doth so easily beset us, and let us run with patience the race that is set before us, looking unto Jesus the author and finisher of our faith; who for the joy that was set before him endured the cross, despising the shame, and is set down at the right hand of the throne of God" [Hebrews 12:1–2]).

Bono was discovering that the Christian life is a struggle. Paul had described it almost two thousand years ago in words that Bono appreciated.

> I find then a law, that, when I would do good, evil is present with me. For I delight in the law of God after the inward man: But I see another law in my members, warring against the law of my mind, and bringing me into captivity to the law of sin which is in my members. O wretched man that I am! who shall deliver me from the body of this death? I thank God through Jesus Christ our Lord. So then with the mind I myself serve the law of God; but with the flesh the law of sin. (Romans 7:21–25)

"Right in the centre of a contradiction, that's the place to be," Bono later said. "There I was. Loyal, but in my imagination filled with wanderlust; a heart to know God, a head to know the world; a rock star who likes to run amok and a sinner who knows he needs to repent."[111]

Song: "I Still Haven't Found What I'm Looking For"

Artist: U2

Single: A-side: "I Still Haven't Found What I'm Looking For" / B-side: "Spanish Eyes," "Deep in the Heart"

Release: May 25, 1987

Album: *The Joshua Tree*

Studio: Danesmoate House, Dublin, Ireland

Personnel: Bono (lead vocals), Edge (lead guitar), Adam Clayton (bass guitar), Larry Mullen (drums)

Writers: U2 (music), Bono (lyrics)

Producers: Daniel Lanois, Brian Eno

Label: Island

Highest Chart Position: 1 (USA), 6 (UK)

Other Significant Recordings: The Chimes (1990), Cher (1999), Celtic Thunder (2010)

Also by U2: "When Love Comes to Town" (1988), "Grace" (2000), "Yahweh" (2004)

THE MERCY SEAT

73

NICK CAVE AND THE BAD SEEDS

1988

While an Anglican cathedral choirboy for four years in Australia, Nick Cave absorbed the words, images, and stories of the Bible, and has spent his musical and literary career trying to understand them and spin them into his own sung tales of violence, death, religion, and redemption.

At times he has claimed to believe in God; at others to believe only in "God" as a symbol for something beyond language that he glimpsed in love, music, and art. At various periods of his life he has visited and worshiped in churches, and during others he has distanced himself both from Christianity and all organized religion.

He unashamedly writes of God, Jesus, the devil, mercy, sin, damnation, heaven, hell, saints, angels, apostles, and prayer. In 1996, he gave a lecture on BBC Radio titled "The Flesh Made Word" where he unpacked the relationship between him, his work, and Christianity.[112] Two years later, he wrote the introduction to Canongate's pocketbook publication of the *Gospel According to Mark*.

In the BBC talk, he explained how the Bible provided him with a vocabulary and stories of conflict that helped him as a songwriter when exploring his experiences. "I soon found in the tough prose of the Old Testament a perfect language, at once mysterious and familiar, that not only reflected the state of mind I was in at the time, but actively informed my artistic endeavors. I found there the voice of God, and it was brutal and jealous and merciless. For every bilious notion I harbored about myself and the world—and there were a lot of those—there in the Old Testament was its equivalent leaping off the pages with its teeth bared."

"The Mercy Seat" features a murderer on death row who is reviewing his life. He ponders on the biblical injunction, "And thine eye shall not pity; but life shall go for life, eye for eye, tooth for tooth, hand for hand, foot for foot" (Deuteronomy 19:21).

Society believes this to be true. He has murdered, so he in turn must be killed. Yet, when Jesus quoted the "eye for eye" verse, it was to replace the old principle of retaliation with a new principle of mercy: "Ye have heard that it hath been said, An eye for an eye, and a tooth for a tooth: But I say unto you, That ye resist not evil: but whosoever shall smite thee on thy right cheek, turn to him the other also" (Matthew 5:38–39).

Cave doesn't directly address the issue of justice versus mercy, but he has the prisoner musing on "How Christ was born into a manger / And like some ragged stranger / Died upon the cross."

The "mercy seat" was the gold lid with its two cherubim that covered the ark of the covenant, where the stone tablets on which God wrote the Ten Commandments were kept in the holy of holies, an area of the temple only accessible to the high priest once a year on the Day of Atonement (Exodus 25:10–22; Leviticus 16). After burning incense, the priest would sprinkle the blood of a bull on the mercy seat on behalf of himself, his family, and all Israel.

In Cave's song, the mercy seat is the electric chair ("Down here it's made of wood and wire"), and the irony is that it offers no mercy. Those who sit on it are there to pay for their own sins. All requests for mercy have been exhausted. The only burning here comes from flesh, not incense. The blood is boiled, not sprinkled.

The song doesn't make it clear whether the condemned man committed the crime he's being executed for. "I always thought it was clear that the guy did it," Cave once said. "What's in question is the concept of guilt and innocence, in the sense that he may have done it but that doesn't mean he's a guilty person in a broader sense. My version is more conflicted. Which is pure Nick Cave, I suppose. . . . It [the song] remains mysterious and ambiguous but genuinely thoughtful."[113]

Song: "The Mercy Seat"

Artist: Nick Cave and the Bad Seeds

Album: *Tender Prey*

Release: September 19, 1988

Studio: Vielklang Studios and Hansa Tonstudio, Berlin; Trident Studios and Strongroom Studios, London

Personnel: Nick Cave (vocals, Hammond organ), Thomas Wydler (drums), Roland Wolf (guitar), Gini Ball, Audrey Riley, and Chris Tombling (strings), Blixa Bargeld (slide guitar), Mick Harvey (bass loops, piano)

Writers: Nick Cave (lyrics), Nick Cave and Mick Harvey (music)

Producers: Tony Cohen, Flood, Nick Cave and the Bad Seeds

Label: Mute

Highest Chart Position: 86 (UK)

Other Significant Recordings: Johnny Cash (2000), the Red Paintings (2006), Camille O'Sullivan (2009)

Also by Nick Cave: "Mercy" (1988), "Mutiny in Heaven" (1993), "Into My Arms" (1997)

74

THE END OF THE INNOCENCE

DON HENLEY

1989

I n her song "Woodstock," Joni Mitchell optimistically envisioned a dawning new age where people would be reunited with the earth and live out their "golden" destinies, but the Eagles' more jaundiced view was that life is corrupt, thrills are short-lived, and dreams inevitably shatter. "Hotel California" portrayed the fun-loving members of what Tom Wolfe called "The Me Generation" as prisoners of their own desires in a bleak and lonely landscape.

The Eagles' main lyricist, Don Henley, an English and philosophy major from North Texas State University (Denton), retained some foundational theology from his years attending First Baptist Church in Linden, Texas. His father didn't belong to the church and his mother was irregular in her worship, but Henley was baptized there (by the father of Texan painter Anthony Martin) and only left when he moved out of the town. Some of his earliest musical memories were of his mother singing gospel songs and his grandmother singing hymns.

"The End of the Innocence," recorded for Henley's third solo album, reflects on his disenchantment with contemporary American political and social life, which he believed was becoming more fractious, litigious, greedy, polluted, violent, and celebrity obsessed. "We live in a time of great mistrust," he said in an interview with the *New York Times* on the eve of the album's release. "The feeling that we are one as a nation is rapidly disappearing, and that carries over into people's private personal lives. I mention lawyers several times on the album. That's because of the pervasive sense of every man for himself and every woman for herself. These days you see more men and women suing each other. It's a very insidious thing."[114]

To underpin his argument, he uses two biblical images. The first is the image of swords and ploughshares employed by the prophet Isaiah to illustrate peace: "And he shall judge among the nations, and shall rebuke many people: and they shall beat their swords into ploughshares, and their spears into pruninghooks: nation shall not lift up sword against nation, neither shall they learn war any more" (Isaiah 2:4).

In the biblical vision, weapons of war (swords, spears) and therefore of death and destruction are recycled as farm implements (ploughshares, pruning hooks) and thus of life and growth. Henley sees the opposite happening—independent farmers being forced out of business and military budgets increased ("But now those skies are threatening / They're beating ploughshares into swords").

The second image is that of cleansing by water. To the anonymous girl addressed in the lyrics he says, "But I know a place where we can go / And wash away this sin." This echoes such Bible verses as, "Wash me thoroughly from my iniquity, and cleanse me from my sin!" (Psalm 51:2 ESV) and "And now why do you wait? Rise and be baptized and wash away your sins, calling on his name" (Acts 22:16 ESV).

Henley is not talking about sin as that which separates people from God but the deleterious effects of human choices on nature: "But I know a place where we can go / That's still untouched by man." His cleansing refers to an escape from such things as pollution, environmental destruction, and the damage of wildlife habitats. The innocence that has ended is not the absolute purity of the Garden of Eden but the relative purity of an unspoiled landscape that existed before we developed the internal combustion engine, plastic, and industrial agriculture.

Song: "The End of the Innocence"

Artist: Don Henley

Single: A-side: "The End of Innocence" / B-side: "If Dirt Were Dollars"

Release: June 1989

Album: *The End of the Innocence*

Studio: A&M Studio, Hollywood, CA

Personnel: Don Henley (vocals, drums), Michael G. Fisher (percussion), Bruce Hornsby (piano, keyboards), Jai Winding (keyboards), Danny Kortchmar (guitar), Wayne Shorter (soprano saxophone)

Writers: Bruce Hornsby, Don Henley

Producers: Bruce Hornsby, Don Henley

Label: Geffen Records

Highest Chart Position: 48 (UK), 8 (USA)

Also by Don Henley: "The Unclouded Day" (1982), "Building the Perfect Beast" (1984), "The Heart of the Matter" (1989)

75

WILL YOU BE THERE

MICHAEL JACKSON

1991

Katherine Jackson was baptized into the Jehovah Witnesses religion in 1963. She had previously been a Lutheran and a Baptist, but switched her allegiance when she discovered that her ministers in both denominations had been caught having extramarital affairs. Her husband, Joe, never became a Jehovah's Witness.

Two years after her conversion, her seven-year-old son, Michael, became a member, and throughout his childhood and teens studied the Bible at home five days a week and attended meetings at the local Kingdom Hall. Even at the height of his fame with the Jackson 5, he was devotedly following the religion's teachings, and when he was a major solo artist with albums like *Off the Wall* and *Thriller* in the charts, he was still doing door-to-door evangelism. So that touring wouldn't interrupt his regular church attendance, advance scouts would find the location of the nearest Kingdom Hall.

Jehovah's Witnesses leaders in his local congregation at Woodland Hills, California, and at the national headquarters in Brooklyn, New York, became unhappy that their most celebrated member was better known for his sexualized stage movements, androgynous image, vast wealth, and mass-adolescent worship than for religious devotion and holy obedience. They wanted him to abandon show business for the sake of his soul. As Jackson's biographer J. Randy Taraborrelli observed, "In truth, it's almost impossible to be a Jehovah's Witness and be an entertainer."[115]

Matters worsened when the video of *Thriller* depicted Jackson transforming into a werecat, and then a zombie, before dancing with ghouls in a mist-wreathed graveyard. Jackson tried to head off controversy by prefacing the film with the caution "Due to my strong personal convictions, I wish to stress that this film in no way endorses a belief in the occult."

Jackson was so convinced that his moral behavior was impeccable that he invited any skeptical Jehovah's Witness leaders to accompany him on tour, but ultimately he found the tension unbearable, and in the spring of 1987 he formally withdrew his membership. The organization issued a press release announcing that it "no longer considers Michael Jackson to be one of the Jehovah's Witnesses."[116]

The Jehovah's Witnesses believe that by rejecting the faith you are rejecting Jehovah (God) and can no longer be among the 144,000 saved souls (mentioned in Revelation 7:4–8 and 14:1–5). Those who "willfully abandon" the faith "thereby become part of the 'antichrist,'" as the Jehovah's Witnesses' magazine *Watchtower* put it in 1985. This also meant that his mother, Katherine, as a faithful member, could no longer discuss the Bible with her apostate son.

Jackson was so steeped in the Bible, though, that he couldn't let go of its language, beliefs, and concerns. "Will You Be There" is a song addressed to God in the midst of confusion, distress, and loss of identity. He starts by asking God to hold him "like the River Jordan," to carry him like a brother ("I will carry you. I have made, and I will bear; I will carry and will save" [Isaiah 46:4 ESV]), and to love him like a mother ("How often would I have gathered thy children together, as a hen doth gather her brood under her wings" [Luke 13:34]).

He admits his weakness and begs God to reveal himself. The words are particularly poignant now that we know the conflicts he endured. He wants God to be a brother, mother, and friend, but never asks him to be a father. (His father cheated on his mother while on the road, pressured the Jackson 5, and encouraged his son to be overtly sexual.)

The saddest lines are, "Everyone's taking control of me / Seems like the world's got a role for me." His father had a role for him as a performer, the media had a role for him as Wacko Jacko, and the Jehovah's Witnesses had a role for him as Brother Jackson. The song asks whether God has a role for him where he can just be himself.

The longer album version begins with a sample from Beethoven's Symphony no. 9 where the chorus sings (in German) part of Friedrich Schiller's poem "Ode to Joy":

> Do you fall in worship, you millions?
> World, do you know your creator?
> Seek him in the heavens
> Above the stars must He dwell.[117]

At the end of this version, there is extra confession asking God if he will be with him through despair, trials, tribulations, doubts, frustrations, fear, anguish, pain, and sorrow. His conclusion is, "I'll never let you part / For you're always in my heart." When performing it on tour, the final couplet would be sung while an angel enveloped Jackson in its wings.

Song: "Will You Be There"

Artist: Michael Jackson

Single: A-side: "Will You Be There" / B-side: "Will You Be There" (Instrumental)

Album: *Dangerous*

Release: November 26, 1991

Studio: Ocean Way Studios, Santa Monica, CA

Personnel: Michael Jackson (vocals), Greg Phillinganes (keyboards), Brad Buxer (keyboards, drums), Michael Boddicker (synthesizers), Rhett Lawrence (synthesizer programming), Bruce Swedien (drums and percussion), Andraé Crouch Singers (vocals), Andraé Crouch (vocal arranger), Sandra Crouch (vocal arranger), Cleveland Orchestra, George Szell (orchestra conductor), Cleveland Orchestra Chorus, Robert Shaw (chorus director)

Writer: Michael Jackson

Producers: Michael Jackson, Bruce Swedien

Label: Epic / Sony

Highest Chart Position: 7 (USA), 9 (UK)

Other Significant Recordings: Boyce Avenue (2010)

Also by Michael Jackson: "Man in the Mirror" (1987), "Keep the Faith" (1991), "Earth Song" (1995)

76

TEARS IN HEAVEN
ERIC CLAPTON
. . . .
1992

On March 20, 1991, Eric Clapton's four-year-old son, Conor, fell out of a fifty-third floor apartment window on East 57th Street in New York City where he was staying with his mother, Lory Del Santo, and was killed when he landed on the roof of a four-story building next door. Clapton, who was no longer living with Del Santo at the time, happened to be in New York to reunite with the son he hardly knew. He had taken him to a circus the day before and was due to take him to the Central Park Zoo when he received the news by phone that he was dead.

It was a painful blow for Clapton who, according to Del Santo, had not been involved in the boy's life up until then, but had taken him out alone for the first time the day before and had vowed to be more committed in the future.

"Tears in Heaven" was his anguished response to the tragedy. Working on the soundtrack for the movie *Rush* with Texan songwriter Will Jennings (who would go on to write "My Heart Will Go On" for the movie *Titanic*), he introduced the partly written song as a possible candidate. He had the tune and the first verse, and asked Jennings to complete it in the studio.[118]

"[The first verse] to me, is all the song," Jennings explained. "But he wanted me to write the rest of the verse lines and the release ('Time can bring you down, time can bend your knees'), even though I told him that it was so personal he should write everything himself. Finally, . . . there was nothing else for me to do but to do as he requested, despite the sensitivity of the subject."[119]

The opening verse appears to restate an age-old theological question: Will we recognize loved ones in the afterlife? But there is a deeper level at which Clapton is confronting his guilt as an absentee father. As Conor had barely seen Clapton in life, is there a chance he won't remember him in death? The last six words of his lyrical contribution express his disappointment with himself: "I don't belong here in heaven."

If Jennings's recollection is correct, he is the author of the line that the song got its title from. "I know there'll be no more tears in heaven" is drawn from the heavenly vision of John on Patmos: "And God shall wipe away all tears from their eyes; and there shall be no more death, neither sorrow, nor crying, neither shall there be any more pain: for the former things are passed away" (Revelation 21:4).

When asked about the persistent theme of spiritual transcendence in his songs, Jennings said, "Well, I grew up in rural east Texas. . . . My paternal grandfather was a Methodist preacher. And all my aunts and uncles sang. So I grew up on all the old-time hymns. Plus, I grew up within hearing of a black Baptist church. . . . And I heard them on Sunday mornings and Sunday evenings. So those are the first songs I can remember hearing, and I'm sure that had a lot to do with forming part of what I do."[120]

Song: "Tears in Heaven"

Artist: Eric Clapton

Single: A-side: "Tears in Heaven" / B-side: "Tracks and Lines"

Release: January 8, 1992

Album: *Rush: Music from the Motion Picture Soundtrack*

Studio: Village Recorder, Santa Monica, CA

Personnel: Eric Clapton (vocals, guitar, dobro), Randy Kerber (synthesizer), JayDee Maness (pedal steel guitar), Nathan East (bass guitar), Gayle Levant (Celtic harp), Lenny Castro (percussion), Jimmy Bralower (drum machine)

Writers: Eric Clapton, Will Jennings

Producer: Russ Titelman

Label: Warner Reprise

Highest Chart Position: 5 (UK), 2 (USA)

Other Significant Recordings: James Galway (1994), Mary J. Blige (2005), Ann Peebles (2006)

Also by Eric Clapton: "Hold Me Lord" (1981), "Holy Mother" (1986), "Sinner's Prayer" (1994)

77

CLEANSED BY FIRE
ALICE COOPER

....

1994

W hen Alice Cooper emerged, his songs and stage act were calculated to offend parents and guardians of morality. He was a man bearing a woman's name and a performer in ghoulish makeup who performed mock executions and was rumored to have killed birds on stage. In the post-Altamont world, he appeared as the personification of all that was dark, cynical, and exploitative. He shocked, but with no bigger cause in view.

Today, things couldn't be more different. Alice Cooper still performs the old hits but argues that it's only a show and points out that even in the days of "shock rock" he had always portrayed evil as truly evil and good as good. He's now a Republican, a churchgoing Christian, and an avid golfer.

It was never a secret that Vincent Furnier was the son of a pastor and had strayed from Christianity. It was assumed that the persona of Alice Cooper was part of his rebellion against his PK (preacher's kid) inheritance. Less widely known was that his descent into alcoholism and cocaine addiction was followed by an unannounced return to Christianity in the late 1980s.

The Last Temptation album sees Cooper working to fuse his reenergized faith with a hard rock sound and the theatricality for which he was known. It tells the story of Steven, a boy who is persistently enticed by a showman to join the "theater of the real" where he need never grow up. Fantasy presents itself as reality, and reality is mocked for being unreal. Popular British author Neil Gaiman was commissioned to write a three-part comic series that fleshed out the story.

"Cleansed by Fire" is the album's final track. It's addressed to the showman who is now exposed as the devil. "You offer me the world and all its wealth" alludes to the offer made to Jesus by the devil. After tempting him to perform a miracle by changing stones to bread and to create a spectacle by leaping from the top of the temple, he offered him temporal power in return for worship.

> Again, the devil taketh him up into an exceeding high mountain, and sheweth him all the kingdoms of the world, and the glory of them; and saith unto him, All these things will I give thee, if thou wilt fall down and worship me. Then saith Jesus unto him, Get thee hence, Satan: for it is written, Thou shalt worship the Lord thy God, and him only shalt thou serve. Then the devil leaveth him, and, behold, angels came and ministered unto him. (Matthew 4:8–11)

Cooper refers to his antagonist as "a fallen star"—a reference to the devil as the fallen angel, Lucifer:

> How art thou fallen from heaven, O Lucifer, son of the morning! how art thou cut down to the ground, which didst weaken the nations! For thou hast said in thine heart, I will ascend into heaven, I will exalt my throne above the stars of God: I will sit also upon the mount of the congregation, in the sides of the north: I will ascend above the heights of the clouds; I will be like the most High. Yet thou shalt be brought down to hell, to the sides of the pit. (Isaiah 14:12–15)

The fire in the song is to be inflicted on the devil as punishment—"Burn this sucker to the ground"—not purgation:

Thine heart was lifted up because of thy beauty, thou hast corrupted thy wisdom by reason of thy brightness: I will cast thee to the ground, I will lay thee before kings, that they may behold thee. Thou hast defiled thy sanctuaries by the multitude of thine iniquities, by the iniquity of thy traffick; therefore will I bring forth a fire from the midst of thee, it shall devour thee, and I will bring thee to ashes upon the earth in the sight of all them that behold thee. All they that know thee among the people shall be astonished at thee: thou shalt be a terror, and never shalt thou be any more. (Ezekiel 28:17–19)

In Cooper's moral fable, it's the devil who peddles fantasy, and he succeeds by convincing people that this is reality. But, Cooper says, he is not telling the whole story. "What about death?" he asks. "What about sin? / What about the web you're trying to spin? / What about truth? / What about life? / What about glory? / What about Christ?"

Song: "Cleansed by Fire"

Artist: Alice Cooper

Album: *The Last Temptation*

Release: July 12, 1994

Studio: Music Grinder Studios Hollywood, CA; Sony Recording Studios, Santa Monica, CA

Personnel: Alice Cooper (vocals), Stef Burns (guitar), Greg Smith (bass guitar), Derek Sherinian (keyboards), David Uosikkinen (drums)

Producer: Andy Wallace

Writers: Alice Cooper, Mark Hudson, Stephen Dudas, Robert Pfeifer

Label: Epic / Sony

Also by Alice Cooper: "I Just Wanna Be God" (2001), "Spirits Rebellious" (2003), "Salvation" (2008)

78

EARTH SONG
MICHAEL JACKSON

1995

Michael Jackson's most environmentally conscious song is addressed to God rather than to the perpetrators of the damage. Written in the style of a psalm, it begs God to explain why he's allowed us to destroy his world.

In the first verse, he asks, "What about all the things / That you said we were to gain." He could have had in mind the creation story where Adam and Eve were commanded to "be fruitful, and multiply, and replenish the earth, and subdue it: and have dominion over the fish of the sea, and over the fowl of the air, and over every living thing that moveth upon the earth" (Genesis 1:28), or Jesus's warning, "For what shall it profit a man, if he shall gain the whole world, and lose his own soul?" (Mark 8:36).

The Genesis text stresses human stewardship. Jesus warned that stewardship can be corrupted and become greed and domination. Jackson seems to see a link between the human drive to exploit natural resources and another type of loss of soul.

In the last line, he asks God if he's noticed "the crying Earth." Paul wrote about creation awaiting its redemption in similar language of anguish:

For the creation was subjected to vanity, not of its own will, but by reason of him who subjected it, in hope that the creation itself also shall be delivered from the bondage of corruption into the liberty of the glory of the children of God. For we know that the whole creation groaneth and travaileth in pain together until now. (Romans 8:20–22 ASV)

In the second verse, Jackson becomes more specifically Christian. He asks, "What about all the peace / That you pledge your only son . . ." "Only son" is a term used in the Gospel of John: "For God so loved the world, that he gave his only begotten Son" (3:16). The "peace" could be a reference to the prophecy that the Messiah will be known as "Wonderful Counselor, Mighty God, Everlasting Father, Prince of Peace" (Isaiah 9:6 NIV) or to the promise of Jesus, "Peace I leave with you; my peace I give unto you: not as the world giveth, give I unto you. Let not your heart be troubled, neither let it be fearful" (John 14:27 ASV).

"Where is this promised peace?" is the question Jackson poses. If the coming of Jesus was an historical intervention, why is there not more evidence in changed human behavior? Why do we still have genocide, murder, pollution, greed, and starvation?

Song: "Earth Song"

Artist: Michael Jackson

Album: *HIStory: Past, Present, and Future, Book 1*

Release: November 27, 1995

Studio: The Hit Factory, New York, NY

Personnel: Michael Jackson (vocals), David Paich (keyboards), Guy Pratt (bass guitar), Steve Ferrone (drums), Steve Porcaro, (synthesizer programming), Andraé Crouch Choir, London Philharmonic Orchestra

Writer: Michael Jackson

Producers: Michael Jackson, David Foster, Bill Bottrell

Label: Epic

Highest Chart Position: 1 (UK)

Also by Michael Jackson: "Man in the Mirror" (1987), "Heal the World" (1991), "Heaven Can Wait" (2001)

NEW TEST LEPER

79 R.E.M.

1996

This song was inspired by a transvestite whom singer/lyricist Michael Stipe saw on a daytime TV show themed "People judge me by the way I look." Stipe saw the line of questioning and the curiosity value of the guest as an exercise in ritual humiliation. It made him think of the lepers of biblical times who were social outcasts.[121]

"Leprosy" in the Bible was a serious and contagious skin disease resulting in scabs, crusts, and white patches. According to Leviticus 13, those showing these symptoms were required to be examined by a priest. If they were found to be lepers, they were declared unclean and were forced to live separately until they were found healed of the disease:

> And the leper in whom the plague is, his clothes shall be rent, and his head bare, and he shall put a covering upon his upper lip, and shall cry, Unclean, unclean. All the days wherein the plague shall be in him he shall be defiled; he is unclean: he shall dwell alone; without the camp shall his habitation be. (Leviticus 13:45–46)

Although an actual disease, leprosy was often used by biblical writers to illustrate the effect of sin. Spiritually the default human condition was disfigurement and the consequences was alienation (from God, others, and ourselves). When Jesus approached and healed lepers, it was an enactment of grace. He was touching the untouchable, cleaning the unclean.

Stipe, raised as a Methodist and named John Michael Stipe after John Wesley, the father of Methodism, was aware of these subtleties, which is why his song was named "New Test Leper" (for New Testament) rather than simply "Leper." He also wanted to write a song that mentioned Jesus in its opening line because he regarded such a move as taboo breaking. He thought that the only precedent in rock music was Patti Smith's rendering of "Gloria," in which she opened with the statement, "Jesus died for somebody's sins but not mine." He was wrong about this. The Velvet Underground had already broken the taboo in 1969 with its album track "Jesus," which started, "Jesus, help me find my proper place."

"New Test Leper," written in the voice of the transvestite, starts by saying that although he couldn't claim to love Jesus, he was aware that Jesus once said, "Judge not, that ye not be judged" (Matthew 7:1). The studio audience—judging by their hostile reaction—appears to disagree, and so he asks, "Have his lambs all gone astray?" a reference to the prophecy by Isaiah: · "All we like sheep have gone astray; we have turned every one to his own way" (Isaiah 53:6). In a 2006 interview with Beliefnet, Stipe said:

> If it's the teachings of Jesus that you're following, it's really
> easy to cut to the chase and get down to what did this man's
> life really represent. And how much of that is acknowledged
> in the Bible? I think a lot. How much of that can get
> muddied by people's interpretation of the Bible and perhaps
> not recognizing that a lot of it is allegory. . . . If there's a
> schism in this country, it might be not between the people
> who have faith and the people who don't have faith, but
> people who have faith that is, in my opinion, pure to the
> teachings of Jesus and people who have taken that and turned
> it into something for other reasons, be that power, be that

intolerance or ignorance. And that's where a schism might have occurred in this country presently.[122]

Song: "New Test Leper"

Artist: R.E.M.

Album: *New Adventures in Hi-Fi*

Release: September 9, 1996

Studio: Bad Animals Studio, Seattle, WA

Personnel: Michael Stipe (vocals), Bill Berry (drums), Peter Buck (lead guitar), Mike Mills (bass guitar, keyboards)

Writers: Michael Stipe, Bill Berry, Peter Buck, Mike Mills

Producers: Scott Litt, R.E.M.

Label: Warner Brothers

Also by R.E.M.: "Burning Hell" (1985), "The End of the World (As We Know It)" (1987), "Losing My Religion" (1991)

80

JOY
WHITNEY HOUSTON
1996

The soundtrack to *The Preacher's Wife* is the best-selling gospel album of all-time, selling over six million copies worldwide. The movie, based on the 1947 film *The Bishop's Wife* that had starred Cary Grant, Loretta Young, and David Niven, tells the story of a troubled New York preacher (Rev. Henry Biggs, played by Courtney B. Vance) and his wife, Julia (played by Whitney Houston), who are visited by an angel named Dudley (played by Denzel Washington). The role of Julia, a former nightclub singer who becomes the star of the church choir, gave Houston (1963–2012) the opportunity to sing unadulterated gospel and for the movie to showcase a seam of American music that is much admired although rarely celebrated or honored.

Houston had impeccable gospel roots. She began singing in the junior gospel choir of New Hope Baptist Church in Newark, New Jersey. Her mother, Emily "Cissy" Houston, had been a gospel singer with the family group the Drinkard Singers that released a live gospel album on the RCA label in 1958. Later, as the Sweet Inspirations, they would back Solomon Burke, Aretha Franklin, Elvis, and Van Morrison.

"Joy" was written by twenty-five-year-old Kirk Franklin, the latest song-writer to rejuvenate gospel with outside influences, in his case with funk, rap, disco, and new jack swing. He'd first recorded it with a local Forth Worth church choir in 1989 to put on a demo tape. Years later, someone working on *The Preacher's Wife* heard it and contacted him.

It's a simple Christmas song about "the child / who can make you whole" lying in a manger. The emphasis (and the title)—the "joy down in my soul"—comes from Luke's account of the angelic visitation to the shepherds: "And the angel said unto them, Fear not: for, behold, I bring you good tidings of great joy, which shall be to all people" (Luke 2:10).

Song: "Joy"

Artist: Whitney Houston

Album: *The Preacher's Wife: Original Soundtrack Album*

Release: November 26, 1996

Studio: Trinity United Methodist Church, Newark, NJ

Personnel: Whitney Houston (vocals), Georgia Mass Choir

Writer: Kirk Franklin

Producers: Mervyn Warren, Whitney Houston

Label: Arista

Highest Chart Position: 22 (US) (in 2012)

Other Significant Recordings: Georgia Mass Choir, featuring Kirk Franklin (1992)

Also by Whitney Houston: "I Know Him So Well" (1988), "Jesus Loves Me" (1992), "I Go to the Rock" (1996)

FORGIVE THEM FATHER

81 LAURYN HILL

1998

The *Miseducation of Lauryn Hill,* the album that featured "Forgive Them Father," sold over eight million copies, won five Grammys, and sold more in the first week than any previous album by a solo female artist. Hill's confidence and honest self-exploration inspired a whole generation of women, as did her blend of pop, R&B, reggae, gospel, and rap.

From a middle-class Baptist family in New Jersey, Hill had excelled at school and went on to be part of the Fugees with Wyclef Jean and Pras Michel. She left the group following disagreements about her behavior and the breakup of a romance with Wyclef. She wanted the freedom to express herself. Her next partner was Bob Marley's son, Rohan (with whom she would have several children), and her relationship with Marley determined her new musical direction.

The words of "Forgive Them Father" are directed at her former bandmates, who she feels have done her wrong. It is drenched in biblical references. "Gospel music is music inspired by the Gospels," she said in 1999. "In a huge respect, a lot of this music turned out to be that. During this album, I turned to the Bible and wrote songs that I drew comfort from."[123]

The substance of the song—asking God to forgive her transgressors—comes from words spoken by Jesus during his crucifixion. Looking down at his Roman executioners, he said, "Father, forgive them; for they know not what they do" (Luke 23:34). She also quotes from the Lord's Prayer: "Forgive us our trespasses as we forgive those who trespass against us" (see Matthew 6:9–13; Luke 11:2–4).

Hill doesn't pursue the theme of generous forgiveness consistently. She can't resist the temptation to name all the sins she allegedly wants God to forgive. Yet she still invokes the Bible. Those who've sinned against her are "cats that don't turn the other cheek," as Jesus taught people to do (Matthew 5:39). They are "wolves in sheep coats," as Jesus described false prophets "who come to you in sheep's clothing, but inwardly are ravening wolves" (Matthew 7:15 ASV).

When accusing her enemies of diminishing her role (presumably in the Fugees), she asks, "Why for you to increase, I must decrease?" This is oddly antiquated language to describe a spat among urban R&B rappers, but, again, it comes from the Bible. The words were spoken by John the Baptist. He was telling his followers that Jesus was more significant than he was, and that they needed to submit to Jesus's authority even at the expense of John's ministry and their own selfish ambition. "He must increase, but I must decrease" (John 3:30).

Song: "Forgive Them Father"

Artist: Lauryn Hill

Album: *The Miseducation of Lauryn Hill*

Release: August 25, 1998

Studio: Tuff Gong Studios, Kingston, Jamaica

Personnel: Lauryn Hill (vocals), Shelly Thunder (vocals), Earl Chinna Smith (guitar), Ronald Robinson (trombone), Everol Ray (trumpet), Chris Meredith (bass guitar), Vada Nobles (drum programming), Che Guevara (drum programming), Julian Marley (guitar)

Writer: Lauryn Hill

Producers: Lauryn Hill, Che Guevara, Vada Nobles

Label: Ruffhouse Records, Columbia Records

Also by Lauryn Hill: "To Zion" (1998), "Oh Jerusalem" (2002), "Adam Lives in Theory" (2002)

FIRE IN THE HOLE

82

VAN HALEN

. . . .

1998

When Gary Cherone replaced Sammy Hagar as lead vocalist in Van Halen for the recording of *Van Halen III*, he brought not only his voice and a fresh approach to lyric writing but a Christian faith that had been awakened by the books of Dallas-area pastor Dr. Charles "Chuck" Swindoll and sustained by the radio broadcasts of theologian R. C. Sproul (whom he would credit in the album's liner notes).

Cherone wasn't a Bible-thumper, but he introduced an introspection, confession, and conscience not normally found in heavy metal. He could also do theology. "Once" doesn't mention the deity, but it is about the Calvinist teaching of "eternal security" or the "perseverance of the saints"—"Once embraced, can't ever be let go / Once revealed, can't ever be not shown." Heavy stuff for heavy metal!

"Fire in the Hole" derives from a New Testament warning about the power of the tongue to destroy. The phrase "fire in the hole" was developed by miners to warn their workmates that a detonation in a confined space was about to take place. The song uses it as a metaphor for the damage that can be done by careless words.

The relevant Bible passage is James 3:5–6: "So the tongue also is a little member, and boasteth great things. Behold, how much wood is kindled by how small a fire! And the tongue is a fire: the world of iniquity among our members is the tongue, which defileth the whole body, and setteth on fire the wheel of nature, and is set on fire by hell" (ASV). In Van Halen's song, this becomes, "Great is the forest, set by a small flame / Like a tongue on fire, no one can tame."

The mention of a rudder and bridle also come from James: "Now if we put the horses' bridles into their mouths that they may obey us, we turn about their whole body also. Behold, the ships also, though they are so great and are driven by rough winds, are yet turned about by a very small rudder, whither the impulse of the steersman willeth" (3:3–4 ASV).

"Fire in the Hole" appeared on the soundtrack of the *Lethal Weapon 4*, the movie starring Mel Gibson, Danny Glover, Rene Russo, Chris Rock, and Joe Pesci.

Song: "Fire in the Hole"

Artist: Van Halen

Album: *Van Halen III*

Release: July 1998

Studio: 5150 Studios, Studio City, CA

Personnel: Gary Cherone (lead vocals), Eddie Van Halen (guitar, keyboards, backing vocals), Michael Anthony (bass guitar), Alex Van Halen (drums, percussion)

Writers: Eddie Van Halen, Michael Anthony, Gary Cherone, Alex Van Halen

Producers: Mike Post, Eddie Van Halen

Label: Warner Brothers

Highest Chart Position: 6 (US)

Also by Van Halen: "One I Want" (1998), "How Many Say I" (1998), "Once" (1998)

RUN ON

MOBY

83

. . . .

1999

H aving been the shaven-headed wunderkind of the New York dance and rave scene as a DJ, mixer, and performer, Moby's career took a nosedive in the mid-1990s after he tried to blend punk with animal rights activism. He came back with the album *Play*, which relied heavily on mixing music sampled from other recordings and turned him into an unlikely pop star, producing eight singles, supplying soundtracks for commercials, and selling over ten million copies.

Moby, born Richard Melville Hall and said to be a distant descendent of the *Moby Dick* author Herman Melville, was an oddity in the world of electro beats, clubbing, and all-around hedonism: a Bible-quoting vegetarian with great intellectual curiosity and a social conscience. As a teenager he identified with the church, but the fundamentals of his faith have changed so much that he's now not even comfortable calling himself a Christian.

His primary skill on *Play* was not singing or playing but manipulating sounds. For "Run On," he took the vocals from a 1949 recording of the song by an almost unknown gospel group, Bill Landford and the Landfordaires, and underpinned it with piano and a drum sample from Melvin Bliss's 1973 single "Synthetic Substitution."

At the time of cutting the record, he was unaware that the song, some-times also known as "You Better Run" or "God's Gonna Cut You Down," was a traditional spiritual that had been recorded by people like the Golden Gate Quartet, Odetta, and Elvis. He just liked what he heard.

The song is told in the voice of someone whom God has given a warn-ing to pass on to all reprobates who might think that they can escape his coming judgment:

> Go tell that lonesome liar
> Go tell that midnight rider
> Tell the gamblin', ramblin' backslider
> Tell them God Almighty gonna cut 'em down
>
> You might run on for a long time
> Run on, ducking and dodging
> Run on, children, for a long time
> Let me tell you God Almighty gonna cut you down

The overall message is that no one ultimately escapes from God and that all will be judged.

> You might throw your rock, hide your hand
> Work in the dark with your fellow man
> Sure as God made you rich and poor
> You're gonna reap just what you sow

These lines derive from Paul's letters: "Have no fellowship with the unfruitful works of darkness, but rather even reprove them" (Ephesians 5:11 ASV), and "Be not deceived; God is not mocked: for whatsoever a man soweth, that shall he also reap" (Galatians 6:7 ASV).

Moby sampled gospel songs on two other tracks on the album: "Trouble So Hard" by Vera Hall on "Natural Blues," and "He'll Roll Your Burdens Away" by the Banks Brothers with the Greater Harvest Baptist Church Back Home Choir on "Why Does My Heart Feel So Bad?"

Years later Adele commented, "There's something that I find really holy about that *Play* album. . . . The way it makes me feel. Even though there's nothing holy or preachy about it. There's just something about it—maybe the gospel samples. But it makes me feel alive, that album, still."[124]

"What attracts me to Christ is that he's so dynamic, aggressive, and courageous. But so much of contemporary Christian culture is fearful," Moby told me in 1994. "The only ones who are courageous are the hate-sellers. A lot of middle-of-the-road Christians are afraid to be one thing or the other. They don't want to be stodgy old Christians and only listen to church music, but they don't want to be too far in advance of popular culture because popular culture is dirty and sinful and they'd rather let the sinners go ahead and make the mistakes so they can choose from their gleanings. I don't know what it is about my nature, but I'd rather go ahead and make a hundred mistakes and look back and think, *That's what I did wrong* than not do anything at all."

Song: "Run On"

Artist: Moby

Single: A-side: "Run On" / B-side: "Spirit," "Running," "Sunday," "Down Slow," and "Memory Gospel"

Release: April 26, 1999

Album: *Play*

Studio: Moby's home studio, New York, NY

Personnel: Moby (guitar, piano)

Writer: Moby

Producer: Moby

Label: Mute / Elektra

Highest Chart Position: 33 (UK)

Other Significant Recordings: Golden Gate Quartet (1947), Bill Landford and the Landfordaires (1949), Elvis Presley (1967), Tom Jones (2010)

Also by Moby: "God Moving Over the Face of the Waters" (1995), "Why Does My Heart Feel So Bad" (1999), "In My Heart" (2002)

84

THE MILLENNIUM PRAYER
CLIFF RICHARD

1999

When Cliff Richard became a Christian in 1965, he was Britain's biggest-selling solo artist, and seven years into his recording career, he still tussled with the likes of the Beatles and the Stones to reach the top spot in the UK singles charts.

However, there was no effective role model for stars converting while still at the top of their game. Terry Dene, one of the earliest of Britain's "answers to Elvis," gave up show business to become a street evangelist, but his career was already well on the wane when this happened.

There were three obvious options: give up his career and join the church or an evangelistic organization, become a gospel singer, or continue his career but keep it separate from his new beliefs and religious practices. Cliff wasn't happy with any of these options, and over the years worked toward integrating his faith with his music—recording gospel albums, raising money for overseas relief projects, authoring books on faith, discussing Christianity in regular interviews, and trying to find songs that reflected his worldview without being overtly religious.

"Millennium Prayer," released to usher in the twenty-first century, was a setting of the words of the Lord's Prayer (from Matthew 6:9–13) to the familiar tune of the Scottish New Year song "Auld Lang Syne." Paul Field put it together in 1997 for a musical, *Hopes and Dreams*, authored by Stephen Deal for church audiences. Stephen Deal threw the idea out almost as a joke. "I couldn't get the idea out of my head," said Field. "I started to tinker around with it. I thought it was the most cheesy, awful idea in the world or it was something that could actually fly. The truth is, it was probably both."[125]

The track was controversial from the get-go. EMI, Cliff's record company since 1958, refused it as a single, so his management went to a small independent label, Papillon. When it was released, leading British radio stations refused to include it on their playlists. BBC Radio 2 didn't think it had "broad enough appeal." George Michael called it a "heinous piece of music." Despite the opposition, it reached the number one spot in the UK charts and raised over £1 million (about $1.5 million) for charity.

Speaking in 2000 on a Chicago radio station, Cliff Richard said that he couldn't understand how people could be so against this song, which is a beautiful lyric about peace and keeping us fed and protecting us from evil. "The lyrics were written virtually by Jesus. And I really found it very confusing. But a Christian friend of mine said to me, 'Look! They crucified Jesus for saying things like this. Of course they're going to be against you for singing it.' So it made me feel a little better."[126]

Song: "The Millennium Prayer"

Artist: Cliff Richard

Single: A-side: "The Millennium Prayer" / B-side: "Two Worlds"

Release: November 15, 1999

Studios: Skratch Studio, Surrey, Whitfeld Street Studios, London

Personnel: Cliff Richard (vocals), Anne Skates (vocal arrangements), David Arch (orchestra arrangements)

Writers: Stephen Deal, Paul Field, David Arch, Anne Skates, Nigel Wright

Producer: Nigel Wright

Label: Papillon Records

Highest Chart Position: 1 (UK)

Also by Cliff Richard: "Little Town" (1982), "Wherever God Shines His Light" (duet with Van Morrison) (1989), "Saviour's Day" (1990)

THE MAN COMES AROUND

85 JOHNNY CASH

2002

J ohnny Cash began and ended his recording career wanting to cut a
standout gospel song. His final producer, Rick Rubin, had a similar
attitude to his first, Sam Phillips, which was: be wary of releasing gospel
tracks because you may alienate your secular audience. His gospel collection,
My Mother's Hymn Book, which was a treasured project, wasn't released until
after his death as part of the five-CD box set titled *Unearthed*.

But knowing he was nearing the end, Cash persisted in composing his
conception of a modern gospel song that would connect with the young
alternative audience he'd built up during the American Recording series of
albums. Producer Rubin had worked hard to focus Cash's energy on making
the music he truly loved while linking him up with new songs and songwriters. He recorded material from seemingly unlikely sources—Tom Petty and
the Heartbreakers, Nine Inch Nails, Nick Cave and the Bad Seeds, Bruce
Springsteen, and Depeche Mode—and made their songs sound as though
they had been written for him alone.

One of the early indications of this turn to the contemporary was a
track he recorded in Dublin with U2 for the band's 1993 *Zooropa* album.
Bono's lyrics for "The Wanderer" drew from the book of Ecclesiastes. The

song planted a seed in Cash's mind that a new type of gospel song might be needed for a new age.

He worked on some ideas over the intervening years that didn't come to fruition, but at the end of 2000 he had embarked on the text of what eventually became "The Man Comes Around." It was a song about death and final judgment that was made poignant by his physical failings. He could barely sing above a whisper, print had to be enlarged due to his loss of sight, and his lines had to be recorded line by line because of respiratory difficulties.

The song was bookended by two quotations from the sixth chapter of Revelation that gave the song its context. The first is about a white horse ridden by a man with a bow, crowned, and going forth conquering (v. 2) and the last references a pale horse that bore "Death, and Hell followed with him" (v. 8). "There's a man goin' 'round takin' names," the first words of the song proper, were quoted from an old spiritual recorded by Josh White in the 1930s, Lead Belly in the 1940s, and many other artists, ranging from the Golden Gate Quartet to Jessye Norman. The allusion was to the idea that our names are recorded in a book in heaven, and that the condemned are those whose names have been erased from it: "He that overcometh, the same shall be clothed in white raiment; and I will not blot out his name out of the book of life, but I will confess his name before my Father, and before his angels" (Revelation 3:5). The man who was "goin' 'round" was Jesus.

The rest of the song was densely packed with at least seventeen biblical references, illustrating not only Cash's deep and abiding interest in theology but also his evangelistic zeal. He was warning his contemporaries in the same way that Dylan had warned his friends with "You Gotta Serve Somebody." The hen calling its chicks was taken from Luke 13:34; the wise men casting down their crowns from Revelation 4:10; the virgins with their candles from Matthew 25:1–13; the Alpha and Omega from Revelation 1:8, 21:6, and 22:13. The version of the song he recorded was trimmed down from around forty completed verses.

Even though Cash's voice had been reduced in power and range, and the tune was not much more than a support for his recitation, it built in intensity as the song described the cast being assembled for the great apocalypse. There was marching and crying, singing and drumming, birth and death, righteousness and filth. It was both an intensely cerebral song that emerged from detailed Bible study and an intensely visceral song that made its listeners see, hear, feel, and smell the coming judgment.

On August 20, 2003, he told a TV interviewer:

> I expect my life to end pretty soon, you know. I'm 71 years old. And, um, I have great faith though. I have an unshakable faith. I have never been angry with God. I've never been, um, I've never turned my back on God, so to speak. I've never, ah, I never thought that God wasn't there. That I knew, I knew that he's my counselor, he's my wisdom. All the good things in my life come from him.[127]

He died three weeks later.

Song: "The Man Comes Around"

Artist: Johnny Cash

Single: A-side: "The Man Comes Around" / B-side: "Personal Jesus"

Release: May 24, 2002

Album: *American IV: The Man Comes Around*

Studio: Cash Cabin Studio, Nashville, TN

Personnel: Johnny Cash (vocals), Randy Scruggs (guitar), Gregory "Smokey" Hormel (guitar), Benmont Tench (piano, organ)

Writer: Johnny Cash

Producer: Rick Rubin

Label: American Recordings

Other Significant Recordings: Jorma Kaukonen (2007)

Also by Johnny Cash: "Redemption" (1994), "Meet Me in Heaven" (1996), "I Came to Believe" (2006)

SACRED LOVE

86

STING

. . . .

2003

S acred Love" is part of a long tradition of poetry and lyric writing comparing spiritual and sexual union. Many Christians have regarded the Song of Solomon as a metaphorical courtship between God and his chosen people. The New Testament portrays Jesus as a bridegroom awaiting marriage to his bride. Poets as varied as St. Teresa of Avila and John Donne have played with the parallels between fleshly rapture and divine ecstasy.

Sting was brought up in a Catholic family in Newcastle, England, and attended a Catholic school. "Every day you're taught in front of the image of a man who has been tortured, has blood pouring from his wounds, has had his legs broken and has thorns in his head," he told me in 1986. "That symbolism of heaven, hell, and eternal suffering obviously has a profound effect on a child. It's an effect I don't regret, though. I'm very grateful for the rich reservoir of symbolism it gave me."

Sting began writing the songs for *Sacred Love* in the aftermath of the 9/11 terror attacks on America. The event stiffened his resolve to write about the serious and eternal nature of love in the light of the often trivial and transient encounters celebrated in rock and pop.

He argued "the idea that sex could be considered a sacred act [seems] too much for a world media attuned to the minutiae of trivia. Sex is either scandalous—when, for example, politicians are caught *in flagrante delicto*—or, it's used to sell cars and aftershave. In both cases, eroticism, the most powerful force in our human nature, is devalued to the point of worthlessness."[128]

On the surface, "Sacred Love" deifies Sting's wife (who lost a friend in the World Trade Center on 9/11). She was the answer to his prayers (although, noticeably, his prayers were addressed to "the moon and the stars" rather than to God), and his relationship with her satisfied him in the way that religion is expected to fulfil people —"You're my religion, you're my church."

But deeper down, Sting is saying that the love of his wife was a conduit for divine love. In presenting this case, he is appropriating biblical imagery: the spirit moves on the water (Genesis 1:2), the word becomes flesh (John 1:14), the angels bow down (Revelation 7:11), the sky darkens and the earth shakes (Joel 2:10).

"Sacred" comes from the Latin word meaning "holy." The online Google dictionary defines it as "connected with God (or the gods) or dedicated to a religious purpose and so deserving veneration." Sting's conclusion that "it all comes down to love" is akin to Paul's poetic comments written to the church in Corinth: "But now abideth faith, hope, love, these three; and the greatest of these is love" (1 Corinthians 13:13 ASV). Sting told the press agency UPI:

> I wanted to try to redefine the word love. I think the word has
> been abused and misused; in pop music, love tends to be a little
> sentimental and violins playing and birds tweeting. But love
> can be a very aggressive and violent emotion, too. It needed
> to grow in my head into something bigger, something scarier,
> something more all-encompassing. The whole thing about love
> is if you ever want to be loved again you have to take the risk
> that you can be destroyed by love—and be willing to because
> the reward is worth the risk.[129]

Song: "Sacred Love"

Artist: Sting

Album: *Sacred Love*

Release: September 29, 2003

Studio: Studio Mega, Paris

Personnel: Sting (guitar, vocals), Christian McBride (double bass), Dominic Miller (guitars), Kipper [Mark Eldridge] (keyboards and programming), Jeff Young (Hammond organ), Vincent Colaiuta (drums), Rhani Krija (percussion), Joy Rose, Katreese Barnes, Ada Dyer, Donna Gardier (backing vocals)

Writer: Sting

Producer: Sting, Kipper

Label: A&M

Also by Sting: "Jeremiah Blues (Part 1)" (1991), "When the Angels Fall" (1991), "Saint Augustine in Hell" (1993)

87

ALL THE TREES OF THE FIELD WILL CLAP THEIR HANDS
SUFJAN STEVENS

2004

All the Trees of the Field Will Clap Their Hands" took its unusual title (and central image) from the prophet Isaiah: "For ye shall go out with joy, and be led forth with peace: the mountains and the hills shall break forth before you into singing, and all the trees of the field shall clap their hands" (Isaiah 55:12).

The song seems to be about Stevens's approach to his art. Written in the form of a prayer of submission, it asks to be a part of what God is doing on earth—"I'm joining all my thoughts to you"—acknowledging that God's artistry is expressed in creation, and that trees and mountains naturally worship him simply by being.

Stevens, who made his first solo album in 2000, was never secretive about his Christian identity but made it clear that he was no musical missionary. His commitment was to making good work and facing technical challenges that would stretch him. The things that he believed in would percolate their way through everything he created.

I suppose my process of making art is driven less by
abstractions of faith or politics and more by practical theory:
composition and balance and color. . . . On an aesthetic
level, faith and art are a dangerous match. Today, they can
quickly lead to devotional artifice or didactic crap. This would
summarize the Christian publishing world or the Christian
music industry. If you are an artist of faith (a Methodist or a
Jew), then you have the responsibility to manage the principles
of your faith wisely lest they be reduced to stereotype, which
is patronizing to the church and to the world, and, perhaps, to
God. . . . It's not so much that faith influences us as it lives in
us. In every circumstance (giving a speech or tying my shoes),
I am living and moving and being. This absolves me from ever
making the embarrassing effort to gratify God (and the church)
by imposing religious content on anything I do. I mean, I've
written songs about stalkers. Is that any less religious than a
song about an ordained pastor? No way.[130]

The album *Seven Swans* was intended as a quieter and more personal
album than its predecessor, the ambitious *Michigan*. In an interview just after
its release, he explained some of the influences. "I was interested in . . .
themes that were about family and love, and about church and God, and
about relationships between these things, and about the earth. And a little bit
of mythology is in there, I think, as well. I had been reading a lot of literature
that was somewhat invested in religious themes—like Flannery O'Connor
[novelist and short story writer], some William Blake [poet] and some of the
other English Romantics, and Thomas Merton [poet, diarist, spiritual author,
and monk], . . . and William Faulkner [novelist]."[131]

The album *Seven Swans* was a huge critical success. The *Guardian* (London),
which awarded it four out of five stars, said, "It almost sounds as if it could
have been recorded 100 years ago, in a remote Shaker community, untainted
by outside influence. Indeed, it's hard to think of another singer able to engage
with the articles of faith with both a childlike sense of wonder and such emotional sophistication. *Seven Swans* feels like an entirely magical visitation."[132]

Song: "All the Trees of the Field Will Clap Their Hands"

Artist: Sufjan Stevens

Album: *Seven Swans*

Release: March 16, 2004

Studio: Home studio of Daniel Smith, New Jerusalem Rec Room, Clarksboro, NJ

Personnel: Sufjan Stevens (guitar, vocals), Andrew Smith (drums), Daniel Smith (bass)

Writer: Sufjan Stevens

Producer: Daniel Smith

Label: Sounds Familyre

Other Significant Recordings: Bonnie "Prince" Billy (2011)

Also by Sufjan Stevens: "Year of Our Lord" (2001), "The Transfiguration" (2004), "No Shade in the Shadow of the Cross" (2015)

88

JESUS WALKS

KANYE WEST

2004

W hen Kanye West did his first demos of "Jesus Walks" in 2000, the studio staff and session musicians laughed at his boldness in attempting to marry rap with overt gospel. When he shopped the recording to record companies, the reaction was the same. As predicted in the lyrics: "They said you can rap about anything except for Jesus / That means guns, sex, lies, video tape / But if I talk about God my record won't get played / Huh?"

The scoffers were wrong. The record did get played. It reached number 11 in the Billboard charts, and his debut album, *The College Dropout*, went on to sell over eight million copies around the world and won the Grammy for Best Rap Album.

West is both controversial and paradoxical. "Jesus Walks" was unusual in making a defiantly Christian statement in a genre better known for songs of violence, misogyny, obscenity, consumerism, and braggadocio. Yet West was not always consistent in his beliefs. He admitted to porn addiction and would later distance himself from the label "Christian" by claiming to admire all religions and was only Christian because of an accident of birth. "I guess I'm religious because I really do believe that Jesus died for our sins," he said in 2005. "But that's because it was instilled in me. If I had been raised as a Muslim I wouldn't believe that Jesus died for our sins."[133]

Four years later he said, "Christianity is embedded in who I am, so I will still say things like this is a blessing, amen, and still say prayers; things that your grandmother embedded in you. I'm always gonna have a little Chicago in me, a little hood in me, and a little Christianity in me."[134]

The title "Jesus Walks" suggests images of Jesus walking on the waters of Galilee but is about Jesus walking alongside the weak, sinful, and poor. West's lyrical drift took its impulse from the recording he sampled of "Walk with Me," recorded in 1997 by the ARC (Addicts Rehabilitation Center) Gospel Choir based in Harlem, New York. "Walk with Me" was a simple plea addressed to Jesus that resonated with addicts.

The New Testament doesn't actually speak of Jesus walking "with" us, but there are several commands to walk after him, to "follow in his steps" (1 Peter 2:21), to walk "in him" (Colossians 2:6), and to walk "even as he walked" (1 John 2:6).

In "Jesus Walks," West begins by adopting the persona of an addict who is "at war" with himself. He begs for guidance because he fears that "the Devil's tryin' to break me down." The rest of the song is delivered in his own voice—that of the rapper who claims to need Jesus.

New Testament writers such as James, Peter, John, and Paul mention the idea that the devil attacks the followers of Jesus. He is pictured as someone out to impede, hurt, deceive, and even destroy with his "fiery darts" (Ephesians 6:16). In speaking of being "broken down" by the devil, West may have been thinking of "Be sober, be vigilant; because your adversary the devil, as a roaring lion, walketh about, seeking whom he may devour" (1 Peter 5:8).

When West writes, "I walk through the valley of Chi where death is," he is referring to "the valley of the shadow of death" (Psalm 23:4) and interpolating it with a reference to his hometown of Chicago, where murders topped six hundred in 2003, the year the song was written.

His persistent plea that his "feet don't fail" him could have been inspired by Old Testament assurances that God can guide our footsteps and keep us from stumbling. "My help cometh from the LORD, which made heaven and earth. He will not suffer thy foot to be moved" (Psalm 121:2–3).

Discussing the song in 2013, West said, "You know what's awesome about Christianity? We're allowed to portray God. We're allowed to draw an image of him. We're allowed to make movies about him. Other religions, you're not allowed to do that. . . . [What] I wanted to get across with that message is that you can have a relationship with Jesus, that you can talk to Jesus in the same way as someone can have [a] 'Jesus is my homeboy' [T-shirt], that is the way I would express it."[135]

Song: "Jesus Walks"

Artist: Kanye West

Single: A-side: "Jesus Walks" / B-side: "Heavy Hitters"

Release: December 3, 2004

Album: *The College Dropout*

Studio: Sony Music Studios, New York, NY; the Record Plant, Los Angeles, CA

Personnel: Kanye West (vocals), John Legend (vocals), Miri Ben-Ari (violin), ARC Gospel Choir (vocal sample), Curtis Lundy (choir director)

Writers: Kanye West, Che Smith, Curtis Lundy, Miri Ben-Ari

Producer: Kanye West

Label: Roc-A-Fella, Def Jam

Highest Chart Position: 11 (USA)

Also by Kanye West: "Sweet Baby Jesus" (2011), "New God Flow" (2015), "Ultralight Beam" (2016)

JESUS WAS AN ONLY SON

89

BRUCE SPRINGSTEEN

. . . .

2005

lthough "Catholic beauty and poetry"[136] had always been part of Bruce
Springsteen's songs, this was the first time he had tackled the subject of
Jesus head-on. During his various introductions to it on his 2005 tour,
he revealed his motivations. It was a song about parent-child relationships—a
strong theme on the *Devils & Dust* album on which it appeared—but it was
also about dedication to a vision and the sacrifices this entailed.

In Seattle, he said, "I wrote a lot of songs about parents and children on
this record, and so I thought, well, you know, I'm going to try to write something from the standpoint of Jesus as someone's child, as someone's—and
what it's like to have your children choose their own destiny, as they do."[137]
In East Rutherford, he added, "My mind wandered . . . to imagining Jesus as
Mary's son."[138]

The description "only son," "only begotten," or "only begotten son" is
used of Jesus five times in the King James Version of the New Testament,
four in the Gospel of John and once in 1 John, but each time in relation to
God rather than to his earthly parents. The best known of the references
is John 3:16: "For God so loved the world, that he gave his only begotten
Son, that whosoever believeth in him should not perish, but have everlasting

278

life." The phrase "only son" is similarly used to the Apostle's Creed (fourth century) in its affirmation, "I believe in Jesus Christ, God's only Son, our Lord . . ."

But as a Catholic by upbringing, Springsteen will have had in mind the phrase as it is expressed in *The Catechism of the Catholic Church* (1994, USA): "Jesus is Mary's only son, but her spiritual motherhood extends to all men whom indeed he came to save."[139]

The Catholic church believes Mary to be the Aeiparthenos, "Ever-virgin," who did not conceive any children after the miraculous birth of Jesus. It teaches that the mentions of other children of Mary, such as, "Is not this the carpenter's son? is not his mother called Mary? and his brethren, James, and Joses, and Simon, and Judas?" (Matthew 13:55), with the term "brethren" refers to Jesus's wider family. So Springsteen's song title: "Jesus Was an Only Son." (Perhaps he was also aware of the spiritual "The Virgin Mary Had A-One Son" that Joan Baez had sung at her Newport Folk Festival debut in 1959.)

He picks up the story as Jesus walks up "Calvary hill," a name mentioned only in Luke's gospel (the other Gospels use "Golgotha," which, like "Calvary," has roots in the word for "skull"): "And when they were come to the place, which is called Calvary, there they crucified him, and the malefactors, one on the right hand, and the other on the left" (Luke 23:33).

Springsteen imagines Mary walking beside Jesus and remembering her protective feelings toward him as a child. Both the walk and the thoughts are reasonable speculation but are not based on gospel accounts. John's Gospel, however, does attest that Mary was present at the crucifixion: "But there were standing by the cross of Jesus his mother, and his mother's sister, Mary the wife of Clopas, and Mary Magdalene" (John 19:25 ASV).

Then Springsteen goes back to events immediately preceding the trial and crucifixion. The focus is now on the human emotions of Jesus. At East Rutherford, he introduced the song by saying, "The choices we make are given meaning by the things that we give up, the things that we sacrifice for others. That's what gives them weight and meaning."[140]

He imagines Jesus confronted with the choice of an easy life and one of sacrifice: "You have to be thinking—see, Galilee is pretty nice this time of year," he said before going into the third verse. "A little bar. I could manage it.

Mary Magdalene could tend bar. I could do the preaching on the weekends, and have some kids, get to notice the sun on their faces, get to feel the breath in your lungs."[141]

In the "garden at Gethsemane," Springsteen sings, Jesus prays "for the life he'd never live." He reveals him begging God to remove "the cup of death from his lips." This scene is based on the Synoptic Gospels—Matthew, Mark, and Luke—two of which describe Jesus suffering anguish in a "place called Gethsemane" (Matthew 26:36), and "a place which was named Gethsemane" (Mark 14:32), where he had retreated with his disciples to pray.

Jesus begged to be spared the agonies that awaited him at the crucifixion but ultimately submitted himself to the will of God:

> He took with him Peter and the two sons of Zebedee, and began to be sorrowful and sore troubled. Then saith he unto them, My soul is exceedingly sorrowful, even unto death: abide ye here, and watch with me. And he went forward a little, and fell on his face, and prayed, saying, My Father, if it be possible, let this cup pass away from me: nevertheless, not as I will, but as thou wilt. (Matthew 26:37–39 ASV)

Springsteen rounds off his song with another imagined scene where Jesus kisses Mary and says, "Mother, still your tears." This may be loosely based on the scene described by John where Jesus spoke to her from the cross and said, "Woman, behold thy son!" (John 19:26) and then said to "the disciple . . . whom he loved" (generally understood to be John), "Behold thy mother!" (John 19:27). As a result, the disciple in question took Mary into his home to care for her. The Catholic church takes these words of Jesus to mean that Mary thereby became the mother of all Christian disciples, not just the one addressed.

Song: "Jesus Was an Only Son"
Artist: Bruce Springsteen
Album: *Devils & Dust*

Release: April 26, 2005

Studio: Thrill Hill Recording, Colt's Hill, NJ; Thrill Hill Recording, Los Angeles, CA (Springsteen's home studios)

Personnel: Bruce Springsteen (guitar, vocals, keyboards, bass, drums), Patti Scialfa (backing vocals), Soozie Tyrell (backing vocals), Lisa Lowell (backing vocals)

Writer: Bruce Springsteen

Producer: Brendan O'Brien

Label: Columbia

Highest Chart Position: *Devils & Dust* album – 1 (US), 1 (UK)

Also by Bruce Springsteen: "My City of Ruins" (2002), "Devils & Dust" (2005), "Land of Hopes and Dreams" (2012)

90

JERUSALEM (OUT OF DARKNESS COMES LIGHT)
MATISYAHU

2006

I t was one of the most unlikely pairings in contemporary rock—Hasidic Judaism and rap-informed reggae. Into a genre dominated either by African American wannabe gangstas or Caribbean Rastafarians came a young white guy from Plains, New York, with a full beard, earlocks, tzitzis, yarmulke, and black silk bekishe, rapping about Moses (Moshe Rabbeinu), King David, and the messiah (*mashiach*), sometimes in Hebrew.

Matisyahu was born Matthew Miller into a nonorthodox Jewish family and didn't become religious until his late teens. He spent eight weeks in Israel studying Jewish identity, and after committing to the Chabad-Lubavitch Hasidic community in 2001, he dug deep into the Torah for two years.

In the records of Bob Marley, he discovered music that combined the passion for popular culture he'd had in his teens with the reverence for the Pentateuch, Psalms, and words of the prophets he found in his Jewish religion. He began writing songs that could only be described as "Hasidic hip-hop reggae," and eventually gained permission from his rabbi to perform and record them.

To the music industry and media, he was a curiosity. When he appeared on *Jimmy Kimmel Live* in 2004,[142] all the questions he was asked revolved about him being a fish out of water: Was there East Coast versus West Coast rivalry in Hasidic hip-hop? Who was the Hasidic Tupac? Was he allowed to use curse words? What things couldn't he do? How easy was it to grow a beard?

All of his songs were informed by his religious beliefs. Some were reflections on the Bible, some were contemporary prayers, and some were reports on his struggle to deal with God in the midst of twenty-first-century life.

"Jerusalem" was initially recorded for his second studio album, *Youth*, and then remixed by the Jamaican production team of Robbie Shakespeare and Sly Dunbar for a downloadable digital release as a single. Subsequently, Matisyahu filmed a music video using the remix, released September 31, 2006.[143]

The song is based on Psalm 137, the psalm that inspired "Rivers of Babylon," but it takes up where Boney M. left off. The fourth verse of the psalm asks, "How shall we sing the LORD's song in a strange land?" but adds the vows, "If I forget thee, O Jerusalem, let my right hand forget her cunning. If I do not remember thee, let my tongue cleave to the roof of my mouth; if I prefer not Jerusalem above my chief joy" (vv. 5–6). In "Jerusalem," this became, "Jerusalem, if I forget you / Fire not gonna come from me tongue / Jerusalem, if I forget you / Let my right hand forget what it's supposed to do."

Since recording "Jerusalem," Matisyahu has edged away from the orthodoxy that characterized his first two studio albums. In 2007, he disassociated himself from the Lubavitch movement, and four years later shaved off his beard and stopped wearing black Hasidic clothing. To a young Jewish audience who looked to him for assurance that it was possible to combine traditional beliefs with contemporary forms of cultural expression, this move was a huge disappointment.

He explained that he still regarded Judaism as a source of inspiration, but not as the sole truth. In 2013, he told the *Times of Israel* that he had felt locked into a particular vision of the world. "I needed to go back to my choices and make decisions about my life," he said. "I still believe there is a lot of truth in Orthodox Judaism, but not the whole truth. Each person has his truth that he has to discover. You don't necessarily have to mold yourself to another idea of who you are."[144]

Song: "Jerusalem (Out of Darkness Comes Light)"

Artist: Matisyahu

Album: *Youth*

Release: March 7, 2006

Single remix: *Matisyahu—The Sly & Robbie Sessions*

Release: September 19, 2006

Studio: Orange Music Sound Studio, West Orange, NJ

Personnel: Matisyahu (vocals), Aaron Dugan (guitar), Josh Werner (bass guitar, keyboards), Jonah David (drums)

Writers: Matthew "Matisyahu" Miller, Ivan Corraliza, Jimmy Douglass, Gregory Prestopino, Matthew Wilder

Producers: Sly Dunbar, Robbie Shakespeare

Label: JDub / Epic

Also by Matisyahu: "Lord Raise Me Up" (2005), "Fire of Heaven/ Altar of Earth" (2006), "King Crown of Judah" (2012)

WHY DO I KEEP COUNTING?

91

THE KILLERS

2006

Brandon Flowers of the Killers is a Mormon, born in Nevada and raised in Utah. He's also afraid of death. This could be because of his upbringing, where it was stressed that salvation was partly dependent on having lived a good life. He could never be totally assured that he was "saved."

Not surprisingly, under the circumstances, he has a fear of flying. In this powerful song, he translates his anxiety into a prayer begging God for a safe landing: "Father / Help me get down." He wants to be assured that he will have more opportunities to prove himself and that he will live to have children. "Basically it's a bargain with God," he told *NME* in 2006. "I have a big problem with flying and the first thing I do if there's something wrong is I pray."[145]

Yet, at the same time, as a member of the Church of Jesus Christ of Latter-Day Saints, he is aware of the contradiction between his worries and the foundational belief that God is in charge. Specifically, he asks, "And if all our days are numbered / Then why do I keep counting?"

Flowers is accused by the Hebrew Bible verse, "Seeing his days are determined, the number of his months are with thee, thou hast appointed his bounds that he cannot pass" (Job 14:5), and the words of Jesus, "But even the very hairs of your head are all numbered. Fear not therefore; ye are of more value than many sparrows" (Luke 12:7). He is also aware of the question posed by Jesus: "And which of you by being anxious can add a single hour to his span of life?" (Matthew 6:27 ESV).

"It's something that's become a real problem for me since we got successful," he told *NME* at the time of the album's release. "But I feel as though if I talk about it in interviews, it lessens the chance of my fears actually happening. Like, I've talked about it, so it would have to be a huge coincidence for it to actually happen to me. Does that make sense?"[146]

Song: "Why Do I Keep Counting?"

Artist: The Killers

Album: *Sam's Town*

Release: October 2, 2006

Studio: Studio at the Palms, Paradise, NV; Criterion Studios, London

Personnel: Brandon Flowers (vocals, keyboards), Dave Keuning (lead guitar, rhythm guitar), Mark Stoermer (bass guitar), Ronnie Vannucci Jr. (drums, percussion), Corlene Byrd (backing vocals)

Writers: Brandon Flowers, Dave Keuning, Mark Stoermer, Ronnie Vannucci Jr.

Producers: Flood, Alan Moulder, the Killers

Label: Island Records

Also by the Killers: "All These Things That I've Done" (2004), "The World We Live In" (2008), "The Calling" (2017)

92

VIVA LA VIDA

COLDPLAY

2008

C hris Martin once described his religious views as "alltheist," meaning that he believed in something from every religion he'd encountered so far. This may explain why many of Coldplay's songs have a spiritual veneer comprised of words associated with religious texts but rarely deliver a cohesive theology or takeaway message.

Martin's background in evangelicalism (he attended the nondenominational Belmont Chapel in Exeter as a child and teenager) explains his particular partiality for biblical language just as his chosen university subject, ancient history, may explain his preoccupation with armies, kings, and kingdoms.

"Viva La Vida" (Spanish for "live life") is crammed with pointers to biblical texts, few of which have anything to do with one another. For example, the deposed king of the song surveys his former territory and declares his castles fell because they were built on "pillars of salt, pillars of sand." The reference to sand is from a story told by Jesus about the importance of having firm foundations. A wise person builds on rock, a foolish person on sand: "And every one that heareth these sayings of mine, and doeth them not, shall be likened unto a foolish man, which built his house upon the sand: And the rain descended, and the floods came, and the winds blew, and beat upon that house; and it fell: and great was the fall of it" (Matthew 7:26–27). The phrase "pillars of salt" comes from the story of the destruction of Sodom and Gomorrah. Instead of turning her back on the burning cities as directed, Lot's wife turned around for a final glance "and she became a pillar of salt" (Genesis 19:26). It has nothing to do with foundations.

The identity of the central character in the song is unclear. He describes himself as a king who once ruled the world but also claims the supernatural power of controlling sea levels. Some have suggested Napoleon, yet he never fought in Jerusalem. Some feel Jesus fits the bill.

Could Martin have had the devil in mind? He is variously described as "the god of this world" (2 Corinthians 4:4), "the prince of the power of the air" (Ephesians 2:2), and "the prince of this world" (John 12:31). He shows Jesus "all the kingdoms of the world" and bargains with him, saying, "All these things will I give thee, if thou wilt fall down and worship me" (Matthew 4:8–9). Jesus doesn't dispute his claim of ownership.

If so, the song could be spun around the idea of the devil's defeat in "the day of the Lord." Why else would bells ring out in Jerusalem?

> In that day shall there be upon the bells of the horses, HOLINESS UNTO THE LORD; and the pots in the LORD's house shall be like the bowls before the altar. Yea, every pot in Jerusalem and in Judah shall be holiness unto the LORD of hosts. (Zechariah 14:20–21)

However, it could be Martin admires the power of biblical words and knows that they add a luster of splendor and timelessness to lyrics that isn't lent by the artifacts of contemporary culture. He more or less admitted this to *Observer* journalist Craig McLean when he said, "God is just a nice word to sing. But it isn't any specific god."[147]

When he says that he fears that "Saint Peter won't call my name," he is referring to the idea of the apostle Peter being heaven's gatekeeper based on the words of Jesus to him: "And I will give unto thee the keys of the kingdom of heaven: and whatsoever thou shalt bind on earth shall be bound in heaven: and whatsoever thou shalt loose on earth shall be loosed in heaven" (Matthew 16:19).

When asked by *Q* magazine what he was referring to by this line, Martin answered:

> You're not on the list. . . . I was a *naughty* boy. It's always fascinated me that idea of finishing your life and then being analysed on it. . . . That is the most frightening thing you could possibly say to somebody. Eternal damnation. I know about this stuff because I studied it. I was into it all. I know it. It's mildly terrifying to me. And this is serious.[148]

Song: "Viva La Vida"

Artist: Coldplay

Album: *Viva La Vida or Death and All His Friends*

Album Release: June 12, 2008

Single Release (US): May 25, 2008 (download only)

Single Release (Europe): A-side: "Viva La Vida" / B-side: "Death Will Never Conquer"

Studio: The Bakery, London

Personnel: Chris Martin (vocals, guitar, keyboards), Guy Berryman (bass guitar), Jonny Buckland (lead guitar), Will Champion (drums)

Writers: Chris Martin, Guy Berryman, Jonny Buckland, Will Champion

Producers: Markus Dravs, Brian Eno, Jon Hopkins, Rik Simpson

Label: Parlophone (UK), Capitol (US)

Highest Chart Position: 1 (US), 1 (UK)

Also by Coldplay: "God Put a Smile upon Your Face" (2003), "A Message" (2005), "Fix You" (2005)

93

FAITH
KENDRICK LAMAR

....

2009

R ight from the get-go, rapper Kendrick Lamar was explicit in his language and explicit about his beliefs. "Faith" starts with him seated in church but with his mind drifting. He challenges God to reveal the purpose of life and receives the answer that it is to live like Jesus, experience his power, and spread the gospel: "I said alright, enthused that my Lord gave a listen / I opened my Bible in search to be a better Christian / And this from a person that never believed in religion."

The rest of the song charts the difficulties of keeping the faith in a tough and unjust world. A close friend who is murdered shakes his certainties. A single mother with four children faces eviction for nonpayment of rent. A violent man muses over the efficiency of guns versus the efficiency of love.

Running through the song is the refrain, "All you need is the size of a mustard seed," which was the response of Jesus to the shallowness of his disciples' faith: "If ye have faith as a grain of mustard seed, ye shall say unto this mountain, Remove hence to yonder place; and it shall remove; and nothing shall be impossible unto you" (Matthew 17:20).

Born and raised in Compton, south of downtown Los Angeles, he witnessed murders as a child, and his father was a former gang member. His songs reflect this background but also deal with the conversion he says he experienced after the grandmother of a friend prayed for him in the parking lot of a local food store.

"I am always inquisitive on life, God, and Jesus himself," he said. "I'm not saying that I'm an actual saint, but this is me. This is who I am. . . . My music reflects my actual life, so I will always continue to put that type of message . . . in my music no matter what I'm doing. This is me as a person. My personal beliefs."[149]

Song: "Faith"

Artist: Kendrick Lamar

Album: *Kendrick Lamar* (EP)

Release: December 31, 2009

Studio: TDE Red Room, Carson, CA

Personnel: Kendrick Lamar (vocals), BJ the Chicago Kid (vocals), Punch (vocals), sample from "Tired of Fighting" by Menahan Street Band

Writer: Kendrick Lamar

Producer: King Blue

Label: Top Dawg Entertainment

Also by Kendrick Lamar: "Heaven and Hell" (2010), "Kush and Corinthians" (2011), "Sing about Me, I'm Dying of Thirst" (2012)

ROLL AWAY YOUR STONE

94 MUMFORD & SONS

2009

The vast difference between attitudes about Christianity and popular music in the middle of the twentieth century and the start of the twenty-first century could be illustrated by the career of Mumford & Sons. Two of the group met through a central London churchyard. Marcus Mumford, who sometimes played in a worship band, was the son of a high-profile evangelical pastor, and biblical themes suffused their work. They didn't conceal these themes, but neither did they foreground them.

Aware of the baggage that comes with specific faith labels, Mumford often goes out of his way to distance himself. In 2012, he told an interviewer, "I don't even call myself a Christian. Spirituality is the word we engage with more. We're fans of faith, not religion."[150] Five years later, at a leadership conference organized by Holy Trinity Brompton (a leading evangelical church in London) at London's Royal Albert Hall, he announced from the stage, "I really love Jesus, I always have and always will."[151]

When the band's songs were overtly spiritual, it was not to preach but rather to work out unresolved issues. Mumford was exhorting himself rather than the audience. "We're just writing songs that ask questions," he said. "Sometimes the best way to go about exploring a question, things we wouldn't necessarily talk about in conversation, is by writing a song. That's why it's quite hard . . . unpacking your songs. You write them in moments of privacy and . . . inadequacy. Inarticulation. When you can't really express how you're feeling, so you write it down with poetic license and vent as much as you want."[152]

"Roll Away Your Stone" is just such an exercise. As with his interviews, it isn't clear whether the song is about submission, rebellion, or a vacillation between the two positions. The words appear to be addressed to God and detail an attempt to rededicate his life. But this is an argument still taking place rather than one that had been resolved.

He likens opening up his life to God to the opening up of Jesus's tomb—the title referring to the gospel account of the resurrection: "And behold, there was a great earthquake; for an angel of the Lord descended from heaven, and came and rolled away the stone, and sat upon it" (Matthew 28:2 ASV). He expresses concern at "what I will discover inside."

He's been stuffing his soul with "darkness" and "things unreal," yet still fears that if he allows himself to be cleansed he'll be left with nothing. God assures him that this is "exactly how this grace thing works." He then invokes the story of the prodigal son to make the point that it's not the walk back home that makes the difference but the welcome of the father (Luke 15:11–32).

In the latter part of the song, he expresses his further doubts and informs God that he remains too fond of his desires to abandon them. He introduces a line spoken by Shakespeare's *Macbeth* (Act1, Scene 4) when he tries to avert his eyes from his own murderous ambition.

> Stars, hide your fires;
> Let not light see my black and deep desires:
> The eye wink at the hand, yet let that be
> Which the eye fears, when it is done, to see.

In saying, "I won't give them up to you this time around," he's letting God know, "This far, but no further." So following the initial determination to submit, he concludes by telling God, "You have neither reason nor rhyme / With which to take this soul that is so rightfully mine."

Of course, as Mumford once pointed out, "You put these thoughts down, but they are not Trip Advisor reports on the destination you've reached. It's more like a travel journal."[153] His spiritual formation, as he reminded *Rolling Stone* in 2013, remains a "work in progress."[154]

Song: "Roll Away Your Stone"

Artist: Mumford & Sons

Single: A-side: "Roll Away Your Stone" / B-side: "White Blank Page" (live)

Release: June 3, 2010

Album: *Sigh No More*

Album Release: October 2, 2009 (UK), February 16, 2010 (US)

Studio: Eastcote Studios, London

Personnel: Marcus Mumford (vocals, mandolin, guitar), Winston Marshall (vocals, banjo, guitar), Ben Lovett (vocals, keyboards, accordion), Ted Dwane (vocals, double bass, drums)

Writers: Marcus Mumford, Winston Marshall, Ben Lovett, Ted Dwane

Producer: Markus Dravs

Label: Universal / Island

Highest Chart Position: 141 (US)

Other Significant Recordings: Noah Guthrie (2014)

Also by Mumford & Sons: "Awake My Soul" (2009), "Sigh No More" (2009), "Below My Feet" (2012)

95

WHO AM I LIVING FOR?
KATY PERRY

2010

Katy Perry was born into a home where churchgoing was compulsory, secular rock was banned, and concerts by artists like Madonna and Marilyn Manson were picketed. Her parents, Keith and Mary, were hippie converts to Pentecostalism. She began by singing gospel, and at sixteen came to Nashville and recorded for a small company that subsequently went out of business. Her debut album, released under her birth name, Katy Hudson, although respectably reviewed in the Christian press, consequently sold only an estimated two hundred copies.

She was a feisty performer who wrote her own songs, wore pigtails, and connected effectively with a young female audience looking for role models who were apparently bold and daring but who would receive the parental seal of approval. Her lyrics gave no pat answers, and she was unafraid to expose her doubts and fears. "I write what I think needs to be written," she said during her first gospel tour in 2001. "I write what I deal with. Actually, I write what I want to say to people that I can't say through my mouth, I guess."[155]

It took another nine years of false starts (two aborted attempts with Island and Columbia) before she was signed by Capitol Records to make her big label debut, *One of the Boys*. By then she had left home and also the

295

religious precepts of her childhood. "God is very much still a part of my life," she told *Rolling Stone*. "But the way the details are told in the Bible— that's very fuzzy. . . . I still believe that Jesus is the Son of God, but I also believe in extraterrestrials, and that there are people who are sent from God to be messengers, and all sorts of crazy stuff."[156]

Most of her second album for Capitol, *Teenage Dream*, was free of the beliefs that had once been central to her existence, but "Who Am I Living For?" was an exception. In the midst of songs about drinking, partying, dancing, spending money, and having commitment-free sex, it not only references the Bible but revives past questions of purpose, integrity, devotion, and persecution.

Her Christian fans can read the song as a declaration of her determination to follow God, whatever the cost. Given the context on an album devoted to fleshly pleasures, however, it may have a more subversive intent. The answer to the question posed in the title could be "Katy Perry," and the battle she outlines is between authenticity and conformity. When she speaks of taking the "road less traveled" (a reference to Robert Frost's poem "The Road Not Taken"), she could mean the road of pop stardom rather than the straight and narrow, and the "cross" she had "to bear" could be Christian disapproval rather than persecution by unbelievers. Her reference is to the command of Jesus: "If anyone would come after me, let him deny himself and take up his cross and follow me. For whoever would save his life will lose it, but whoever loses his life for my sake will find it" (Matthew 16:24–25 ESV).

She speaks of being "called" and "chosen," but could mean the lure of show business and the election of fame rather than the "many are called, but few are chosen" that Jesus spoke of (Matthew 22:14 ESV). She pictures herself staring at the heavens (the glory of stardom or the abode of God?), and yet she could still hear "the flames calling out my name" (the flames of condemnation by the church or the furnace of hell?).

Christians hearing her sing of the "light that's inside of me" will imagine she refers to the presence of God ("The light of the body is the eye: if therefore thine eye be single, thy whole body shall be full of light" [Matthew 6:22]), but she may refer to aspirations that she felt had been quashed by her strict background. She claims it is growing into a bolt of lightning and "one spark will shock the world." Elsewhere on the album she employs light and fire as metaphors for yearnings that she's been afraid to encourage and explore.

Toward the end of the song she writes, "So I pray for favor like Esther," referring to the young Jewish woman raised in Persian captivity who, according to the Bible, was chosen by King Ahasuerus to be his queen: "And Esther obtained favour in the sight of all of them that looked upon her. . . . And the king loved Esther above all the women . . . so that he set the royal crown upon her head" (Esther 2:15–17).

Ahasuerus failed to realize she was Jewish, and she was able to use her position to relieve the mistreatment of Jews in Persia. It was an unusual Bible character for Perry to identify with. Did she choose her as an example of someone who worked on behalf of God from within enemy territory (like a Christian in the secular music industry), or simply because she was a woman of power? "Heavy is the head that wears the crown," she sings. "Don't let the greatness get you down."

She said the song is "probably one of the most introspective songs on the record . . . a song that is about my own personal convictions . . . thoughts that race through my mind every day concerning my upbringing and my future . . . what do I want written at the end of it all? Who am I? What do I want to achieve? Hopefully it's more than just all of this and so I guess that's kind of me putting my heart on my sleeve and singing for the world."[157]

Song: "Who Am I Living For?"

Artist: Katy Perry

Album: *Teenage Dream*

Release: August 24, 2010

Studio: Henson Recording Studios, Los Angeles, CA

Personnel: Katy Perry (vocals), Christopher "Tricky" Stewart (keyboards)

Writers: Katy Perry, Christopher Stewart, Brian Thomas, Lamont Neuble

Producers: Christopher Stewart, Kuk Harrell

Label: Capitol

Also by Katy Perry: "Faith Won't Fail" (2001), "By the Grace of God" (2013), "Bigger Than Me" (2017)

96

JUDAS
LADY GAGA

2011

L ike Madonna before her, Lady Gaga caused controversy by mingling the language of Christian devotion and spiritual surrender with expressions of rebellion and sexual abandon. The Catholic League responded to the video of "Judas" by referring to her as a "backslider" and accused her of "playing fast and loose with Catholic iconography."

Born in Manhattan, New York, brought up in a Catholic family, and educated at an all-girls Catholic school, Stefani Germanotta embraced the downtown New York arts and music scene but never totally left behind her foundational beliefs. In 2010, she told interviewer Larry King, "I am very religious. I was raised Catholic. I believe in Jesus. I believe in God."[158]

Yet her beliefs were often at odds with the official teachings of the Catholic church. In "Judas," she portrays herself as befriending the disciple best known for identifying Jesus in the Garden of Gethsemane so that the authorities could arrest and eventually execute him: "Satan entered into Judas who was called Iscariot" (Luke 22:3 ASV), and Jesus referred to him as "the son of perdition" (John 17:12 ASV). The Gospels don't portray him as someone who suffered a momentary lapse of judgment but as someone who knowingly schemed.

Lady Gaga doesn't celebrate him as an anti-Christian crusader but as a symbol of the dark side of our natures: "I believe that it's the darkness in your life that ultimately shines and illuminates the greater light that you have upon you," she explained. "So the song is about washing the feet of both good and evil and understanding and forgiving the demons from your past in order to move into the greatness of your future."[159]

The song pictures her ready to "wash his feet with my hair if he needs," thereby sourcing another story from the Gospels. The woman who wet the feet of Jesus with her tears "and wiped them with the hair of her head, and kissed his feet, and anointed them with the ointment" (Luke 7:38 ASV) was a "sinner" (Luke 7:37, 39) whose sins he forgave, saying, "Your faith has saved you; go in peace" (Luke 7:50 ESV). She was not befriending her "dark side" but opening herself to the light.

The song works on two levels. On one level it is about confronting past mistakes, in particular past choices of relationship. She confesses to having been drawn back to men who had mistreated her in the past. "'Judas' is about constantly walking towards the light in my life but always pushing on to the light while peering towards the Devil in the back," she told Kevin Simmons of the *Skorpion Show*. "So, I sing about what a holy fool I am in that although moments of my life are so cruel and relationships can be so cruel I'm still in love with Judas. I still go back, and back again."[160]

On another level, Lady Gaga's logic is that if we're to love our enemies—as Jesus loved his enemies—we first need to love the enemy within. In her words, "The song is about honoring your darkness in order to bring yourself into the light."[161]

Song: "Judas"
Artist: Lady Gaga
Single Release: "Judas" (CD single or digital download)
Release: April 15, 2011
Album: *Born This Way*
Album Release: May 23, 2011
Studio: Gang Studios, Paris

Personnel: Lady Gaga (lead vocal), RedOne (programming, backing vocals, vocal arrangements, instrumentation)

Writer: Stefani Germanotta (Lady Gaga)

Producer: Lady Gaga, RedOne

Label: Interscope Records

Highest Chart Position: 4 (US), 8 (UK)

Other Significant Recordings: Vitamin String Quartet (2011)

Also by Lady Gaga: "Born This Way" (2011), "Hair" (2011), "Sinner's Prayer" (2016)

97

DO UNTO OTHERS
BILLY BRAGG

. . . .

2013

T he year 1611 saw the first publication of a translation of the Bible commissioned by King James I of England. It became known as the King James Version (KJV) or Authorized Version of the Bible. It is acknowledged as being one of the greatest influences on subsequent English language literature, from its memorable images and its cadences to its vocabulary and finely wrought prose.

Its quartercentenary was celebrated in 2011 with events, academic books, TV programs, radio series, and services of thanksgiving. In London, Josie Rourke, artistic director of the Bush Theatre, designed a long show titled *Sixty-Six Books*, for which she gave one book of the Bible to sixty-six writers and asked them to create a work that engaged with the text. Writers ranged from then-Archbishop of Canterbury Rowan Williams to controversial American playwright Neil LaBute and British poet laureate Carol Ann Duffy.

The British singer-songwriter Billy Bragg, best known for his acoustic punk/folk/protest music and his allegiance to a range of left-wing causes from Red Wedge in the 1980s (a campaign to get young people to become politically active and hopefully vote for Labour) to the Occupy Movement in 2011, was sent the Gospel of Luke.

He found support for his interest in social justice and the fate of the poor in some of the sayings of Jesus. Ironically, in spite of the fact that he was celebrating the publication of the KJV, he seems to have used the New International Version for the chorus (and title) of his song. The saying, "And as ye would that men should do to you, do ye also to them likewise" (Luke 6:31), is "Do to others as you would have them do to you" in the NIV, the closest to Bragg's translation of "Do unto others as you would have them do to you."

The context is Jesus addressing his twelve disciples. Bragg's eye may have been caught by the preceding verses, in which the poor, hungry, rejected, and suffering were offered hope, and the rich and respected were warned of the dangers inherent in wealth, comfort, and popularity.

> Looking at his disciples, he said: "Blessed are you who are poor, for yours is the kingdom of God. Blessed are you who hunger now, for you will be satisfied. Blessed are you who weep now, for you will laugh. Blessed are you when people hate you, when they exclude you and insult you and reject your name as evil, because of the Son of Man. Rejoice in that day and leap for joy, because great is your reward in heaven. For that is how their ancestors treated the prophets. But woe to you who are rich, for you have already received your comfort. Woe to you who are well fed now, for you will go hungry. Woe to you who laugh now, for you will mourn and weep. Woe to you when everyone speaks well of you, for that is how their ancestors treated the false prophets." (Luke 6:20–26 NIV)

Then Jesus preached love, tolerance, and forgiveness.

> "But to you who are listening I say: Love your enemies, do good to those who hate you, bless those who curse you, pray for those who mistreat you. If someone slaps you on one cheek, turn to them the other also. If someone takes your coat, do not withhold your shirt from them. Give to everyone who asks you, and if anyone takes what belongs to you, do not

demand it back. Do to others as you would have them do to you." (vv. 27–31 NIV)

Bragg begins the song by referring to the giving of the Ten Commandments by Moses, an event recounted in Exodus 19–20, and then adds, "But the greatest commandment of all / Is in the book of Luke as I recall / Do unto others as you would have them do to you."

He cheats slightly because discussion of the "greatest commandment" comes from Mark and Matthew, not Luke, and Jesus's answer was not "Do unto others as you would have them do to you" but the more thorough, "Thou shalt love the Lord thy God with all thy heart, and with all thy soul, and with all thy mind. This is the first and greatest commandment. And the second is like unto it, Thou shalt love thy neighbour as thyself. On these two commandments hang all the law and the prophets" (Matthew 22:37–40).

Bragg then chides those who might dismiss any advice from the Bible on the grounds that "the story of Adam and Eve" clashes with science. He is referring to the story of creation and fall presented in the first three chapters of Genesis. He doesn't get into a science versus religion debate but suggests, "In the cold light of day / Peaceful words still point the way."

Before he concludes, there are two further lines taken from the Bible. "So just lift up your eyes," he sings. "Don't pass by on the other side." There is one reference to lifting up one's eyes in Luke: "And when these things begin to come to pass, then look up, and lift up your heads; for your redemption draweth nigh" (21:28), but it's more likely that Bragg was remembering the popular psalm that starts, "I will lift up mine eyes unto the hills, from whence cometh my help. My help cometh from the LORD, which made heaven and earth" (Psalm 121:1–2).

The advice not to "pass by on the other side" comes from the parable of the good Samaritan, a story Jesus told to answer the question, "Who is my neighbour?" (Luke 10:29). In the parable, a man traveling from Jerusalem to Jericho was attacked, robbed, and stripped of his clothes by bandits who preyed on travelers during the long, lonely stretches on the road.

And by chance there came down a certain priest that way: and when he saw him, he passed by on the other side. And likewise a Levite, when he was at the place, came and looked on him, and passed by on the other side. But a certain Samaritan, as he journeyed, came where he was: and when he saw him, he had compassion on him, and went to him, and bound up his wounds, pouring in oil and wine, and set him on his own beast, and brought him to an inn, and took care of him. (Luke 10:31–34)

It was the least likely of the passersby who performed in a neighborly way. The priest and the Levite, who would have known by heart the laws about love, were too intent on their religious duties to get involved with a dying man. They were put to shame by their cultural and theological foe, the Samaritan.

Introducing the song in Milwaukee in 2013, Bragg said, "I can't help but notice that those people volunteering down at the food bank tend to be more inspired by their faith than they are by Karl Marx, and I have to respect that. Personally I'm not comfortable with the fundamentalist atheism of the likes of Richard Dawkins with his idea that all people of faith are stupid. . . . That's not something that sits very well with me."[162]

Song: "Do Unto Others"

Artist: Billy Bragg

Release: March 18, 2013 (UK), March 19, 2013 (US)

Album: *Tooth & Nail*

Studio: The Garfield House Studio, South Pasadena, CA

Personnel: Billy Bragg (acoustic guitar, vocals), Greg Leisz (steel pedal guitar), David Piltch (bass), Patrick Warren (keyboards), Jay Bellerose (drums)

Writer: Billy Bragg

Producer: Joe Henry

Record Label: Cooking Vinyl

Also by Billy Bragg: "Blake's Jerusalem" (1990), "King James Version" (1996), "I Ain't Got No Home" (2013)

98

DEVIL PRAY

MADONNA

2014

H aving been raised as a Catholic, Madonna has used the faith of her early years as a foil for her art. Sometimes she has attacked it for placing restraints on her appetites; at other times she has used the language, symbols, and theological framework as tools for exploration.

"Catholicism feels like my alma mater," she told *Billboard* in 2015. "It's the school I used to go to, and I can go back any time I want and take whatever I want from it because I suffered all the oppression and all the abuse—and also enjoyed all the pomp and circumstance, the drama and the confusion and the hypocrisy and the craziness. I feel like I can say whatever I want and do whatever I want."[163]

In "Devil Pray," she addresses the issue of whether drugs are a viable means of achieving spiritual transcendence. Is there a fast-track chemical way to God that avoids the need for repentance, prayer, ritual, and discipline? "I'm saying you can do all of these things [drugs] to connect to a higher level, but ultimately you're going to be lost," she explained to *Rolling Stone*. "People who are getting high are instinctively also trying to connect to a higher level of consciousness, but are doing it in a way that will not sustain them."[164]

She framed the discussion in Christian terms from the opening line of "Take my sins and wash them away" (reminiscent of "Wash me thoroughly from mine iniquity, and cleanse me from my sin" [Psalm 51:2]) to the closing lines of "the devil's here to fool ya" (surely drawn from the observation of Jesus: "When he speaketh a lie, he speaketh of his own: for he is a liar, and the father of it" [John 8:44]).

It is a confessional prayer. She admits to drowning, going astray, and being "stranded here in the dark," and calls out to God to "save my soul." The implication is that although drugs can supply a variety of wild experiences that some describe as "spiritual," they don't deal with sin or supply something or someone to have faith in. As she explained to magician David Blaine, "A lot of people drop acid or do drugs, because they want to get closer to God. But there's going to be a short circuit, and that's the illusion of drugs, because they give you the illusion of getting closer to God, but ultimately they kill you. They destroy you. I mean, I tried everything once, but as soon as I was high, I spent my time drinking tons of water to get it out of my system."[165]

Song: "Devil Pray"

Artist: Madonna

Single: "Devil Pray" (digital download)

Release: December 2014

Album: *Rebel Heart*

Album Release: March 6, 2015

Studio: Henson Recording Studios, Hollywood, CA

Personnel: Madonna (vocals), Avicii (keyboards, programming), Carl Falk (keyboards, guitar, programming)

Writers: Madonna, Ash Pournouri, Carl Falk, Dacoury Natche, Michael Tucker, Rami Yacoub, Savan Kotecha, Tim Bergling

Producers: Madonna, Avicii, DJ Dahi, Michael Diamonds

Label: Interscope

Also by Madonna: "Like a Prayer" (1989), "Girl Gone Wild" (2012), "Holy Water" (2015)

HOW GREAT

CHANCE THE RAPPER

2016

99

C hance the Rapper, born Chancelor Johnathan Bennett, is a rapper/
singer/producer from Chicago whose third collection, *Coloring Book*,
was the first streaming-only album to win a Grammy (Best Rap
Album, 2017).[166]

Just before recording *Coloring Book*, Chance became a Christian—and
his new material reflected the change. Mentored by rapper Kanye West and
gospel artist Kirk Franklin, he often writes directly about Jesus and uses
choirs. On January 31, 2016, he announced on Twitter, "Today's the last
day of my old life. . . . Headed to church for help. All things are possible
thru Christ who strengthens me,"[167] the last line being a slight paraphrase
of "I can do all things through Christ who strengthens me" (Philippians
4:13 NKJV).

This made him one of a new breed of rapper who was at the same
time cutting edge, credible, Christian, and commercially and critically successful. On a track that didn't make the final cut—"Grown Ass Kid"—he
had the lines, "Everybody can finally say it out loud / My favorite rapper—a
Christian rapper," causing the *Chicago Tribune* to comment, "It may not have
seemed like a big deal but there it was, out in the open, possibly the most

overt declaration of Christian faith from a secular rapper since Kanye West's seismic single 'Jesus Walks.'"[168]

"How Great" launches itself with a rendering of the song "How Great Is Our God" that was cowritten and recorded by Contemporary Christian Music artist Chris Tomlin in 2004, and that had rapidly become one of the most performed worship songs in America. Christian Copyright Licensing International reported in 2017 it was still the third most used song in American churches.[169] Chance the Rapper heard it at a christening and at two family funerals.

On "How Great," Nicole Steen performs part of the song solo and is then joined by a twelve-strong choir. The words "How great is our God" are taken from "Great is the LORD" and "Worthy of all praise" is from the next statement in the verse: "highly to be praised" (Psalm 145:3 NASB). "Name above all names" comes from Paul's words about the resurrected and ascended Jesus: "For this reason also, God highly exalted Him, and bestowed on Him the name which is above every name" (Philippians 2:9 NASB).

A long rap follows that wanders, because of its free-association style of composition, but is packed with biblical references. Continuing in the spirit of the worship song, it uses the words "magnify" and "exalt," probably suggested by, "O magnify the LORD with me, and let us exalt his name together" (Psalm 34:3); "glorify," probably from the words of Jesus, "Father, glorify thy name" (John 12:28); "lift it on high," which is reminiscent of a saying of Jesus: "As Moses lifted up the serpent in the wilderness, even so must the Son of man be lifted up: that whosoever believeth in him should not perish, but have eternal life" (John 3:14–15); and "let my light shine" is surely a reference to, "Let your light so shine before men, that they may see your good works, and glorify your Father which is in heaven" (Matthew 5:16).

He mentions that he "used to hide from God," an allusion to the behavior of Adam and Eve when they "hid themselves from the presence of the LORD God amongst the trees of the garden" (Genesis 3:8); compares himself to Noah building the ark (Genesis 6–9); and his Muslim rap partner Jay Electronica ends by dwelling on the visions of the book of Revelation citing the New Jerusalem (mentioned in Revelation 21:2), the beast (Revelation 13:1), false messiahs (the beast's representative in Revelation 13:12–13), Babylon (Revelation 18:2), and "the angel in Revelations with a foot on water and a foot on land" that comes from Revelation 10:1–2: "I saw another mighty angel come down from heaven . . . and he set his right foot upon the sea, and his left foot on the earth."

"I never set out to make anything that could pretend to be new gospel, or pretend to be THE gospel," Chance told BBC Radio 1 presenter Zane Lowe at the time of the album's release. "It's music for me as a Christian man. . . . I have imperfections but there's a declaration that could be made out of, you know, going through all . . . that I went through in the past two years."[170]

Song: "How Great"

Artist: Chance the Rapper

Album: *Coloring Book*

Release: May 13, 2016

Studio: Chicago Recording Company, Chicago, IL; Conway Recording Studios, Hollywood, CA

Personnel: Chance the Rapper (lead vocals), Jay Electronica (lead vocals), Nicole Steen (lead vocals), Chicago Children's Choir, Francis Starlite (harmonizer)

Writers: Chancellor Bennett (Chance the Rapper), Timothy Thedford, Nate Fox, Carter Lang, Ed Cash, Christopher Tomlin, Jesse Reeves, Peter Wilkins

Producer: The Social Experiment

Label: Self-released

Highest Chart Position: (Album) 8 (US)

Other Significant Recordings: (As "How Great Is Our God") Chris Tomlin (2004), Hillsong Church UK (2006), Don Moen (2007)

Also by Chance the Rapper: "Blessings" (2016), "Angels" (2016), "Joy" (2016)

BLINDED BY YOUR GRACE, PT. 2

100

STORMZY, FEATURING MNEK

2017

I t's an arresting title because the best-known song about grace is about the power of grace to restore sight to the blind: "I was blind but now I see" (John 9:25 NIV). This song reverses the process. In the case of Saul of Tarsus, his experience of God's grace initially robbed him of sight. The brightness of the light he saw on the road to Damascus left him unable to see: "And they led him by the hand, and brought him into Damascus. And he was three days without sight, and did neither eat nor drink" (Acts 9:8–9 ASV). For UK grime artist Stormzy, grace can be as unsettling as it can be reassuring.

Of Ghanaian parentage but born and raised in South London, Stormzy (birth name Michael Owuo) experienced hard times as a child and was exposed to urban gang culture. "Blinded by Your Grace, Pt. 2" was partly an amazed response at his elevation to star status. He had gained the respect, fulfilment, and financial reward that gang members seek by other means. He saw it as part of God's plan.

He refers to himself as "God's son," and says that this is "not by blood and it's not by birth," all of which comes from the words of the Gospel of John: "But as many as received him [Jesus], to them gave he the right to become children of God, even to them that believe on his name: who were born, not of blood, nor of the will of the flesh, nor of the will of man, but of God" (John 1:12–13 ASV).

On *Gang Signs & Prayer*, "Blinded by Your Grace, Pt. 2" sits among a collection of songs that are decidedly earthy. The cover parodies Leonardo da Vinci's painting *The Last Supper*, with Stormzy standing as Jesus while he is flanked by "disciples" wearing the full-face black balaclavas often associated with bank robbers and terrorists. The lyrics on the album use curse words liberally, and there are frequent mentions of drugs and violence where you can't be sure if Stormzy is a participant or a nonjudgmental observer.

Some reviewers saw these incongruities as evidence of a multidimensional individual. Others saw it as inconsistent or even hypocritical. Yolisa Mkele, writing for the *Times of South Africa*, noted that "a dark song about people pretending to be real gangsters" was followed by a song "which could easily be played in the youth chapter of a church." Mkele stated that "the two don't gel very well."[171]

Asked about "Blinded by Grace, Pt. 2" by BBC Radio 1, Stormzy explained, "It's a song that means so much to me both in terms of my faith and what God means to me but also for my artistry as well. . . . It's a little bit of an anthem in the weirdest way. It's a little soulful, a little gospel. I've played it at festivals and everyone's hands are in the air like [they were] drunk and I don't know if it goes but it's working and it's beautiful and it's amazing. Everyone kinda comes together for it."[172]

Song: "Blinded by Your Grace, Pt. 2"

Artist: Stormzy, featuring MNEK

Single: "Blinded by Your Grace, Pt. 2" (digital download)

Single Release: October 27, 2017

Album: *Gang Signs & Prayer*

Album Release: February 24, 2017

Studio: Matrix Studio Complex (My Audio Tonic Productions), London

Personnel: Stormzy (vocals), MNEK (vocals), Adam Wakeman (Hammond organ), Dion Wardle (piano, keyboards), Ben Epstein (bass guitar), Fraser T. Smith (guitar, programming), Dexter Hercules (drums), Rasul A-Salaam (choir arranger)

Writers: Stormzy, Fraser T. Smith, MNEK

Producer: Fraser T. Smith

Label: Merky Records

Highest Chart Position: 7 (UK)

Also by Stormzy: "100 Bags" (2017), "21 Gun Salute" (2017), "Lay Me Bare" (2017)

ACKNOWLEDGMENTS

....

T hanks to curator Amy Van Dyke, who when inviting me to contribute a foreword to the catalogue of an exhibit on John Newton and his song "Amazing Grace," introduced me to Museum of the Bible.

Through Amy I met the museum's then head of research, editorial, and publications, Stacey L. Douglas, whose idea this book was. It was only later that I learned that he'd always imagined me being attached to the project, so I'm grateful to him for both the concept and for personally rooting for me. It was a great pleasure to work with someone who loves both the Bible and music, and I valued his observations, recommendations, and corrections. He not only knows his KJV from his RSV, but his ASCAP from his BMI.

Knitting the project together by liaising between me, Museum of the Bible, and Worthy Publishing was writer, consultant, and motivational speaker Wayne Hastings, who was always reliable, speedy, and straight to the point. He made things happen. Like Stacey, he too was a lover of Scripture and music.

My hands-on editor at Worthy was Kyle Olund, who delighted me by letting me know that the book covered a lot of the songs that were his personal favorites and had been embdedded in his growing-up experience.

One of the great things about working on this book has been the personal enthusiasm of those involved who would offer me their professional advice but then follow up with a PS that indicated their emotional involvement with the subject matter.

In ending, I need to acknowledge the personal encounters in almost fifty years of reporting on music that have enriched my understanding of the subject of this book. Not only have I listened to the songs but have been privileged to sit with many of the creators and talk to them about their creative processes, the ideas behind their lyrics, and the nature of their spiritual beliefs.

My thanks then to: Ray Charles, Johnny Cash, Thomas A. Dorsey, Jerry Lee Lewis, "Cowboy" Jack Clement, Joan Baez, Pete Seeger, Gerry Marsden, Lamont Dozier, Eddie Holland, Chuck Berry, Roger McGuinn, David Crosby, John Lennon, Paul McCartney, Rick Danko, Robin Williamson, Mike Heron, Van Morrison, Mick Jagger, Keith Richards, Edwin Hawkins, Pete Townshend, Tim Rice, Larry Norman, Judy Collins, Noel Paul Stookey, Ozzy Osbourne, Geezer Butler, Randy Newman, Roger Waters, David Gilmour, Bernie Leadon, Andrae Crouch, Eric Clapton, David Bowie, Bruce Springsteen, T Bone Burnett, David Byrne, Brian Eno, Bono, The Edge, Gordon Gano, Leonard Cohen, Nick Cave, Alice Cooper, Moby, Cliff Richard, and Sting.

ABOUT THE AUTHOR

S teve Turner's first feature story about music was published in the *Beatles Monthly* in 1969. Since then he has written extensively about music, popular culture, travel, and religion in a variety of publications from *Rolling Stone* and *New Musical Express* to *The Times* (London), *Mail On Sunday*, and *Christianity Today*. He is the author of biographies of musicians including Johnny Cash, Marvin Gaye, the Beatles, and Van Morrison, several books of poetry, as well as historical studies of gospel music, the song "Amazing Grace," and the musicians who sailed on the *Titanic*. *People* magazine said that he has "a hipster's eye and a parishioner's faith." He lives in London with his wife, Mo, and has an adult son and daughter.

SCRIPTURE INDEX

· · · · · · · · · · · · · · · · · · · ·

22. **"Turn! Turn! Turn! (To Everything There Is a Season)" by the Byrds** – 1 Kings 4:29–34; Ecclesiastes 1:1–2; 3:1–8

23. **"Girl" by the Beatles** – Genesis 3:16–19

24. **"Blessed" by Simon & Garfunkel** – Psalm 22:1; 33:12; Matthew 5:5; 27:46; Mark 11:10; Revelation 5:12

25. **"God Only Knows" by the Beach Boys** – Psalm 139:1–4; Matthew 24:36

26. **"Within You Without You" by the Beatles** – Matthew 16:24–26; Mark 8:34–37; Luke 9:23–25; 17:20–21

27. **"I Shall Be Released" by the Band** – Matthew 24:27; Luke 21:28

28. **"I Am a Pilgrim" by the Byrds** – 1 Peter 2:11; Matthew 9:20–21; 14:36; 2 Corinthians 5:1, 6; Hebrews 11:13; Revelation 21:2

29. **"All Along the Watchtower" by the Jimi Hendrix Experience** – Isaiah 21:2–9; Jeremiah 5:31; Matthew 24:42–51; 1 Thessalonians 5:2; 1 Peter 5:8

30. **"Job's Tears" by the Incredible String Band** – Matthew 27:35, 48; Mark 16:6; John 19:34; Acts 2:24; 1 Corinthians 13:12; Revelation 3:5; 4:10–11; 21:21

31. **"Astral Weeks" by Van Morrison** – John 3:3–6

32. **"Sympathy for the Devil" by the Rolling Stones** – Isaiah 5:20; 14:12–15; Matthew 26:39; 27:24, 46; 2 Corinthians 11:14; 1 Peter 5:8

33. **"Prodigal Son" by the Rolling Stones** – Luke 15:20–24

34. **"Bad Moon Rising" by Creedence Clearwater Revival** – Joel 2:30–31; Matthew 24:6–7, 29; Luke 17:24; Revelation 6:12

35. **"Oh Happy Day" by the Edwin Hawkins Singers** – 2 Chronicles 15:15; Psalm 51:2; Matthew 26:40–41; Philippians 4:4; 1 John 1:7

36. **"Christmas" by the Who** – Mark 7:32–35; Romans 10:13–14

37. **"Superstar" by Murray Head** – Matthew 26:20–25, 56; Luke 22:3

38. **"I Wish We'd All Been Ready" by Larry Norman** – Matthew 24:6–11, 40–44

39. **"Bridge over Troubled Water" by Simon & Garfunkel** – Psalm 4:8; 23:2; Isaiah 43:2; 66:12–13; Matthew 11:28; John 15:13; Revelation 21:4

40. **"What Is Truth" by Johnny Cash** – John 18:37–38

41. **"Let It Be" by the Beatles** – Psalm 49:3; Luke 1:35, 38; Revelation 21:4

42. **"Woodstock" by Joni Mitchell** – Isaiah 2:4

43. **"Amazing Grace" by Judy Collins** – Luke 15:24; John 9:25; Romans 7:24; 1 Chronicles 17:16

44. **"Wholy Holy" by Marvin Gaye** – Isaiah 6:3–4; John 14:1; Revelation 4:8

45. **"Wedding Song (There Is Love)" by Noel Paul Stookey** – Genesis 2:24; Matthew 19:4–6; 18:20

46. **"After Forever" by Black Sabbath** – Romans 14:11–12

47. **"God's Song (That's Why I Love Mankind)" by Randy Newman** – Genesis 4:2–16, 25; 19:24; 2 Samuel 12:19–20; Luke 3:38

48. **"Go Like Elijah" by Chi Coltrane** – 2 Kings 2:8–11

49. **"Eclipse" by Pink Floyd** – Ecclesiastes 1:14; 3:1, 8; Ephesians 5:15–20

50. **"Desperado" by the Eagles** – Genesis 9:8–17; Ecclesiastes 1:8; 4:8–9; 12:1, 13; Luke 15:13, 17

51. **"Jesus Is the Answer" by Andraé Crouch and the Disciples** – Matthew 11:28; John 14:6, 13, 27; Philippians 2:9; 1 Thessalonians 5:24

52. **"Give Me Strength" by Eric Clapton** – Psalm 86:1–7, 15–17

53. **"Word on a Wing" by David Bowie** – Exodus 2:22; Deuteronomy 10:19

54. **"Anarchy in the U.K." by the Sex Pistols** – Matthew 25:32–33; Mark 16:19; Acts 7:55–56; Romans 8:34; Colossians 3:1

55. **"Exodus" by Bob Marley and the Wailers** – Genesis 1:29; 2 Kings 24–25; Psalm 9:9; 18:8; Isaiah 43:25; 61:1; Luke 4:21; Revelation 22:2; 7:9–17

56. **"Waiting for the End of the World" by Elvis Costello** – Matthew 13:39–42

57. **"Adam Raised a Cain" by Bruce Springsteen** – Genesis 4:12, 16; Numbers 14:18; Romans 5:12

58. **"Privilege (Set Me Free)" by the Patti Smith Group** – Psalm 23:1–4; Luke 1:38; 2 Timothy 4:7

59. **"Rivers of Babylon" by Boney M.** – Psalm 19:14; 137:1, 3–4

60. **"Precious Angel" by Bob Dylan** – Genesis 3:1; Matthew 7:26; John 8:44; 2 Corinthians 4:4; Ephesians 6:12; 1 Thessalonians 5:3; 1 John 1:7; Revelation 9:6

61. **"Power of Love" by T Bone Burnett** – Luke 19:8; John 11:43–44; Philippians 2:9

62. **"The Jezebel Spirit" by David Byrne and Brian Eno** – Matthew 18:18; John 14:14; Revelation 2:20

63. **"Dweller by a Dark Stream" by Bruce Cockburn** – John 8:34–36; 19:5; 1 Corinthians 15:26; Hebrews 7:27; Revelation 1:1, 10; 21:1–5

64. **"Every Grain of Sand" by Bob Dylan** – Genesis 22:17; Psalm 77:19; Jeremiah 17:9; Matthew 11:25; Luke 12:6–7; 1 Corinthians 13:7

65. **"The Number of the Beast" by Iron Maiden** – Revelation 12:12; 13:18

66. **"Yah Mo Be There" by James Ingram and Michael McDonald** – Psalm 50:15; Matthew 24:12; John 8:12; Romans 10:13

67. **"40" by U2** – 1 Samuel 13:14; Psalm 6:3; 40:1–3; Acts 13:22; Ephesians 4:22–24; Philippians 2:3

68. **"Jesus Walking on the Water" by Violent Femmes** – Matthew 14:22–34; Mark 6:45–53; John 6:16–21

69. **"Hallelujah" by Leonard Cohen** – Exodus 20:7; Judges 16; 1 Samuel 16:22–23; 2 Samuel 11; Psalm 51; Revelation 19

70. **"Pie Jesu" by Sarah Brightman and Paul Miles-Kingston** – Matthew 11:28; John 1:29; 3:16

71. **"The Cross" by Prince** – Matthew 24:3; Mark 13:35–37; Luke 9:23; Romans 5:8; 1 Corinthians 2:2; Revelation 7:16–17

72. **"I Still Haven't Found What I'm Looking For" by U2** – Psalm 107:14; Proverbs 5:3; 6:27; Matthew 6:10; Luke 11:2; Acts 12:7; Romans 7:21–25; 1 Corinthians 13:1; Hebrews 12:1–2

73. **"The Mercy Seat" by Nick Cave and the Bad Seeds** – Exodus 25:10–22; Leviticus 16; Deuteronomy 19:21; Matthew 5:38–39

74. **"The End of the Innocence" by Don Henley** – Psalm 51:2; Isaiah 2:4; Acts 22:16

75. **"Will You Be There" by Michael Jackson** – Isaiah 46:4; Luke 13:34; Revelation 7:4–8; 14:1–5

76. **"Tears in Heaven" by Eric Clapton** – Revelation 21:4

77. **"Cleansed by Fire" by Alice Cooper** – Isaiah 14:12–15; Ezekiel 28:17–19; Matthew 4:8–11

78. **"Earth Song" by Michael Jackson** – Genesis 1:28; Isaiah 9:6; Mark 8:36; John 3:16; 14:27; Romans 8:20–22

79. **"New Test Leper" by R.E.M.** – Leviticus 13:45–46; Isaiah 53:6; Matthew 7:1

80. **"Joy" by Whitney Houston** – Luke 2:10

81. **"Forgive Them Father" by Lauryn Hill** – Matthew 5:39; 6:9–13; 7:15; Luke 11:2–4; 23:34; John 3:30

82. **"Fire in the Hole" by Van Halen** – James 3:3–6

83. **"Run On" by Moby** – Galatians 6:7; Ephesians 5:11

84. **"The Millennium Prayer" by Cliff Richard** – Matthew 6:9–13

85. **"The Man Comes Around" by Johnny Cash** – Matthew 25:1–13; Luke 13:34; Revelation 1:8; 3:5; 4:10; 21:6; 22:13

86. **"Sacred Love" by Sting** – Genesis 1:2; Joel 2:10; John 1:14; 1 Corinthians 13:13; Revelation 7:11

87. **"All the Trees of the Field Will Clap Their Hands" by Sufjan Stevens** – Isaiah 55:12

88. **"Jesus Walks" by Kanye West** – Psalm 23:4; 121:2–3; Ephesians 6:16; Colossians 2:6; 1 Peter 2:21; 5:8; 1 John 2:6

89. **"Jesus Was an Only Son" by Bruce Springsteen** – Matthew 13:55; 26:36–39; Mark 14:32; Luke 23:33; John 3:16; 19:25–27

90. **"Jerusalem (Out of Darkness Comes Light) " by Matisyahu** – Psalm 137:5–6

91. **"Why Do I Keep Counting?" by the Killers** – Job 14:5; Matthew 6:27; Luke 12:7

92. **"Viva La Vida" by Coldplay** – Genesis 19:26; Zechariah 14:20–21; Matthew 4:8–9; 7:26–27; 16:19; John 12:31; 2 Corinthians 4:4; Ephesians 2:2

93. **"Faith" by Kendrick Lamar** – Matthew 17:20

94. **"Roll Away Your Stone" by Mumford & Sons** – Matthew 28:2; Luke 15:11–32

95. **"Who Am I Living For?" by Katy Perry** – Esther 2:15–17; Matthew 6:22; 16:24–25; 22:14

96. **"Judas" by Lady Gaga** – Luke 7:37–39, 50; 22:3; John 17:12

97. **"Do Unto Others" by Billy Bragg** – Psalm 121:1–2; Matthew 10:31–34; 22:37–40; Luke 6:20–31; 21:28

98. **"Devil Pray" by Madonna** – Psalm 51:2; John 8:44

99. **"How Great" by Chance the Rapper** – Genesis 3:8; 6–9; Psalm 34:3; 145:3; Matthew 5:16; John 3:14–15; 12:28; Philippians 2:9; 4:13; Revelation 10:1–2; 13:1, 12–13; 18:2; 21:2

100. **"Blinded by Your Grace, Pt. 2" by Stormzy, Featuring MNEK** – John 1:12–13; 9:25; Acts 9:8–9

NOTES

·······················

1   Details of this project and its recordings may be found online at https://folkways.si.edu/
    anthology-of-american-folk-music/african-american-music-blues-old-time/music/album/
    smithsonian, https://www.discogs.com/Harry-Smith-Anthology-Of-American-Folk-Music/
    master/568903.
2   See Tom Piazza, "A Folk Album That Awakened a Generation," *New York Times*, August 24,
    1997, accessed June 29, 2018, https://nyti.ms/2KBvFEg, and details of the "Social Music"
    tracks online at https://www.discogs.com/Harry-Smith-Anthology-Of-American-Folk-Music
    -Volume-Two-Social-Music/release/2848587.
3   Jann Wenner, "Bono: The Rolling Stone Interview," *Rolling Stone*, November 3, 2005,
    accessed March 21, 2018, https://www.rollingstone.com/music/news/bono-the-rolling
    -stone-interview-20051103.
4   Ibid.
5   George Gallup Jr. and Jim Castelli, *The People's Religion: American Faith in the 90's* (New York:
    Macmillan Publishing Company, 1989), 60.
6   George Barna, *The Second Coming of the Church* (Nashville, TN: Word, 1998), 21–22.
7   George Steiner, "The Good Books," *New Yorker*, January 11, 1988, 94.
8   Rev. Stephen Edington, *Bring Your Own God: The Spirituality of Woody Guthrie* (Bloomington,
    IN: Trafford Publishing, 2012), 31.
9   Robert Santelli, *This Land Is Your Land* (Philadelphia, PA: Running Press, 2012), 85.
10 Jim Longhi, *Woody, Cisco, and Me* (Champaign, IL: University of Illinois Press, 1997), 63.
11 *Billboard*, March 3, 1945, 98.
12 Ron Briley, "Woody Guthrie and the Christian Left," *Journal of Texas Music History* v. 7, no. 1,
    Texas State University (January 2007): 8–21.
13 Joe Klein, *Woody Guthrie: A Life* (New York: Alfred A. Knopf Inc., 1980), 407.
14 Ace Collins, *Untold Gold: The Stories Behind Elvis's #1 Hits* (Chicago: Chicago Review Press,
    2005), 55–56.
15 Tony Heilbut, *The Gospel Sound: Good News and Bad Times* (New York: Anchor Books, 1975),
    35.
16 Johnny Cash, *Man in Black* (Grand Rapids, MI: Zondervan, 1976), 78.
17 Robert Hilburn, *Johnny Cash: The Life* (London: Weidenfeld & Nicholson, 2013), 104.
18 Robert Palmer, "The Devil and Jerry Lee Lewis," *Rolling Stone,* December 13, 1979.
19 Greil Marcus, *Mystery Train: Images of America in Rock 'n' Roll Music* (New York: E. P.
    Dutton & Co., 1976), 261–64. The audio can also be heard at https://www.youtube.com/
    watch?v=fto2NZsPJ7E.
20 Robert Palmer, "The Devil and Jerry Lee Lewis."
21 Terry Teachout, *Duke: A Life of Ellington* (New York: Gotham Books, Penguin Group, 2013), 328.
22 Flip Schulke, ed., *Martin Luther King, Jr.: A Documentary . . . Montgomery to Memphis* (New
    York: W. W. Norton & Company Inc., 1976), 222–24.
23 Tony Heilbut, *The Gospel Sound: Good News and Bad Times.*
24 Interview filmed January 22, 1986, available at www.youtube.com/watch?v=rss9XMrdRaA.
25 Interview with Mark Myers by Mike Stoller, May 31, 2012, www.jazzwax.com/2012/05/.
26 http://www.hrc.utexas.edu/multimedia/video/2008/wallace/hammerstein_oscar_t.html.

27 "California: Is It Still America's Promised Land?," *Time*, November 18, 1991.

28 *Chuck Berry: The Autobiography* (London: Faber & Faber Ltd. 1988), 2.

29 Author interview with Lamont Dozier, London, December 7, 1983.

30 Donnie Simpson interviews Curtis Mayfield for "Standing the Tests of Time," BET, June 1995, www.youtube.com/watch?v=d6FsJWHWd-s.

31 Interview with biographer Alec Wilkinson, March 2009, http://www.openculture .com/2009/04/pete_seeger_on_turn_turn_turn.html.

32 Jeffrey Pepper Rodgers, "Pete Seeger: How Can I Keep from Singing?" *Acoustic Guitar*, vol. 13, no. 1 (July 2002).

33 Jann S. Wenner, "Lennon Remembers—Part Two," *Rolling Stone* no. 74, February 4, 1971.

34 Francis Wyndham, "Close-Up: Paul McCartney as Songwriter," *London Life*, December 4–10, 1965, 26.

35 Theodor Reik, *Masochism in Modern Man*, trans. Margaret H. Beigel and Gertrud M. Kurth (New York: Grove Press, 1941), 341–42.

36 Ibid.

37 From an interview with British music journalist Karl Dallas and cited in Jim Abbott, *Jackson C. Frank: The Clear, Hard Light of Genius* (Brooklyn, NY: Ba Da Bing Records, 2014), 71.

38 Charles L. Granata, *I Just Wasn't Made for These Times: Brian Wilson and the Making of Pet Sounds* (London: Unanimous, 2003), 100–101.

39 Mike Grant, "Beach Boys News Special," *Rave*, February 1967.

40 Granata, *I Just Wasn't Made for These Times,* 99.

41 D. K. Wilgus talks to Mose Rager in excerpt from "Lyrics and Legends," National Educational TV, www.youtube.com/watch?v=G5i-2Pqs-is.

42 See Shindler's lyrics for "I'm a Pilgrim," online at https://hymnary.org/text/im_a_pilgrim _and_im_a_stranger_i_can_tar.

43 McGuinn converted to evangelical Christianity in 1978. See Mark Moring, "No Ordinary Folk," *Christianity Today* (web only), June 1, 2004, accessed June 29, 2018, https://www .christianitytoday.com/ct/2004/juneweb-only/rogermcguinn-0604.html. Hillman married his wife in 1979, and he converted to Orthodox Christianity sometime after that. See Joey J. Miller, "I Like the Christian Life: The Byrds' Hillman Talks about His Faith," November 4, 2013, accessed June 29, 2018, http://www.patheos.com/blogs/joeljmiller/2013/11/i-like-the -christian-life-chris-hillman-talks-about-his-faith/.

44 Robin Williamson and Mike Heron, *The Incredible String Band: Words, Music, and Chords for 34 Songs*, edited with an introduction by Happy Tram (New York: Penguin Books, 1975), 14.

45 *Baudelaire: Selected Poems,* trans. Joanna Richardson (New York, NY: Penguin Books, 1975), 194–95.

46 Jann S. Wenner "Mick Jagger Remembers," *Rolling Stone*, December 14, 1995.

47 Mark Beaumont, "20 Things You Didn't Know About Sympathy for the Devil," NME.com, November 26, 2012, http://www.nme.com/blogs/nme-blogs/20-things-you-didnt-know -about-sympathy-for-the-devil-766764.

48 David Fricke, "Online Exclusive: Keith Richards Uncut," *Rolling Stone*, September 24, 2002, www.rollingstone.com/music/news/online-exclusive-keith-richards-uncut-20020924.

49 Steve Sullivan, *Encyclopedia of Great Popular Song Recordings,* vol. 3 (Lanham, MD: Rowman & Littlefield, 2017), 91.

50 Pete Welding, "Reverend Robert Wilkins: Interview Part 5," *Blues Unlimited* no. 55, July 1968, 11, accessed June 20, 2018, https://sundayblues.org/wp-content/uploads/2014/03/wilkins -bu.pdf.

51 Michael Goldberg, "Fortunate Son," *Rolling Stone*, February 4, 1993, accessed June 29, 2018, http://riverising.tripod.com/john-interviews/rollingstone2.html.

52 Henry Yates, "The Story Behind the Song: Bad Moon Rising by Creedence Clearwater Revival," *Classic Rock*, May 28, 2017, https://www.loudersound.com/features/story-behind -the-song-bad-moon-rising-by-creedence.

53 "A Conversation with Edwin Hawkins and Erica Campbell" with video, GospelGuru website,

October 20, 2014, accessed June 29, 2018, http://thegospelguru.com/2014/10/watch-conversation-edwin-hawkins-erica-campbell/.

54   Comment made in documentary film *The Harmony Game: The Making of Bridge Over Troubled Water*, directed by Jennifer LeBeau, LeBeau, Sony Music Entertainment, 2011.

55   David Hinckley, "Legendary Singer Claude Jeter Dies," *New York Daily News*, January 8, 2009, http://www.nydailynews.com/entertainment/music-arts/legendary-singer-claude-jeter-dies-article-1.421227.

56   Peter Ames Carlin, *Homeward Bound: The Life of Paul Simon* (New York: Henry Holt and Company, 2016), 194.

57   *J. S. Bach: The Complete Cantatas*, translated by Richard Stokes (Lanham, MD: Scarecrow Press, 1999), 93.

58   Philip Norman, "Johnny Cash: Jailhouse, Jesus and H. G. Wells," *Sunday Times*, 1971, accessed June 29, 2018, https://www.rocksbackpages.com/Library/Article/johnny-cash-jailhouse-jesus-and-hg-wells.

59   David Sheff, *The Playboy Interviews with John Lennon & Yoko Ono* (London: New English Library, 1982), 170–71.

60   John Edge, "Do the Beatles Believe in God?" *The Beatles Are Back* (magazine special), MacFadden-Bartell Corporation, 1964, 59–63.

61   Barry Miles, *Paul McCartney: Many Years from Now* (New York: Henry Holt and Company, 1997), 538.

62   Ray Connolly, "The First Woman to Break Paul McCartney's Heart," *MailOnline*, February 28, 2013, http://www.dailymail.co.uk/tvshowbiz/article-2285670/The-woman-break-Paul-McCartneys-heart-The-Beatle-reveals-dearest-wish-mother-again.html.

63   See poster image online at https://en.wikipedia.org/wiki/Woodstock#/media/File:Woodstock_poster.jpg.

64   Lyrics online at http://jonimitchell.com/music/song.cfm?id=75.

65   Dave Zimmer and Henry Diltz, *Crosby, Stills, and Nash: The Biography* (New York: St. Martin's Press, 1984).

66   Cited in William Ruhlman, "From Blue to Indigo," *Goldmine*, February 17, 1995, http://jonimitchell.com/library/view.cfm?id=115.

67   Ibid.

68   Camille Paglia, "Joni Mitchell: The Trailblazer Interview," *Interview Magazine*, August 2005, http://jonimitchell.com/library/view.cfm?id=1327.

69   *Billboard*, April 18, 1970, 64.

70   *Bootleg,* Larry Norman, One Way Records, Hollywood CA, 1972.

71   Originally published in *The Hollywood Free Paper* in the column "The Way I See It" that Larry started contributing to in September 1970, as quoted in Larry Norman, Why Should the Devil Have All the Good Music songbook (Hollywood, CA: One Way Publications, 1972), 16.

72   Jon Wilde, "Smokey Robinson on Motown, Britain and Cocaine," *Sabotage Times*, March 1, 2016, accessed June 29, 2018, https://sabotagetimes.com/music/my-date-with-smokey.

73   "Wedding Song (There Is Love) with Chords and Lyrics," Noel Paul Stookey, http://www.noelpaulstookey.com/chord%20sheets/Wedding%20Song.html.

74   "Wedding Song (There Is Love) by Noel Paul Stookey," Songfacts, http://www.songfacts.com/detail.php?id=8313.

75   Chad Childers, "Black Sabbath's Geezer Butler: 'If God Could See Us Killing Each Other in His Name, He'd Be Disgusted'" Loudwire, June 11, 2015, http://loudwire.com/black-sabbath-geezer-butler-god-killing-each-other-in-his-name-disgusted/.

76   Paul Elliot, "Black Sabbath's Geezer Butler on Knives, Vegan Food, and Wanking Bandmates," *Classic Rock*, October 6, 2016, http://teamrock.com/feature/2016-10-06/black-sabbaths-geezer-butler-on-knives-vegan-food-and-wanking-bandmates.

77   Iain Ellis, "What Does Randy Newman Say When He Talks With God?" Pop Matters, February 22, 2016, https://www.popmatters.com/what-does-randy-newman-say-when-he-talks-with-god-2495452160.html.

78 Interview with Chi Coltrane by RTV Zwolle FM, a radio station in the Netherlands, https://www.youtube.com/watch?v=jKbGjlHO-pk.

79 "Interview with Andrae Crouch" Gospelflava.com, http://www.gospelflava.com/articles/andraecrouchinterview1.html.

80 Meg Patterson, *Dr. Meg: An Autobiography* (London: Nelson Word, 1994), 127–29.

81 Eric Clapton, *Clapton: The Autobiography* (London: Century, 2007), 164.

82 Ibid., 257.

83 Angus MacKinnon, "The Future Isn't What It Used to Be," *NME*, September 13, 1980, http://www.bowiegoldenyears.com/articles/800913-nme.html.

84 Nicky Horne, *Your Mother Wouldn't Like It*, Capital Radio interview with David Bowie, February 13, 1979, complete audio online at https://vimeo.com/239189909; question about Buddhism starts at 24:40.

85 Daniel Rachel, *Isle of Noises: Conversations with Great British Songwriters* (London: Picador, 2013), 153-54, excerpt online at https://sabotagetimes.com/music/being-john-lydon.

86 John Lydon as told to Pat Gilbert, "John Lydon Relives the Making of Anarchy in the UK," *Mojo*, February 2016, https://www.mojo4music.com/articles/22741/john-lydon-relives-the-making-of-anarchy-in-the-uk.

87 Elvis Costello, *Unfaithful Music & Disappearing Ink* (London: Viking Penguin, 2015), 186.

88 J. D. Considine, "Elvis Costello on Music, Religion and the Act of Writing Songs," *Globe & Mail*, November 2, 2010, https://www.theglobeandmail.com/arts/music/elvis-costello-on-music-religion-and-the-act-of-writing-songs/article1215986/.

89 Bruce Springsteen, *Born to Run* (New York: Simon & Schuster, 2016).

90 *The Million Sellers: The UK's Greatest Hits*, The Official Charts Company (assisted by Alan Jones) (London, Omnibus Press, 2012), eBook edition.

91 Andrew McCarron, "The Year Bob Dylan Was Born Again: A Timeline" Oxford University Press (OUPblog), Janurary 21, 2017, https://blog.oup.com/2017/01/bob-dylan-christianity/.

92 Robert Hilburn and *Los Angeles Times*, "Bob Dylan's Song of Salvation," *Washington Post*, November 24, 1980, https://www.washingtonpost.com/archive/lifestyle/1980/11/24/bob-dylans-song-of-salvation/1fba5ce3-e6fa-40dc-8a17-a384bb537643/?utm_term=.323c74f76a6c.

93 C. S. Lewis, "Is Theology Poetry?" in *The Weight of Glory and Other Addresses* (London: Macmillan Company, 1949).

94 Bill Bentley, "T-Bone Burnett: Born Again, but Still Looking," *L.A. Weekly*, August 8–August 14, 1980, 56.

95 Unpublished author interview with Brian Eno, London, circa 1983.

96 Marcus Boon, "On Appropriation," *CR: The New Centennial Review* 7.1 (2007), http://marcusboon.com/on-appropriation/.

97 Unpublished author interview with Brian Eno, London, circa 1983.

98 Bruce Cockburn, *Rumours of Glory: A Memoir* (New York: HarperCollins, 2014), 150.

99 Booklet included in *Biograph* vinyl box-set, interview by Cameron Crowe, Columbia, 1985.

100 Robert Hilburn, "I Learned Jesus Was Real and I Wanted That," *Los Angeles Times*, November 23, 1980. Contained in Carl Benson, *The Bob Dylan Companion: Four Decades of Commentary* (Schirmer Books, 1998), 164; and in Artur Jarosinski, *Every Mind Polluting Word: Assorted Bob Dylan Utterances* (Don't Ya Tell Henry Publications, 2006), 719, 720.

101 Robert Burns, "Project Gutenberg's Poems and Songs of Robert Burns," (Project Gutenberg, January 25, 2005), eBook, http://www.gutenberg.org/files/1279/1279-h/1279-h.htm#link2H_4_0316.

102 "Yah Mo B There by James Ingram and Michael McDonald," Songfacts, accessed (August 10, 2018), http://www.songfacts.com/detail.php?id=10412.

103 Original cassette recording of talk given by Bono and the Edge for Ghettout Music event at Gaines Christian Centre, Worcester, England, January, 1981. A forty-five-minute sound CD was sold in 2006 as *U2's Vision* (Littlehampton, England: Dream Depot, 2005), but was

withdrawn after complaints from U2's management company, https://www.atu2.com/news/rare-recording-featuring-three-fourths-of-u2-for-sale.html

104 Introduction by Bono, *The Book of Psalms* [Pocket Canons] (Edinburgh, UK: Canongate, 1999).

105 Ibid.

106 Jeff Burger, ed., "Leonard Cohen on Leonard Cohen," *Chicago Review Press*, 2014, 171.

107 Interview with Robert Sward, *Malahat Review*, December 1986. Reprinted in Jeff Burger, ed., *Leonard Cohen on Leonard Cohen*, 164.

108 Paul Zollo, "Leonard Cohen: Inside the Tower of Song," *SongTalk* (National Academy of Songwriters), April 1993. Reprinted in Jeff Burger, ed., Leonard Cohen on Leonard Cohen, 284.

109 Agata Paluch, "The Power of Language in Jewish Kabbalah and magic: How to Do (and Undo) Things with Words," The British Library online, February 29, 2016, https://www.bl.uk/hebrew-manuscripts/articles/the-power-of-language-in-jewish-kabbalah.

110 Unpublished interview with Bono by the author, 1988.

111 Neil McCormick, *U2 by U2* (London: HarperCollins, 2006), 225. There is an interesting interview with Bono in which he talks about the Bible and Jesus online at https://www.youtube.com/watch?v=atMF1mBOtsU.

112 Nick Cave, "The Flesh Made Word," NickCave.it, http://www.nickcave.it/extra.php?IdExtra=44.

113 "The Mercy Seat by Nick Cave & the Bad Seeds," Songfacts, accessed (August 10, 2018), http://www.songfacts.com/detail.php?id=43229.

114 Stephen Holden, "Innocence Ended," *New York Times*, July 5, 1989, https://www.nytimes.com/1989/07/05/arts/the-pop-life-151789.html.

115 J. Randy Taraborrelli, *Michael Jackson: The Magic, the Madness, the Whole Story* (London: Pan MacMillan, 2009), 363.

116 Jehovah's Witnesses, "Michael Jackson's Life as a Jehovah's Witness," JWfact.com, accessed February 27, 2018, at http://jwfacts.com/watchtower/experiences/michael-jackson-jehovah.php.

117 English translation from: https://en.wikipedia.org/wiki/Ode_to_Joy#Lyrics.

118 See interview comments here: https://www.youtube.com/watch?v=tmmBynDJzWw.

119 Will Jennings talking about "Tears in Heaven," the song he wrote with Eric Clapton, Songfacts, http://www.songfacts.com/detail.php?id=1274.

120 Ibid.

121 "Ask Michael Stipe: Finale!," Pop Songs 07–08, September 28, 2008, https://popsongs.wordpress.com.

122 Michael Stipe interview with Beliefnet, "I Just Think We're Better Than That," January 2006, http://www.beliefnet.com/entertainment/celebrities/i-just-think-were-better-than-that.aspx.

123 Greg Kot, "Lauryn Hill: The Album of the Year," *Rolling Stone*, January 21, 1999, accessed February 28, 2018, https://www.rollingstone.com/music/news/the-rolling-stone-music-awards-lauryn-hill-19990121.

124 Brian Hiatt, "17 Things You Learn Hanging Out With Adele," *Rolling Stone*, November 30, 2015, accessed February 28, 2018, https://www.rollingstone.com/music/news/17-things-you-learn-hanging-out-with-adele-20151130.

125 Steve Turner, *Cliff Richard: The Biography* (Oxford, UK: Lion Books, 1993), 343.

126 Details online at http://www.cliffrichardsongs.com/popup.php?data=TheMillenniumPrayer199932_popupplus.

127 Johnny Cash's last interview, August 20, 2003, with Kurt Loder of MTV online at https://www.youtube.com/watch?v=i1zRFnw4jOU. and http://www.mtv.com/news/1632739/on-johnny-cashs-birthday-a-look-back-at-his-final-interview/.

128 Sting, *Lyrics by Sting* (New York: The Dial Press, 1991).

129 Gary Graff, "Sting Finds New Meaning in 'Sacred Love,'" United Press International, https://www.upi.com/Sting-finds-new-meaning-in-Sacred-Love/33571066233646/.

130 Matt Fink, "Interview with Sufjan Stevens," Delusions of Adequacy, September 25, 2006, http://www.adequacy.net/2006/09/interview-with-sufjan-stevens/.

131 Interview on Belgian radio, 2004, https://www.youtube.com/watch?v=YkiXxSu-qso.

132 David Peschek, "Sufjan Stevens, Seven Swans," *Guardian*, March 25, 2004, https://www.theguardian.com/music/2004/mar/26/popandrock.sufjanstevens.

133 Dorian Lynskey, "Natural Born Show-off," *Guardian*, August 4, 2005, https://www.theguardian.com/music/2005/aug/05/kanyewest.

134 Josh, "Kanye West on Religion and Jesus Christ," Phatmass, May 13, 2009, http://www.phatmass.com/phorum/topic/93979-kanye-west-on-religion-and-jesus-christ/.

135 THR Staff, "Kanye West Explains Why He Brings 'Jesus' Onstage during Concerts," *Hollywood Reporter*, October 22, 2015, https://www.hollywoodreporter.com/earshot/kanye-west-explains-why-he-650201.

136 Springsteen recounts the influence of Catholicism in his life and music when introducing "Jesus Was an Only Son" in his Seattle concert, August 11, 2005, available online at https://www.youtube.com/watch?v=Qelew5_k90E. At 2:47 he says, "It sort of worked its way into all my songs." "It" refers to "that institution" of the Catholic church from remarks said just before this (2:28): "For a child, and when you grew up in the shadow of, of, of, of all this, that, that institution, and it was filled with sort of mystery and terror, and there was also great beauty and, and enormous poetry. And, uh, uh, it was, it was, it—It sort of worked its way into all my songs."

137 Ibid.

138 Bruce Springsteen, "Jesus Was An Only Son," intro from his concert in East Rutherford, NJ, November 17, 2005, YouTube video, https://www.youtube.com/watch?v=5cDvbmRU27k.

139 "Catechism of the Catholic Church" on the Vatican Archives, "Paragraph 2. 'Conceived by the Power of the Holy Spirit and Born of the Virgin Mary,'" Part 1, Section 2, Article 3, http://www.vatican.va/archive/ENG0015/__P1K.HTM#$J8.

140 Bruce Springsteen, "Jesus Was An Only Son," intro from his concert, NJ, May 19, 2005, YouTube video, https://www.youtube.com/watch?v=mPrFlbitSro.

141 Ibid.

142 "Episode #3.154," *Jimmy Kimmel Live!*, ABC, August 24, 2004, https://www.youtube.com/watch?v=QHznspbYTT4.

143 Matisyahu, "Jerusalem (Out of Darkness Comes Light) (Video)," official music video, 2009, YouTube, https://www.youtube.com/watch?v=H8ULIw0Zgaw.

144 Daniel Hoffman, "Matisyahu Explains Why He Got Less Religious," *Times of Israel*, March 13, 2013, https://www.timesofisrael.com/matisyahu-explains-why-he-got-less-religious/.

145 "Brandon Flowers Track by Track Guide to 'Sam's Town,'" The Killers News, July 11, 2013, https://thekillersnews.com/post/55215993395/brandon-flowers-track-by-track-guide-to-sams.

146 Mark Beaumont, *The Killers: Days & Ages* (London: Omnibus Press, 2014).

147 Craig McLean, "We're about to Be Fed to the Lions," *Guardian*, May 31, 2008, https://www.theguardian.com/music/2008/jun/01/popandrock.coldplay.

148 Sylvia Patterson, "¡La Vida Loca!" [pictures by Stephan Crasneanscki], Q, July 2008, https://www.flickr.com/photos/27283582@N08/2537635409/in/album-72157605348081812/.

149 Kendrick Lamar, "Kendrick Lamar Talks Jesus and Spirituality in His Music," YouTube, uploaded by Lomax Edits, December 3, 2012, https://www.youtube.com/watch?v=qhVg8H-OR6I.

150 Sylvia Patterson, "Mumford & Sons: 'We're Fans of Faith, Not Religion,'" *The Big Issue*, October 3, 2012, https://www.bigissue.com/interviews/mumford-sons-fans-faith-not-religion/.

151 "Marcus Mumford Interview Segment," video recording at Holy Trinity Brompton's Life Changing Leadership, Leadership Conference 2017, Royal Albert Hall, London, https://alpha.org/lc/talks (statement begins at 1:58).

152 Sylvia Patterson, "Mumford & Sons."

153 Neil McCormick, "Mumford & Sons Come to Australia as One of the World's Most Popular, and Unlikely, Bands," *Sydney Morning Herald*, October 22, 2015, https://www.smh.com.au/entertainment/music/mumford--sons-in-the-domain-20151020-gke3m1.html.

154 Brian Hiatt, "Mumford & Sons: Rattle and Strum," *Rolling Stone*, March 28, 2013, https://www.rollingstone.com/music/news/mumford-sons-rattle-and-strum-20130328.

155 Jim Standridge, "Katy Perry Uncensored Raw Talent," *Vimeo* video, https://vimeo.com/104457629.

156 Vanessa Grigoriadis, "Sex, God, and Katy Perry," *Rolling Stone*, August 19, 2010, https://www.rollingstone.com/music/news/sex-god-katy-perry-rolling-stones-2010-cover-story-20110607.

157 "Katy Perry Wiki," Fandom, "Who Am I Living For? (Song)," http://katyperry.wikia.com/wiki/Who_Am_I_Living_For%3F_(song).

158 Larry King, "Top Entertainer–Lady Gaga!" *Larry King Live!*, aired June 1, 2010, CNN transcript, http://transcripts.cnn.com/TRANSCRIPTS/1006/01/lkl.01.html; video accessed March 2, 2018, https://www.youtube.com/watch?v=HCW3v5gbxrY; statement at 8:56.

159 Kevin Ritchie, "Pop Culture as Religion," MSN Canada, April 26, 2011, https://ipfs.io/ipfs/QmXoypizjW3WknFiJnKLwHCnL72vedxjQkDDP1mXWo6uco/wiki/Judas_(Lady_Gaga_song).html.

160 Kevin Simmons, *The Skorpion Show*, February 2011. Discussion of "Judas" begins at around 3 minutes, https://www.youtube.com/watch?v=bQO3V99KydE.

161 Marissa Mayer, "Google Goes Gaga," March 2011. Discussion of "Judas" starts at around 39 minutes, https://www.youtube.com/watch?v=hNa_-1d_0tA.

162 Billy Bragg, "'Do Unto Others," introduction and song at Turner Hall, Milwaukee, WI, September 24, 2013, Youtube video, https://www.youtube.com/watch?v=rtjpeXEVcqo.

163 Vanessa Grigoriadis, "Madonna Talks 'Fifty Shades of Grey' ('Not Very Sexy'), the Pope, and Why the 'Word Police Can F--- Off,'" *Billboard*, February 2, 2015, accessed March 2, 2018, https://www.billboard.com/articles/news/6472671/madonna-interview-rebel-heart-50-shades-of-grey-pope-word-police.

164 Caryn Ganz, "'Rebel Heart': Madonna Reveals the Story behind Six Surprise Songs," *Rolling Stone*, December 21, 2014, https://www.rollingstone.com/music/features/rebel-heart-madonna-reveals-the-story-behind-six-surprise-songs-20141221.

165 David Blaine, "Madonna," *Andy Warhol's Interview*, November 26, 2014, accessed March 2, 2018, https://www.interviewmagazine.com/music/madonna-1.

166 Lyndsey Havens, "Chance the Rapper's 'Coloring Book' Is First Streaming-Only Album to Win a Grammy," *Billboard*, February 13, 2017, https://www.billboard.com/articles/news/grammys/7686341/chance-the-rapper-coloring-book-first-streaming-only-album-grammy.

167 Chance the Rapper (@chancetherapper), Twitter, January 31, 2016, 10:28 a.m., https://twitter.com/chancetherapper/status/693833227987980290?lang=en.

168 Allison Stewart, "Gospel and Faith Merge with Rap, in Song," *Chicago Tribune*, June 2, 2016, http://www.chicagotribune.com/entertainment/music/ct-rap-music-gospel-ae-0605-20160602-story.html.

169 "CLCI Top 100," Song Select, https://songselect.ccli.com/search/results?List=top100.

170 Aidan Smith, "Chance The Rapper—Zane Lowe Interview on Beats 1 (360p)," Vimeo video, https://vimeo.com/168865388, statements at 16:30–17:00.

171 Yolisa Mkele, "Hurricane Warning as Stormzy Loads the Bass on UK Rap," *Times (South Africa)*, March 10, 2017.

172 "Watch Stormzy Perform Blinded by Your Grace Pt.2," BBC Radio 1, Live Lounge, [2017], http://www.bbc.co.uk/programmes/articles/56cVKLL0HxhYBXwZYgmTNzc/stormzy-covering-sweet-like-chocolate-is-the-track-you-didnt-know-you-needed-in-your-life.

SPOTIFY PLAYLIST

LISTEN AS YOU READ

· ·

Want to listen to the music
as you read the stories
behind the songs?
All but two songs are
available on Spotify.

"Turn, Turn, Turn – The Book" Playlist*

www.bit.ly/turnturnturnthebook

*Link active as of August 16, 2018